THE CURRENT INFLATION

The Current Inflation

Proceedings of a Conference held at the London School of Economics on 22 February 1971

Edited by

H. G. JOHNSON

and

A. R. NOBAY

Macmillan
St Martin's Press

First published 1971 by
THE MACMILLAN PRESS LTD
London and Basingstoke
Associated companies in New York Toronto Dublin Melbourne Johannesburg and Madras

Library of Congress catalog card no. 73–171602

SBN 333 13112 6

Printed in Great Britain by
WESTERN PRINTING SERVICES LTD
Bristol

Contents

Acknowledgements

Chapter 1, 'Some Aspects of the Present Inflation and the National Institute Model' by Michael Artis, is reproduced by permission of the National Institute of Economic and Social Research.

The editors would like to thank Diana Marshallsay for her invaluable help in proof-reading.

Introduction

HARRY G. JOHNSON*

By the early autumn of 1970 it had become evident to economic observers and commentators in the academic world, finance and journalism that this country was experiencing an inflation unprecedented in the post-Second World War period. The inflationary process was most obviously manifest in a sharp increase in the percentage wage increases demanded by the union movement, and won in collective bargaining with employers. This had begun towards the end of 1969, and was an issue in the General Election of June 1970. The continuance of accelerated cost and price inflation throughout the rest of the year produced an extremely confused situation among informed observers. On the one hand, those who thought they understood how the economy worked were baffled by the combination of exceptionally high unemployment, unprecedented rates of wage and price increase, and an extremely favourable balance of payments, so favourable in fact as to require special measures to stave off unwanted capital inflows. On the other hand, there developed deep divisions in the policy debate among those who favoured an incomes policy, those who favoured demand management and had no faith in incomes policy, and those who favoured demand management but felt that it had failed and that an incomes policy was now required as an emergency measure.

In these circumstances, a number of economists came to the conclusion that a conference of experts was required, to take stock of the existing body of economic knowledge about the workings of the British economy with special reference to its bearing on the current inflationary situation, and to discuss the policy alternatives for government in the light of this knowledge. It was my privilege to propose the convening of such a conference on behalf of the academic community and to organise

* Harry G. Johnson is Professor of Economics at both the London School of Economics and Political Science and the University of Chicago.

the Conference itself, which took place on 22 February 1971 at the London School of Economics. It was my good fortune to be able to enlist the assistance of Bob Nobay of Southampton University to handle the administrative details, which he did perfectly in spite of the postal strike that began almost immediately after the Conference was planned, and of Mr Alan Peters of Shell International, who arranged for the necessary finances.

Participants in the Conference included academics from universities all over the United Kingdom, representatives of the Treasury, the Bank of England, the National Economic Development Office, the National Institute of Economic and Social Research, the National Board for Prices and Incomes, and the clearing banks, with observers attending from the Trades Union Congress, the Confederation of British Industry, the Social Science Research Council, the Bank for International Settlements, and Shell International.

The Conference was held *in camera*, to permit frank expression of ideas by the participants. However, it was agreed in advance that the academic papers could be published for the benefit of a wider audience; and it was fortunately also agreed subsequently that the panel papers on the policy problem of inflation raised no issues of confidentiality and could also be published.

To accommodate the diverse facets of the problem and the interests of the participants, the Conference was organised in three sessions corresponding to the three parts of this book. The first was concerned with the wage and price relationships employed in the large macro-economic forecasting models that have been developed by economists and econometricians working outside the Government. Three such models exist in various stages of perfection: the National Institute Model, the London Business School Model, and the Southampton University Model. Representatives of the teams responsible for these models were asked to discuss the way in which wage and price determination is handled in their respective models. In addition, Professor J. D. Sargan of the London School of Economics, who has been working with his students specifically on wage determination in the United Kingdom, was asked to describe this work.

The problem of inflation in the United Kingdom, and very largely elsewhere as well, has been approached since 1958, when the concept was first invented by Professor A. W. Phillips (then at the London School of Economics), in terms of the empirical relationship customarily described as the 'Phillips curve'. This curve depicts a statistical relationship between the percentage rate of wage increase and the percentage of unemployment (and in more sophisticated versions, other variables as well). The traditional Phillips curve for Britain clearly does not fit the recent facts. The question is why, and whether the reason makes the Phillips curve an obsolete or merely an overly naïve concept. This question was the theme of the second session of the Conference (the second part of this book) which surveys the literature and recent work on the Phillips curve and includes a critique of the foundations of the aggregate curve in the behaviour of individual labour markets. In addition, we have included a paper by Professor Albert Hines, whose comments from the floor on the other papers excited wide interest among the participants.

The Conference concluded (the third part of the book) with a panel discussion of the current inflation and the policy alternatives. Leslie Dicks-Mireaux was asked to discuss the question suggested by the December 1970 report by the Secretary-General of the Organisation for Economic Co-operation and Development on *Inflation: The Present Problem*, of whether the current inflation in Britain should be viewed as a domestic problem with special domestic causes or as a local manifestation of a world-wide problem with world-wide causes. Michael Parkin was asked to discuss the bearing of the empirical evidence reviewed in the preceding two sessions of the Conference on the problem for policy posed by the current inflation. Sir Frederick Catherwood, of the National Economic Development Office, and Mr Ralph Turvey, of the National Board for Prices and Incomes, were asked to present their own views of the policy problem as seen from their respective vantage-points.

A conference of this kind is intended to remind the participants of what is known already or widely believed, and to focus attention on where the outstanding issues lie, rather than to produce a consensus on theoretical analysis and policy recommendations. The reader of the proceedings must read and form his own judgement.

The discussions as distinct from the papers presented remain confidential. In my private role as a participant, however, I may perhaps be permitted to offer three thoughts, one per session, that I drew from it. The first is that the inability of the 'big models' to deal more satisfactorily with wage, and therefore price, behaviour may be less a consequence of the inherent difficulties of the problem than of the probability that, for both government and private business, it is quantities of output and employment rather than the money price tags put on them that it is really important to forecast. If so, the implication is that inflation is by no means as serious an economic problem (I do not say social problem) as the conventional wisdom proclaims, certainly not as serious as the problem of unexpectedly slack demand and high unemployment.

The second, prompted by a certain tendency of the Conference participants to settle on the frustration of workers' expectations of rising real consumption levels as the explanation of the recent shift in (or disintegration of) the Phillips curve, is that this aspect of labour market behaviour is important to investigate – and that it may require increased attention to the 'real' as compared to the 'monetary' elements in labour market behaviour. More specifically, the argument implies that what the unions are after is the increase in *real* wages that experience has taught them they should be able to get, given the normal rise in productivity, rather than the increase in *money* wages past experience has taught them they can get with a given level of overall pressure of demand for labour. Perhaps it would be more accurate to say that wage bargaining is influenced by the relation of the actual to the marginal productivity real wage as well as by the relation of demand for labour to supply of labour at the existing level of real wages.

The third point, related to the second by a more complicated theoretical analysis than can be expounded here, is that British economists may have made a fundamental theoretical mistake in attempting to explain British inflation in terms of purely domestic factors – and been lucky until the past few years inasmuch as neither domestic British policy (the devaluation of 1967) nor the outside world environment was transmitting strong inflationary pressures into the British economy. The prevailing mood of the Conference seemed to be to dismiss a change in the external influences in favour of a change in the internal influences, as the primal causal factor in the current inflation. It may be that in a year's time Britain's economists will be discussing how to isolate the economy from inflationary forces coming from the outside environment – as European policy-makers have been doing for some time, though without noticeable policy results.

PART ONE

Price and Wage Relationships in Macro-economic Models

1. Some Aspects of the Present Inflation and the National Institute Model

MICHAEL ARTIS*

Editors' note: The contribution by Michael Artis dealt with wage and price relationships in the National Institute's forecasting system. The discussion of wages drew largely upon material which was subsequently published in chapter iii, 'Some Aspects of the Present Inflation', in the *National Institute Economic Review*, no. 55 (Feb. 1971). The whole of this chapter, with only minor editorial amendments, has been reprinted below. In addition, a short section has been added, covering some details of the principal pricing equation employed in the National Institute's forecasting procedures.

INTRODUCTION

Recent experience of forecasting at the National Institute throws up three main propositions about wage and price relationships which are relevant in the present context. The first two propositions are contrasting in nature, in so far as they concern the stability of relationships. For whilst, on the one hand, it is clear that there are now no usable econometric relationships for forecasting wages, the position with respect to prices, on the other hand, is quite different. Here it seems that price relationships are behaving in what may be regarded as a normal way, given the behaviour of wages. The third proposition is that in view of the form of the price relationships, and given the parameters of the tax and consumption functions

* Michael Artis is a Senior Research Officer of the National Institute of Economic and Social Research, and is Editor of the *National Institute Economic Review*.

applicable to the British economy, errors in wage forecasting are of a second order of importance when it comes to generating predictions for 'real' magnitudes, e.g. the volume of consumers' expenditure. This point was put in the National Institute's *Economic Review* for February 1970 (pp. 26–7) and is explored again in further detail below.

The lack of usable relationships for predicting wages was not a phenomenon new in 1970. Although, in many respects, the National Institute has been the home of the empirical Phillips curve and of extensions of it,[1] the usefulness of formal wage relationships had been in doubt since the mid-1960s. Two specific factors which deserve mention in this regard are the attempts to use various forms of income policy in the latter half of the decade, which could be expected to modify 'normal' wage behaviour, and then the apparent shift in labour market relationships, evident from 1967 onwards, which affected particularly the correlation between movements in unemployment and movements in vacancies and for which no clearly agreed explanation is available. Partly because of these factors, wage forecasting had been, for most of the period from the mid-1960s to 1970, an *ad hoc* affair. The only exception was a brief period of about a year spanning 1968 and 1969, when it was found that an equation predicting the total wage and salary bill (equation (4) in Table 3 on p. 10) worked reasonably well. Some further work conducted at the Institute[2] began to suggest that equations in average earnings of a standard 'Phillips' type, but substituting vacancies for unemployment, might give good results; but this discovery soon proved misleading (see the discussion of Table 3 below), and no systematic method of wage forecasting was available for use in 1970. The procedures of wage forecasting now necessarily place a large premium on intuitive feel for the trend of wage bargaining and the impact of government policy. Considerable care goes into formulating the best possible data background for making the necessary judgements, of course, which involves processing large amounts of settlements and claims data, inspecting settlements/claims ratios and the trend of wage drift.

Some of the salient features of the recent inflation were published in the National Institute's February 1971 *Review*, in a chapter which, on the kind suggestion of the editors of the present volume, is reprinted in full below. The chapter gives some formal expression to the proposition that formal wage relationships which fit the past quite well are quite inadequate to explain the events of 1970, and as well as providing other material also gives some account of the connection between the wage–price process and the 'real' magnitudes in the economy. As it excluded any formal account of the behaviour of price relationships, a short tailpiece has been added to cover this point.

THE SIZE OF THE PROBLEM

Table 1 shows a set of cost and price indices, indicating their percentage rate of change in the four most recent years and their trend rate of increase in the preceding seven.

The G.D.P. deflators may perhaps be regarded as the most comprehensive indicators of inflation in the economy and a measure of the present inflation may be obtained from their 1970 rate of increase of some 6½–7 per cent. This compares with a trend rate of rise over the period 1959–66 of around 3 per cent. The retail price index, too, moved up at over twice its trend rate in 1970, though the national accounts index of consumer prices failed to register quite such a strong acceleration.

The lower part of the table gives some details which bear on the question of the proximate cause of the acceleration in inflation. It shows that in 1970 basic hourly wage rates rose by 10¼ per cent, and wages and salaries per employee by an estimated 12½ per cent, compared with trend values of 5 per cent and just under 5½ per cent respectively, while output per head increased by only just over 2 per cent. This meant that costs per unit of output were over 10 per cent up, a rise well in excess of three times the trend increase.

The table also shows that the rate of price inflation was markedly above trend in 1968 and 1969. In those years, however, the rise in wage rates and in wage costs per unit of output was relatively modest, but the rises in import prices (in 1968) and in indirect taxes (both in 1968 and in 1969) were well above normal. Both of these rises were of course in large part the result of devaluation and the demand management policy associated with it.

TABLE 1. MOVEMENTS IN COSTS AND PRICES
(per cent annual rates of change)

	1959–66 trend	1966–7	1967–8	1968–9	1969–70
Retail prices	3·2	2·5	4·7	5·4	6.9
Consumer prices[1]	3·1	2·5	4·5	5·3	5·3[6]
G.D.P. deflator (factor cost)	2·9	3·7	2·7	3·5	6·9[7]
G.D.P. deflator (market prices)	3·2	3·2	3·8	5·1	6·4[7]
Hourly wage rates	5·0	4·1	6·8	5·4	10·2
Wages and salaries per head[2]	5·4	5·4	7·7	7·8	12·6[6]
Output per head[3]	2·3	2·3	4·6	2·4	2·1[6]
Wages and salaries per unit of output	3·1	3·1	3·0	5·2	10·3[6]
Import prices[4]	1·3	1·3	11·5	2·6	4·8[7]
Indirect taxes[5]	5·3	−0·1	11·0	14·7	2·5[7]

Source: *Economic Trends*

[1] Implicit deflator of the constant price consumers' expenditure series.
[2] Wages and salaries per employee in employment.
[3] G.D.P. (average estimate) per employee in employment.
[4] Implicit deflator of the constant price series of imports of goods and services.
[5] Implicit deflator of the constant price factor cost adjustment series.
[6] Estimates derived from the *National Institute Economic Review*, no. 55 (Feb 1971) tables 1 and 5, pp. 23 and 27.
[7] Average of first three quarters of 1970 (seasonally adjusted) compared with average 1969.

COST CONTRIBUTIONS

It would be helpful to be able to isolate the contributions of the various cost components to the overall rise in prices in some way. Unfortunately, this can only be done in a rather approximate manner; but for what it is worth, the results of an attempt to isolate the contributions of cost factors to the rise in the consumer price index are set out in Table 2. Information contained in the 1963 input–output tables was used to arrive at the figures shown. The procedure was to apply the 1963 primary input coefficients of consumers' expenditure to the rise in the most appropriate price indices available. In the case of imports and indirect taxes the implicit deflators of the constant price estimates of imports of goods and services and of the factor cost adjustment were used, and, in the other cases, indices of employment incomes and of non-employment factor incomes per unit of total output were employed. The aim was to 'explain' the rise in consumer prices (the implicit deflator of the constant price consumers' expenditure series or C.P.I.) between the third quarters of the years 1967 to 1970. The results seem fairly reasonable; the unexplained margin of price increase was largest in the 1968–9 period (when it was nearly ½ per cent) and in the 1969–70 period the error is in the expected direction inasmuch as the recorded rise in the C.P.I. relative to the retail price index seems then to have been abnormally low. For 1967–8 the overall residual is negligible.

TABLE 2. POSSIBLE CONTRIBUTIONS TO THE RISE IN PRICES[1]
(per cent rates of change)

	1968(III)– *1967*(III)	*1969*(III)– *1968*(III)	*1970*(III)– *1969*(III)
Consumers' price index	5·30	4·95	5·35
of which, accounted for by:			
Import prices	1·63	0·39	0·71
Indirect taxes[2]	1·71	2·57	−0·28
Unit labour costs	0·93	1·51	4·73
Unit non-labour factor costs	0·97	0·07	0·45
Total identified	5·24	4·54	5·61

[1] See text for an explanation of the assumptions underlying the calculations.
[2] Includes S.E.T.

The table indicates that the main factors behind the rise in consumer prices in the 1967–8 period were import prices and indirect taxes; these accounted about equally for some two-thirds of the increase. In 1968–9 indirect taxes alone appear to have accounted for more than one-half of the total increase. In 1970, however, unit labour costs have made the running, accounting for over 80 per cent of the rise. Of course, it must be borne in mind that this arithmetic is just a literal accounting procedure, and no more: it does not tell a full 'causal' story.[3]

THE GENERATION OF THE PRESENT INFLATION

The cost accounting record plainly attributes the source of inflationary pressure in 1970 to rising unit wage costs and the earlier rise in prices to import prices and indirect taxes. In the latter case, it is clear that devaluation and associated policies were the cause. But what is the cause of the wage cost explosion in 1970? Perhaps the most obvious answer is really the same one again: that the rise in the pace of price inflation in the two earlier years, associated with the devaluation, is in fact the proximate cause of the later rise in wage rates.

But one fact of considerable importance has not so far been mentioned, and that is the international character of the present inflation. The O.E.C.D. has recently issued a wide-ranging study of this aspect of the matter[4] and here we need only note that in all the major industrial countries the last two or three years, and 1970 in particular, have been marked by inflation; that inflation was more universal than tight demand conditions, though the United Kingdom combination of low demand pressure and inflation was perhaps the most strikingly out-of-line, and that there has been a general tendency for export prices to rise much faster in relation to domestic price indices than is customary.[5] There are perhaps three main ways in which the international inflation affects the pace of price rises in the United Kingdom. The most straightforward and obvious effects are those induced by the rise in import prices on final prices and costs of production; Table 2 indicates how important this effect was in the post-devaluation period and attributes something to it for 1970. To this should be added the 'permissive' effect on export prices. A less limited description of the process, however, brings in assumptions about wage relativities and differential rates of productivity improvement in different sectors of the economy, to show that the linkage with international inflation is likely to be much more far-reaching than this. The outlines of such a model are sketched in below ('Disaggregated productivity and price movements'). Finally, the 'demonstration effects' of autonomous and successful wage pushes overseas – notably France and Italy – should not be wholly discounted as factors in labour militancy. And, throughout, it needs to be borne in mind that the comparatively low rate of rise of productivity in the United Kingdom automatically magnifies the effect on final prices of any wage push.

The role of import prices and indirect taxes in pushing up the rate of inflation in 1968 and 1969 is generally accepted. There is rather less agreement on the proximate causes of the 1970 unit wage cost explosion. The three main suggestions offered – which to some extent overlap and are not mutually exclusive – are, first, that the explosion represents the after-effects of incomes policy restraint; secondly, that it represents a reaction to frustrated expectations of real income advance; thirdly, that expectations of continued inflation have come to assume a dominant role. 'Proof' and 'disproof' of these propositions, even in the accustomed sense in which these words should be used in economic science, are not easy to come by, principally because the period occupied by the wage 'explosion' is both comparatively short and recent. This fact precludes strong statistical inferences and makes for greater reliance upon intuition, *a priori* theorising and borrowing from overseas experience. An additional complication is that in recent years the relationships between labour market indicators have clearly changed.[6] This makes for additional problems in the specification of relationships governing wage behaviour.

One explanation which does not work, however, is that the wage increases in 1970 were due to increased pressure of demand. The orthodox 'Phillips'-type explanation simply does not apply. Table 3 lists the specification and the underprediction of earnings increases using 'Phillips'-type explanations, but where vacancies, and the change in vacancies, have been substituted for the usual terms in unemployment.[7] Additionally, an equation for the level of wages and salaries is included. Over their estimation periods, all the equations listed performed reasonably well and the prediction errors in 1969 were not large. The 1970 prediction errors, however, were considerable. Against the actual increases in earnings (on the various definitions used in the table), or in wages and salaries, of some $12\frac{1}{2}$–$13\frac{1}{2}$ per cent, the predictions were for a rise of some $6\frac{1}{2}$–$7\frac{1}{2}$ per cent, implying underpredictions several times the standard errors of the equations.

TABLE 3. PREDICTION ERRORS OF WAGE EQUATIONS

Equation no.	*Dependent variable*	*Constant*	*Coefficients of independent variables*[1]			R^2	D.W.	S.E.E.	*Prediction error*[2]	
			v_{t+1}	$\dot{v}_t$	$\dot{p}_t$				*1969*	*1970*
(1)	$\dot{e}_t$ (all industries)	2·039 (0·910)	0·344 (0·117)	3·538 (0·795)	0·382 (0·100)	0·742	1·536	1·093	0·706	7·563
(2)	$\dot{e}_t$ (all industries)	1·931 (0·864)	0·330 (0·109)	2·599 (0·709)	0·463 (0·097)	0·760	2·043	1·003	0·237	5·263
(3)	$\dot{e}_t$ (manu-facturing)	1·918 (0·867)	0·336 (0·110)	2·880 (0·712)	0·423 (0·097)	0·761	2·113	1·007	0·578	6·073
			(log)GDP	(log)WS_{t-1}	t					
(4)	WS_t (log)	0·185 (0·842)	0·296 (0·071)	0·670 (0·086)	0·003 (0·001)	0·999	1·64	n.a.	0·91	6·08

Source: *Employment and Productivity Gazette*; *Economic Trends*; N.I.E.S.R. estimates

See opposite for notes.

The 'expectations' hypothesis has received more formal theoretical attention in this context than have other explanations. The basic idea is that the wage bargain is struck in real terms, i.e. after both parties have allowed for the expected rise in prices. This expectation governs both the money wage claim submitted by the union and the concession which employers feel they can make. This suggestion amounts to saying that the orthodox 'Phillips' explanation is dynamically unstable and in its fully extended form leads to the implication that there is no 'trade-off' between inflation and unemployment in the long run – only a 'natural rate of unemployment'.

Formally, if:

$$\dot{w}_t = f(u) + a\dot{p}^e{}_t \qquad (1)$$

represents the standard Phillips explanation, with the change in money wage rates ($\dot{w}$) dependent upon excess demand (represented by u, the rate of unemployment) and a term in expected price change (usually represented in empirical work by the

---

General notes: Variables are defined as follows: $\dot{e}_t'$ is the rate of change of average hourly earnings, calculated as $(e_{t+1}-e_{t-1})/e_{t-1}$, for April and October earnings survey data. $\dot{e}_t$ is defined as a central difference rate of change, i.e. as $(e_{t+1}-e_{t-1})/e_t$, also using April and October survey data. Other rate of change variables in equations (1), (2) and (3) are defined correspondingly. v represents vacancies, $\dot{v}$ the change in vacancies, and $\dot{p}$ the change in retail prices. WS is the total wage and salary bill, quarterly, t represents a time trend (1966(I) = 0). All other variables have their usual meaning. Periods of fit are: equations (1)–(3), 1952–69; equation (4), 1959(I)–1969(IV). Standard errors are shown in brackets.

[1] Seasonal and incomes policy dummies, included in equations (1)–(3) and not individually statistically significant, are not reported.

[2] For equation (1), the errors in predicting the rate of change in earnings to October 1969 and October 1970; for equations (2) and (3), errors in predicting the rate of change in earnings (central difference definition) at April 1969 and April 1970. The prediction error figures for 1970 in equations (2) and (3) are approximate, being based on 'actual' values for April 1970 which have to be interpolated from the monthly average earnings series. The April 1970 survey was not comparable with earlier and later survey results, necessitating this interpolation. For equation (4) prediction errors are the difference between actual and predicted rates of change year on year (1969–8; 1970–69). The 'actual' figure for 1970(IV) was estimated and corresponds to the figure shown in the *National Institute Economic Review*, no. 55 (Feb 1971) Table 5, p. 27.

actual change in prices), and the coefficient a, on expected prices, is unity, then we arrive at

$$\dot{w}_t - \dot{p}^e{}_t = f(u) \tag{2}$$

so that the Phillips relationship becomes one between the rate of increase in real wages and unemployment.

If the rate of productivity growth, $\dot{q}_t$, is regarded as independent of money wages and prices, then in long-run equilibrium, where inflation is proceeding at a constant rate and $\dot{p}^e{}_t = \dot{p}_t = \dot{p}_{t-1}$ and where prices are determined by a mark-up on wages per unit of output, that is,

$$\dot{p}_t = \dot{w}_t - \dot{q}_t, \tag{3}$$

we end up with

$$\dot{q}_t = f(u), \tag{4}$$

which is the expression for the natural rate of unemployment. This schema, which represents a recrudescence of classical macro-economic theory in a new form, requires empirical support in the shape of evidence to the effect that the coefficient of expected prices is indeed unity. Warren Smith, in a recent article,[8] suggests that in the United States no such evidence has been produced.

A similar conclusion would seem to hold for the United Kingdom, to judge from the results obtained by Solow[9] and by Parkin.[10] Table 4 shows some additional results obtained from a set of regressions in which 'price expectations' were used to help explain the rate of change in earnings, and these also suggest that the coefficient on 'expected prices' is substantially less than unity.

The general framework of the earnings change equations was the same as the one described earlier: using vacancies rather than unemployment, the change in earnings was postulated to depend on the level and rate of change of vacancies and upon expected prices.[11] For the latter, an 'extrapolation' scheme was used, various values being imposed for the extrapolation coefficient.

TABLE 4. PRICE EXPECTATIONS AND WAGE BEHAVIOUR

λ	*Coefficient of independent variable*					
	Constant	v^*_t	$\dot{p}^*_t$	$\dot{v}^*_t$	R^2	D.W.
0·4	0·71	0·23	0·75†	4·90†	0·45	2·561
	(0·62)	(0·17)	(0·34)	(1·11)	(1·26)	
0·5	1·12	0·21	0·67†	4·85†	0·50	2·562
	(0·65)	(0·16)	(0·26)	(1·00)	(1·19)	
0·6	1·49†	0·21	0·60†	4·73†	0·55	2·544
	(0·67)	(0·14)	(0·21)	(0·90)	(1·14)	
0·7	1·83†	0·21	0·55†	4·56†	0·60	2·498
	(0·68)	(0·13)	(0·17)	(0·80)	(1·09)	
0·8	2·13†	0·23†	0·51†	4·39†	0·65	2·422
	(0·68)	(0·11)	(0·14)	(0·72)	(1·06)	
0·9	2·39†	0·24†	0·47†	4·23†	0·69	2·319
	(0·69)	(0·100)	(0·13)	(0·66)	(1·04)	
1·0	2·64†	0·25†	0·45†	4·09†	0·72	2·196
	(0·70)	(0·09)	(0·11)	(0·61)	(1·03)	

Notes: The dependent variable, $\dot{e}^*_t$, is the change in average hourly earnings, defined in central difference form using April and October survey data and transformed, as with other variables listed, in the manner indicated below. v^*_t and $\dot{v}^*_t$ represent vacancies and change in vacancies, $\dot{p}^*_t$ the change in expected prices after transformation. λ is the 'extrapolation' coefficient, values for which were arbitrarily imposed, as shown in the table. Figures shown in brackets are standard errors of coefficients and † indicates statistical significance at 95 per cent level.

The basic equation was $\dot{e}_t = a + bv_t + c\dot{v}_t + d\dot{p}^e_t$ (1)

where $\dot{e}_t$ represents the change in earnings, v_t the level and $\dot{v}_t$ the change in vacancies, $\dot{p}^e_t$ being the expected change in prices; and inflation expectations were postulated as determined by the scheme:

$$\dot{p}^e_t = \lambda \dot{p}_t + (1 - \lambda)\dot{p}^e_{t-1},\ 0 \leqslant \lambda \leqslant 1. \qquad (2)$$

The following equation, for which estimates are given in the table above, can be obtained by lagging (1) once, multiplying it by (1 — λ) and subtracting it from the expression given by substituting (2) in (1):

$$\dot{e}^*_t = \alpha_0 + bv^*_t + c\dot{v}^*_t + d\dot{p}^*_t \qquad (3)$$

where $\dot{e}^*_t = \dot{e}_t - (1 - \lambda)\dot{e}_{t-1}$; $\alpha_0 = a\lambda$; $v^*_t = v_t - (1 - \lambda)v_{t-1}$; $\dot{v}^*_t = \dot{v}_t - (1 - \lambda)\dot{v}_{t-1}$ and $\dot{p}^*_t = \lambda \dot{p}_t$.

The notes to the table indicate the procedures used, and the coefficients quoted there for $\dot{p}^*_t$ represent estimates of the coefficient of expected inflation on this basis. The results (assuming, *inter alia*, that problems of simultaneity, etc., can be ignored) appear to indicate that the best explanation is achieved when the 'extrapolation coefficient' is set at high values, and that at these high values the coefficient of expected prices is well below unity – about 0·5.

Whilst this evidence and other similar experiments appear to cast doubt on the strong form of the expectations hypothesis, some important qualifications are in order. In particular, the difficulty of measuring price expectations needs stressing: it is unreasonable to think that the standard schemes are very realistic and other possibilities need exploring. It may be that 'threshold' effects are important – that only above certain critical levels of current inflation do expectations play a powerful role, and that even mechanical schemes would do better if they brought into the measurement further dimensions of the inflationary process (the rate of change of inflation itself, for example). One would clearly give some weight, then, to the argument that inflationary expectations, initially no doubt stoked up by the rise in import prices and indirect taxes following devaluation and then feeding upon the wage cost-induced price increases, have played a role in sustaining the wages explosion through 1970.

The suggestion that the wage push is due to a frustration of objectives for real income advance is in some respects similar to the price expectations argument, in so far as a rise in real incomes was choked off by higher prices caused by increased indirect taxation and higher import costs. But it is not an identical argument, and different policy conclusions are likely to be drawn from acceptance of one rather than the other. There is no worthwhile statistical evidence to offer on this point, for the core of the argument is precisely that it is the 'austerity' conditions of the recent period, in conjunction with enhanced expectations of real income objectives, which are the root of the problem. None the less the suggestion is clearly a very plausible one.

The argument that the relaxation of incomes policy was the dominant factor seems, if anything, less plausible than either of the two arguments reviewed above, if one were to accept the previous judgements made (by ourselves and others) that incomes policy was having very little net restraining effect (aside from the totally but only temporarily effective period of freeze and severe restraint in 1966–7). Of course, one might revise this judgement, in the light of the wages explosion and, so to speak, job backwards, to arrive at much bigger figures of effectiveness.[12] But this does not seem a very satisfactory line of argument, and the idea that incomes policy 'caused' the wages explosion must rest heavily, not on the ground that incomes policy was in fact exercising a much more severe net restraining influence than was realised, but on the ground that it grossly 'distorted' relativities. But it is not very clear what kind of detailed evidence could be produced to support this assertion.

While this review remains inconclusive as regards the ultimately dominant causes of the wages explosion, there still are some definite statements which can be made. It is quite clear that the orthodox 'Phillips'-type relationship will not explain the 1970 wage developments, even if adjustments are made to its specification to accommodate the developments of the three previous years. It also is clear that the wage push followed two years when prices were rising well above trend due to indirect taxes and import costs; this makes it plausible to believe that inflationary expectations and frustrated anticipations of real income growth played a role, though these cannot be satisfactorily quantified. And, finally, whilst the previous period of incomes policy may have had some part to play in stimulating subsequent wage inflation, it seems unlikely to have been of overwhelming importance.

DISAGGREGATED PRODUCTIVITY AND PRICE MOVEMENTS

The suggestion was made above that the transmission of international to domestic inflation was more complicated than is conveyed by the simple picture of increases in import costs and export prices, perhaps geared up by consequent wage demands. The following simple model, of which a more sophisticated version has appeared in the *Swedish Journal of Economics*,[13] gives an important role to differential productivity movements, combined with universality in domestic money wage movements.

The basic idea is that the economy can be divided into two sectors, a competitive sector in which prices are in the main determined by international competition and a sheltered sector whose output is not traded internationally (the public sector, services, buildings, etc.). In the competitive sector enterprises are assumed to be price-takers, and the price level is then determined by world movements. Given prices determined in this way, wages in the competitive sector rise, by the additional amount of the increase in productivity in that sector, subject to the maintenance of profitability of enterprises. This rise in wages sets the pace for increases throughout the economy. However, in the sheltered sector, productivity as a rule rises less than in the competitive sector; consequently prices will rise more than in the competitive sector. Thus the domestic rate of inflation will be higher than the rate of inflation in internationally traded goods and services.

The general features of this model are familiar in other contexts: in accounting, for example, for the faster rate of rise of the prices of services than of goods[14] and in the rationale for the 'relative price effect' nowadays used in forward estimates of public expenditure. There are two important applications to the model in the present context. First it shows how devaluation could give rise to an increase in money wages through its effects both on import prices and on export prices. Secondly, it shows how for countries operating fixed exchange rates, and with sizeable trade with the rest of the world, any objectives concerning price stability need to be related to world movements. For very small countries no doubt the domestic inflation must just follow the world inflation in the manner indicated by the model. For a larger economy, such as the British, there is a greater tolerance. The penalties for departing, in an upward direction, from the rate of inflation given by world conditions – in terms of its effect on the balance of payments and employment – may be less immediate and apparent in a large economy than in a small one so that there is a range of possible alternative rates of domestic inflation from which a best objective might be selected; but it would appear, however, to be unrealistic to aim for outright stability if the world movement of prices of internationally traded goods and services was rather strongly and persistently upwards.

The central strands of the model cannot be expected to be matched exactly by the facts. A looser requirement than that money wage increases should be uniform, for example, is that their dispersion should be less than that of productivity growth. There is evidence that this is, in fact, the case. Table 5 gives relatives of average earnings, output per head and (where possible) wholesale prices for twenty industrial and services groups on a base 1964 = 100. It can be readily seen that the spread of the average earnings relatives is much less than the spread of productivity relatives, and also rather less than that of prices. Where comparable price data are available, the coefficient of variation for prices is over twice that of average earnings, and that for productivity five times as much. There is no clear association between average earnings and productivity.

It may well be that international movements would make a target of outright stability for British prices unrealistic. Nevertheless it is instructive to use the model to show up the implications of achieving outright stability of prices because the structural implications remain whatever is the target chosen for the average increase of prices in the domestic economy.

Table 6 shows the rates of increase in twenty components of the consumers' price index at factor cost,[15] and Fig. 1 indicates, in the right-hand panel, the size of the individual requirements necessary to stabilise the overall index, the dispersion remaining the same as observed over the period 1964–9.[16] The components are listed in the order of their rate of change in the period 1959–64, and this ranking did not change very much in 1964–9, nor is it very different from the ranking observed over the period 1955–65 (cf. *National Institute Economic Review*, no. 38, Nov. 1966). On the whole, the factor cost price of manufactured goods appears to have risen less than that of services (although there are exceptions, notably books, newspapers and magazines). The fall in the index for cars in the period 1959–64 followed by a slight increase in the following five years is striking. Of course the trend in purchase tax on motor cars has been downwards so that a fall in the market price should not be too surprising, but this is a factor cost index. It is, however, an index which depends on both new and second-hand prices for cars and motor-cycles. We constructed an index of the price of new cars at factor cost for a range of models since 1952. This shows a slight upward trend in the factor cost price over the whole period with a steep acceleration since 1968.

TABLE 5. PRICES, EARNINGS AND OUTPUT PER HEAD BY INDUSTRY GROUP 1964–69
(relatives for 1969, 1964 = 100)

	Average earnings	*Output per employee*	*Wholesale prices*	*Output*	*Employees in employment, Great Britain, June*
Agriculture, forestry, fishing	139·9[1]	143·0	...	106·7	74·6
Mining and quarrying	129·0	119·2	...		
Food, drink and tobacco	139·8	117·1	114·1	116·0	99·1
Chemical and allied	140·0	133·6	106·3	135·9	101·7
Metal manufacture	136·3	108·1	111·7[2]		
Engineering and electrical	135·7	127·1	115·2	132·4	104·2
Shipbuilding	148·1	97·9	...	88·4	90·3
Vehicles	136·8	114·6	101·0[3]		
Metal goods n.e.s.	137·0	104·2	117·0[4]	104·6	100·4
Textiles	139·0	129·9	108·8		
Leather, fur, etc.	129·5	101·4	...	91·3	90·0
Clothing and footwear	134·0	107·7	110·1	98·5	91·5
Bricks, pottery, and glass	136·4	115·4	...	110·7	95·9
Timber, furniture	133·0	98·5	118·4	97·3	98·8
Paper, printing, publishing	138·4	110·2	115·9	112·8	102·4
Other manufacturing	137·3	114·4	...	126·0	110·1
All manufacturing	137·4	116·7	117·7		
Construction	138·5	116·5	120·6[5]	106·8	91·7
Gas, electricity and water	128·1	132·4	124·1[6]		
Transport and communication	144·6	119·5	121·2[7]	112·3	94·0
Miscellaneous services	137·9	105·2	133·9[8]	102·9	97·8
All industries and services					
mean	*137·0*	*115·8*			
standard deviation	*4·7*	*12·1*			
coefficient of variation	*0·034*	*0·104*			
Industries and services for which wholesale prices are available					
mean	*137·2*	*115·3*	*113·8*		
standard deviation	*2·28*	*11·10*	*4·38*		
coefficient of variation	*0·017*	*0·096*	*0·038*		

Source: *Monthly Digest of Statistics*; *National Income and Expenditure*

[1] Agriculture only. [2] Steel only. [3] Factor cost price of cars.
[4] Mechanical engineering. [5] Value of new construction.
[6] Retail price index for gas and electricity (October–October).
[7] Retail price index for transport and vehicles (October–October).
[8] Retail price index for miscellaneous services (October–October).

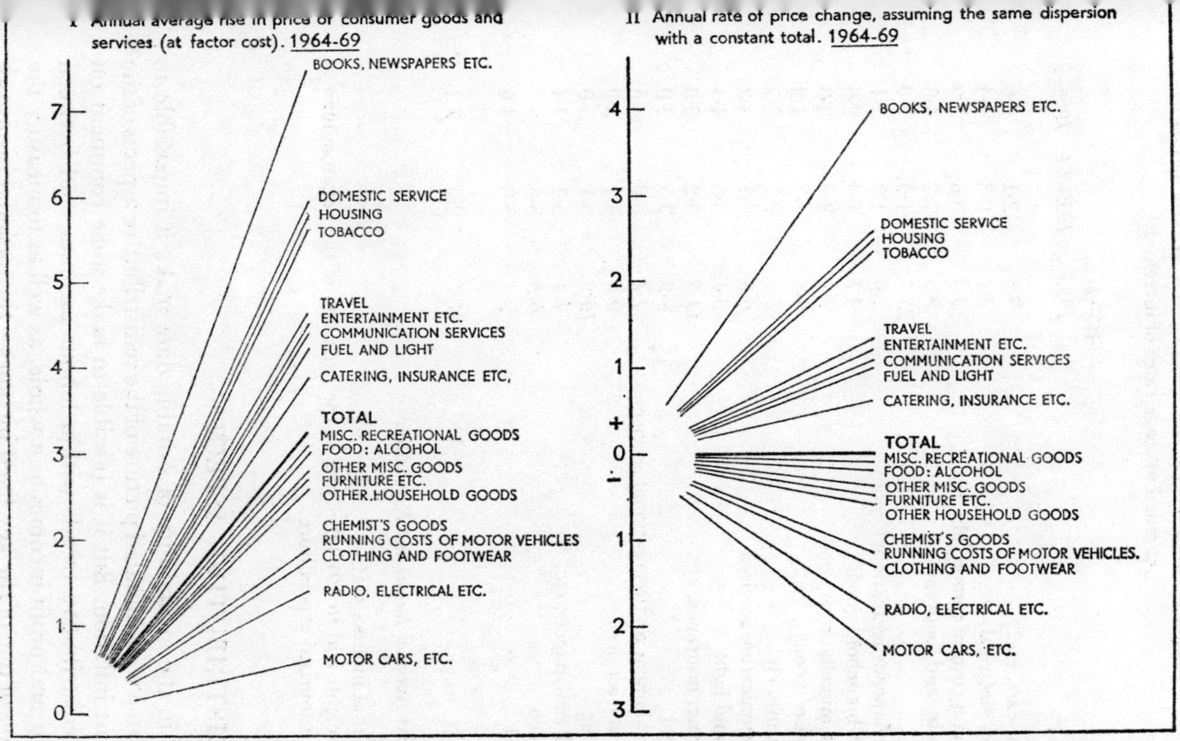

Fig. 1. The dispersion of consumer prices (at factor cost), 1964–69, and the implication of a stable price index. (For an explanation of the methods used to estimate the price indices, see text.)

Source: *National Income and Expenditure*

TABLE 6. CHANGES IN THE COMPONENTS OF THE C.P.I.[1]
(annual average rates of increase)

	Weight in 1963	*1959–64*	*1964–9*
Motor-cars, etc.	*3·2*	–2·1	0·6
Radio, electrical, etc.	*2·4*	0·3	1·4
Running costs of motor vehicles	*3·5*	0·6	1·9
Clothing and footwear	*9·5*	1·2	1·8
Food	*23·8*	1·5	3·0
Miscellaneous recreational goods	*2·0*	1·9	3·1
Other household goods	*3·1*	1·9	2·6
Other miscellaneous goods	*1·3*	2·6	2·8
Chemists' goods	*1·5*	2·7	1·9
Furniture, etc.	*2·4*	2·7	2·7
Communication services	*0·9*	2·7	4·2
Fuel and light	*5·1*	3·0	4·4
Catering, insurance, etc.	*11·9*	3·2	3·9
Alcohol	*6·0*	3·5	3·0
Entertainment and recreational services	*1·7*	3·8	4·5
Domestic service	*0·6*	4·2	5·9
Housing	*10·9*	5·1	5·8
Books, newspapers, etc.	*1·4*	5·2	7·4
Tobacco	*6·5*	5·8	5·7
Travel	*3·4*	5·8	4·6
Total	*101·1*[2]	2·4	3·2

Source: *National Income and Expenditure*

[1] Net of indirect taxes.
[2] Weights add to 101·1 because of the exclusion of the negative item of foreign tourists' expenditure.

REDISTRIBUTIVE ASPECTS

Lags in the availability of suitable data make it impossible to present a well-rounded picture of the redistributive aspects of the present inflation. But it is possible to make some comment on the redistributive trends within labour incomes, and between labour and profit incomes as a whole, as well as to measure the erosion of one of the key fixed incomes – the national insurance retirement pension.

Labour incomes: men, women and juveniles

As between men, women and juveniles, changes in the basic wage rate indices during 1970 indicate a continuing faster rate of rise for juveniles than for adults, and a bigger rise for women than for men. In the latter case, this largely cancelled out an earlier tendency in the opposite direction, while for juveniles the margin above the average rate of increase declined. Table 7

TABLE 7. BASIC WEEKLY WAGE RATES: MEN, WOMEN AND JUVENILES
(per cent rates of increase)

	December 1968–December 1969	*December 1969–December 1970*	*September 1968–December 1970*	
			Total	*Average per annum*
Men (18 and over)	5·8	12·7	22·6	9·5
Women (18 and over)	3·9	15·0	22·0	9·2
Juveniles	9·9	15·3	30·8	12·7
All manual workers	5·8	13·2	23·0	9·6

Source: *Employment and Productivity Gazette*

shows movements in the basic wage indices for the three groups over the period from September 1968 (the date of the New Earnings Survey), and they are given in graphical form in Fig. 2.

Major wage settlements over the period covered appear to have granted percentage wage increases for women which were greater or at least equal to those for men. However, wage negotiating groups for industries which employ predominantly female workers are among those whose wage increases over the period have been relatively low. Of nine major national negotiating groups which are reported to cover more females than men, six (which cover approximately 800,000 females) have had percentage increases in basic wage rates which were below the average for all manual workers. Since well over half of these women will be eligible for increases in their basic wage rates early in 1971, or have wage claims under consideration, it is likely that the index of basic wage rates of female manual workers will grow faster than for men during the early part of 1971, and that the relative position of females will regain and improve on that which existed in September 1968.

Juveniles form the other main group of manual workers. They include boys and girls under the age of eighteen, and constituted at the time of the 1966 Census 4·7 per cent of males and 7·6 per cent of females in employment. Basic wages of this group increased by 30·8 per cent from September 1968 to the

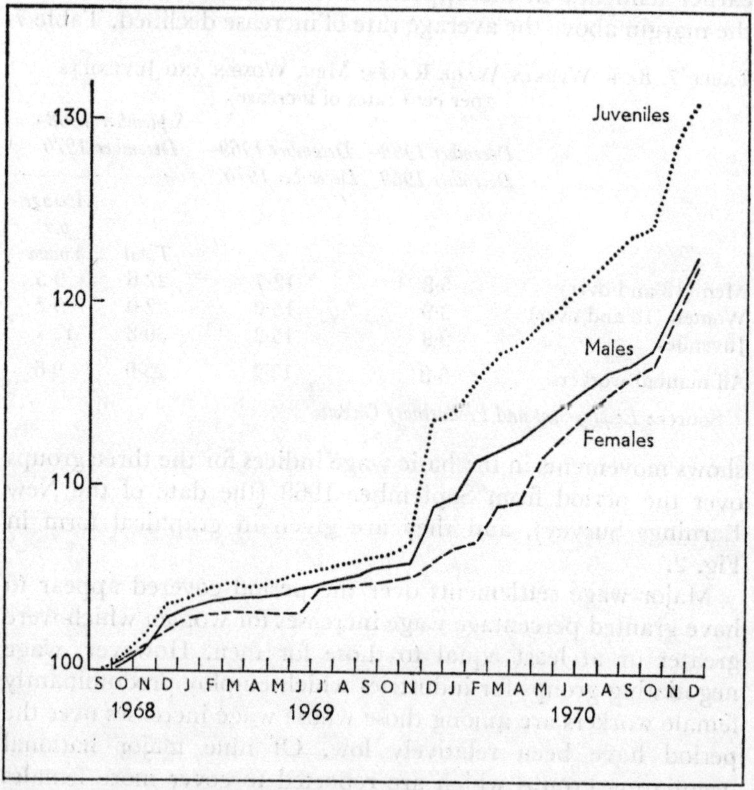

Fig. 2. Indices of basic weekly wage rates of manual workers (September 1968 = 100).

Source: *Employment and Productivity Gazette*

end of 1970, and this increase was considerably higher than for the other groups of manual workers. The main improvement in their relative position occurred in December 1969, and since that time their basic wage rates have increased at approximately the same rates as those for women.

Lowest- and highest-paid workers

Some further impression of the redistribution going on within labour incomes can be obtained by analysing wage settlement data according to the relative rates of increase negotiated for workers on different points in the wage scale (lowest, middle and highest paid or unskilled, semi-skilled, and skilled). The settlement data do not include a record of the number of workers at each point in the wage scale affected by the change, a difficulty which precludes comparisons of the average increases negotiated for workers of different skill levels. However, it is possible to compare the numbers of groups obtaining relatively higher or lower rate increases for skilled and unskilled workers, and to weight these numbers by the estimated total number of workers affected (using weights drawn from the *New Earnings Survey*).[17] The results of this set of calculations are set out in Table 8, and they indicate that over the whole period from September 1968 to December 1970, and within both sub-periods, there was a tendency for the lowest-paid/unskilled worker to fare better than or at least as well in obtaining rises in his basic rate as the highest-paid/skilled workers. This tendency was stronger than appears from the calculations set out in Table 8 if account is additionally taken of the fact that the basic wage of lowest-paid workers varies considerably from one negotiating group to another. For it appears that the tendency to obtain higher rate increases for the lowest-paid/unskilled than for the higher-paid/skilled worker was much stronger in negotiating groups where the rate for the lowest paid was very low than it was for the groups taken as a whole. Thus, groups covering 43 per cent of male workers in the analysis had in September 1968 basic weekly wage rates for their lowest-paid workers which were below £11 per week; and these groups negotiated agreements over the period in which the lowest-paid workers were given higher percentage increases than skilled workers, and lowest-paid workers received percentage wage increases above the average for all manual workers more frequently than did groups with higher basic rates for low-paid workers. Weighting these 'lowest low-paid' groups by the number of males covered, 86 per cent are found to have negotiated increases for lowest-paid workers above the average

TABLE 8. CLASSIFICATION OF NEGOTIATING GROUPS BY RELATIVE INCREASES AWARDED TO SKILLED/UNSKILLED

(groups settling between September 1968 and December 1970)[1]

Increase in basic rates	*1969*		*1970*		*September 1968–December 1970*	
	Number of groups	*Weighted percentage*	*Number of groups*	*Weighted percentage*	*Number of groups*	*Weighted percentage*
Relatively higher for unskilled (or lowest paid)	14	48	20	35	19	51
Same relative increase for all skill levels	14	31	10	27	4	10
Relatively higher for skilled (or highest paid)	13	21	11	38	18	39

Source: Department of Employment and Productivity, *Time Rates of Wages and Hours of Work* (updated by reference to the monthly information on *Changes in Rates of Wages and Hours of Work*); *New Earnings Survey*

[1] Groups covered are those distinguished in the *New Earnings Survey*, Sept 1968.

for all manual workers (compared to 51 per cent for all groups) and 90 per cent negotiated increases for them above those for their skilled workers (which again compares with 51 per cent for all groups).

A further indication of this redistributive effect is afforded by the observation that whereas the (weighted) proportion of groups in 1968 with a lowest-paid basic rate of £11 or less was 43 per cent, in December 1970 the proportion with a lowest paid rate of £13·52½ or less (i.e. 23 per cent, or the average rate of increase, up on £11) was only 10 per cent.[18]

Earnings data are not available on so up-to-date a basis for this kind of analysis, but the figures which are available tend to modify the picture obtained from analysing the movement in basic rates. Table 9 compares rates of increase in average

TABLE 9. INCREASES IN AVERAGE EARNINGS: SEPTEMBER 1968–APRIL 1970 (per cent)

	Manual men	*Manual women*	*Non-manual men*	*Non-manual women*
Lowest decile	13·9	14·3	14·1	9·7
Lowest quartile	14·3	17·8	14·7	11·7
Median	14·3 (12·2)[1]	18·5 (9·3)[1]	12·9	12·8
Upper quartile	14·2	17·6	12·6	12·6
Highest quartile	13·9	15·6	10·9	11·3

Source: *Employment and Productivity Gazette*

[1] Figures in brackets show corresponding increase in average basic weekly rate.

earnings between given points in the distribution of earnings in the two surveys of September 1968 and April 1970. It will be seen that, in general, and with the exception of 'non-manual men', the rate of increase between the lowest decile and lowest quartile points in the two surveys was less than the median, although for all groups the middle of the distribution seems to have fared better than the upper part. In addition, rates of increase in average earnings of women between the two surveys appear to have been higher than for men, so that although women have been losing relative to men in terms of basic wage rate increases up to the first quarter of 1970, the reverse was the

TABLE 10. SHARES OF EMPLOYMENT INCOMES AND GROSS TRADING PROFITS IN DOMESTIC INCOME[1]
(per cent)

	1959	*1960*	*1961*	*1962*	*1963*	*1964*	*1965*	*1966*	*1967*	*1968*	*1969*	*1970*[2]
Employment incomes	67·4	66·7	68·2	68·7	67·9	67·8	68·2	69·5	68·9	69·4	70·6	72·1
Gross trading profits	15·4	15·8	14·4	13·7	14·6	14·8	14·2	12·6	12·9	12·0	10·7	9·7

Source: *Economic Trends*

[1] After allowing for stock appreciation.
[2] First three quarters seasonally adjusted.

case for average earnings. (This comparison must be a tentative one, however, because in the basic wage statistics men include males of eighteen and over, whereas for average earnings, only males of twenty-one or over are included.)

PROFITS

Table 10 shows the shares of employment incomes and of gross trading profits in the total of domestic income (stock appreciation being excluded).[19] It is clear that on top of the normal

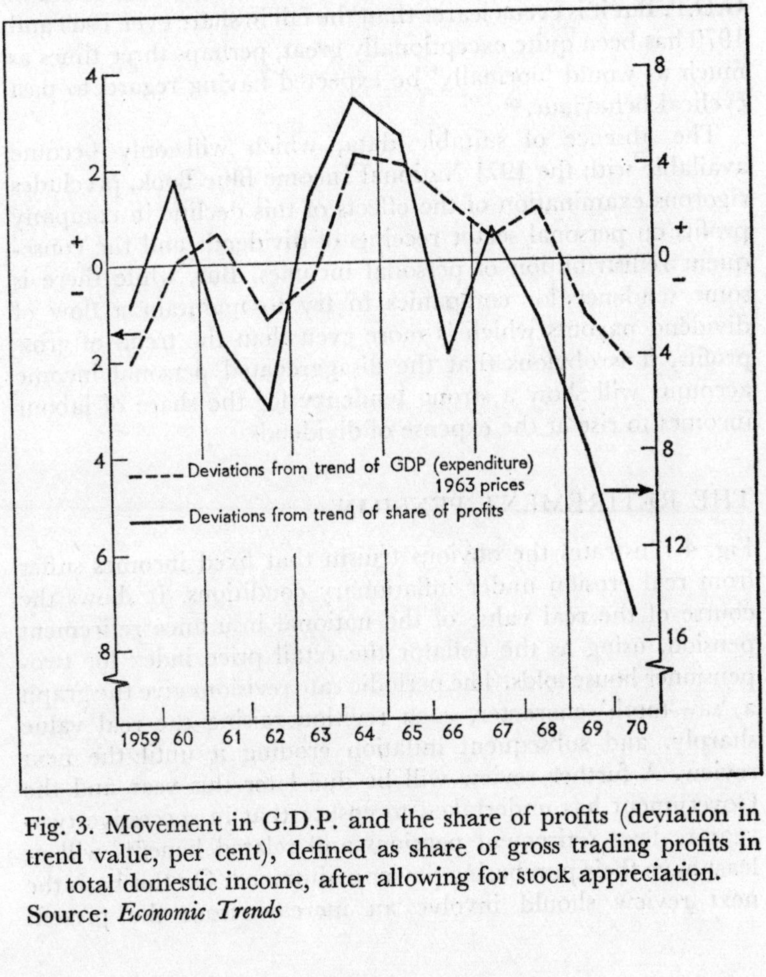

Fig. 3. Movement in G.D.P. and the share of profits (deviation in trend value, per cent), defined as share of gross trading profits in total domestic income, after allowing for stock appreciation.
Source: *Economic Trends*

trends (slightly upwards for employment incomes and downwards for profits) the movement of the shares in the past two years, especially in 1970, has been quite sharply in favour of employment incomes. In absolute terms there was a fall in 1969 of 1½ per cent in profits, and on the average of the first three quarters of 1970 (seasonally adjusted figures) there was no recovery from this decline last year.

Some fall in the share of profits would, it is true, be expected to occur at a time when demand pressure has been falling. This point emerges from Fig. 3 which shows deviations from trend in the profits share side by side with deviations from the trend of G.D.P. But it is even clearer than the fall in share over 1969 and 1970 has been quite exceptionally great, perhaps three times as much as would 'normally' be expected having regard to past cyclical behaviour.[20]

The absence of suitable data, which will only become available with the 1971 National Income Blue Book, precludes rigorous examination of the effects of this decline in company profits on personal sector receipts of dividends and the consequent redistribution of personal incomes. But, while there is some tendency for companies to try to maintain a flow of dividend payouts which is more even than the trend of gross profits, it is obvious that the disaggregated personal income accounts will show a strong tendency for the share of labour incomes to rise at the expense of dividends.

THE RETIREMENT PENSION

Fig. 4 illustrates the obvious truism that fixed incomes suffer from real erosion under inflationary conditions. It shows the course of the real value of the national insurance retirement pension, using as the deflator the retail price index for two-pensioner households. The periodic rate revisions give the graph a 'saw-tooth' character, each revision raising the real value sharply, and subsequent inflation eroding it until the next review. A further review will be due later this year and the Government has undertaken to ensure that in successive two-year reviews retirement pensions and related benefits will at least have their purchasing power maintained. On this basis the next review should involve an increase from the present (married couple) pension rate of £8.10 to something like £9.20.

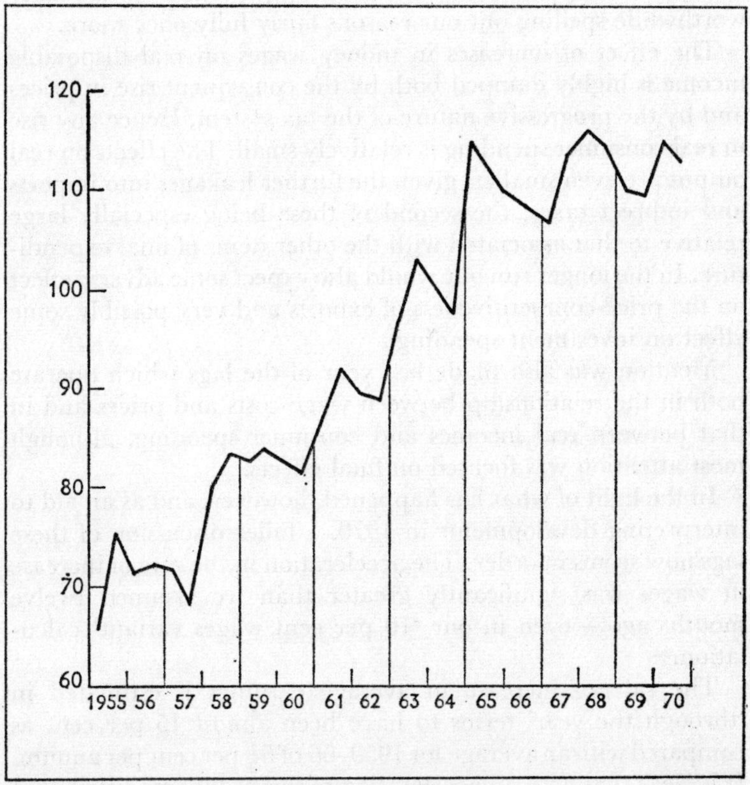

Fig. 4. The real value of the retirement pension (1963 = 100; half-yearly averages), defined as the National Insurance retirement pension rate, for married couples, deflated by the retail price index for two-pensioner households. Figures before 1962 are partly estimated.

Source: *Employment and Productivity Gazette*; *Economic Trends*; *Annual Abstract of Statistics*

MACRO-ECONOMIC ASPECTS

In the issue of the *National Institute Economic Review* for February 1970, we stated that '[we do] not deny that labour incomes are improved in real terms by aggressive wage claims, but at the same time . . . [we consider] that the main result of higher money wages is higher prices, not higher consumption'.[21] Our view on this question remains unchanged but it is probably worthwhile spelling out our reasons fairly fully once more.

The effect of increases in money wages on real disposable income is highly damped both by the consequent rise in prices and by the progressive nature of the tax system. Hence any rise in real consumer spending is relatively small. The effects on real output are even smaller, given the further leakages into imports and indirect taxes, the second of these being especially large relative to that associated with the other items of final expenditure. In the longer run one would also expect some adverse effect on the price-competitiveness of exports and very possibly some effect on investment spending.

Mention was also made last year of the lags which operate both in the relationship between wage costs and prices and in that between real incomes and consumer spending, although most attention was focused on final effects.

In the light of what has happened, however, and as an aid to interpreting developments in 1970, a fuller discussion of these lags now seems in order. The acceleration in the rate of increase in wages was significantly greater than we assumed twelve months ago – even in our '10 per cent wages variant' calculation.[22]

The rate of increase in average earnings is estimated in 'through the year' terms to have been almost 15 per cent as compared with an average for 1959–66 of $5\frac{1}{2}$ per cent per annum. It is clear that with an acceleration of this order any distributed lag relationship (even one in which wage rises were fully compensated for by price increases) will throw up a significant divergence between the rates of increase in costs and prices *in the short run*. Hence a short-run acceleration in real incomes is possible, and this is indeed what appears to have happened in 1970. Fig. 5 shows the gap between increases in wage rates and retail prices and the large rise which occurred (before tax) in real wage rates in 1970.

We have computed an alternative outcome for 1970 using actual values of the exogenous variables such as exports, investments, etc., but assuming that average earnings rose at a steady 6 per cent per annum rate from the fourth quarter of

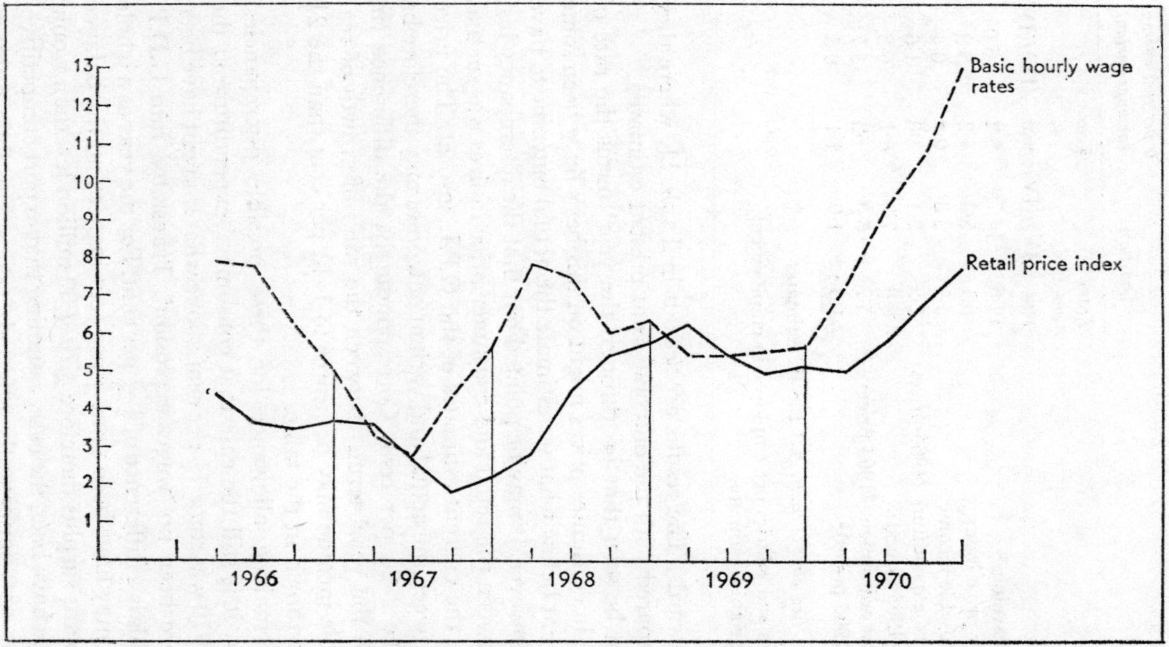

Fig. 5. Wages and prices: annual rates of change in retail prices and basic hourly wage rates, 1966–70 (percentages, quarter on same quarter a year previous).

Source: *Economic Trends*; *Monthly Digest of Statistics*

TABLE 11. 1970 OUT-TURN AND '6 PER CENT WAGE ALTERNATIVE'
(per cent changes)

	Out-turn		*6 per cent average earnings variant*	
	Year-on-year	(IV)/(IV)	*Year-on-year*	(IV)/(IV)
Average earnings[1]	12·6	14·7	6·2	6·0
Consumer price index	6·1	5·3	4·2	3·9
Real disposable income	3·7	3·8	0·9	0·4
Consumers' expenditure (1963 prices)	2·9	3·1	2·0	1·6
Imports (1963 prices)	6·8	7·8	6·1	6·8
Factor cost adjustment (1963 prices)	5·7	6·0	4·3	3·7
G.D.P. (1963 prices)[2]	1·5	1·0	1·1	0·3

Source: *Economic Trends*, N.I.E.S.R. estimates

[1] Wages and salaries per employee in employment.

[2] Compromise estimate.

1969 onwards. The results are set out in Table 11, where they are compared with the outcome as at present estimated.

It can be seen that in 'through the year' terms the rate of increase in consumer prices might on this basis have been some 1½ per cent below what we estimate the actual outcome to have been. However, it may be pointed out that the discrepancy last year between the retail and consumer price indices was such as to make the current estimates of the C.P.I. suspect. The price 'gap' between the actual and variant outcomes may therefore be more like 2–2½ per cent. Correspondingly, the difference (in 'through the year' terms) between the rates of growth of real disposable income may be nearer to 1–1½ per cent than the 2½ per cent shown in the table.

After making allowance for these possible discrepancies, however, it is still the case that consumers' expenditure at the end of 1970 was some 1½ per cent above what it might have been had there been no 'wages explosion'. Translated into G.D.P. terms, this is a difference of ½–¾ per cent. For the year as a whole imports may have been some ¾ per cent higher and the balance of payments surplus therefore £70–£80 million less than would otherwise have been the case, assuming that export competitiveness was not significantly affected, taking the four quarters together.

The matter does not, however, rest here, unless we assume, somewhat implausibly, that wages will continue to accelerate *ad infinitum*. In a sense, the extra 1½ per cent in real incomes at the end of 1970 was 'borrowed' and (given unchanged policies and/or little acceleration in the exogenous demand items)[23] it will have to be 'paid back'. Put more scientifically, this means that while the wage cost increases which have already occurred are still working through into prices, a deceleration in the rate of average earnings increase must lead to a reversal of the real effects experienced while wages were accelerating. Even the modest deceleration which we assume in our main forecast[24] – down to an annual rate of earnings rise of 10½ per cent at the end of this year and 9½ per cent at the end of 1972 – leads to a very modest rise in the total of real disposable incomes this year and a small fall through next year, as prices continue to rise by 7¾ and 6¼ per cent respectively. It is obvious that were earnings to fall back to the rates of increase experienced prior to 1969, this effect would be even stronger.

The income effects (via imports) on the balance of payments are also, of course, reversible, though they are combined with a (not automatically reversible) loss of export price competitiveness, the effects of which are likely to be spread over two or three years. This latter deflationary influence is implicitly included in our forecast in so far as our 'exogenous' export projection includes an allowance for a relative rise in United Kingdom export prices.

The balance of the effects of these developments, past and forecast, on investment, is difficult to determine and we have made no allowance one way or the other in our forecast. The increase in demand last year as a result of wage rises might be thought to have a stimulative effect, which would, however, be reversed as the price lag worked itself out. On the other hand, it seems fairly well established that the wage increases were, at least in part, secured at the expense of profits, and the net acquisition of financial assets by companies has now been negative for an unprecedented three-year period. Hence whilst rising demand may have meant a higher desired level of investment, the means to finance it were not available. We have therefore assumed the net effect (over 1970–2) to be zero.

FORECASTING CONSUMER PRICES

Whilst the wages explosion of 1970 defies econometric explanation, the behaviour of prices – given that of wages – does not appear to have posed comparable problems. This proposition is subject to one caveat, as is made clear below, concerning the reliability of recent official price data.

The chief price index for which estimates are generated in the National Institute's forecasting procedure is the C.P.I., the implicit deflator of the national accounts series of consumers' expenditure. The relationship employed represents a form of mark-up equation, but is sufficiently generally formulated, being a distributed lag relationship, to accommodate alternative views on the speed with which prices are adjusted to changes in unit costs. The results obtained do, however, indicate a relatively rapid adjustment.

Thus, the general form of the relationship is:

$$\text{CPIfc} = a+b(1-\lambda)\sum_{i=0}^{\alpha}(\text{WS/GDP})_{t-i}+c(1-\lambda)\sum_{i=0}^{\alpha}\lambda^{i}(\text{MP})_{t-i}$$

where CPIfc is the C.P.I. at factor cost (i.e. net of indirect taxes),[25] WS/GDP represents unit wage and salary costs (i.e. wages and salaries per unit of output) and MP represents import prices (the unit value index of imports of goods). Transformed in the usual way, and estimated with quarterly data over the period 1958 (I)–1969 (IV), this yields:

$$\text{CPIfc} = \underset{(0{\cdot}0129)}{0{\cdot}0131} + \underset{(0{\cdot}066)}{0{\cdot}763}\text{CPIfc}_{t-1} + \underset{(0{\cdot}02)}{0{\cdot}035}\text{MP}_t + \underset{(0{\cdot}09)}{0{\cdot}315}(\text{WS/GDP})_t$$

$$R^2 = 0{\cdot}998;\ \text{D.W.} = 2{\cdot}52;\ \text{S.E.E.} = 0{\cdot}0044.$$

These results indicate a relatively rapid passing on of costs into prices, a result which was, if anything, strengthened when the estimation was carried out using an Almon lag procedure. About a quarter of the final effect on prices would come through in the same quarter as the increase in costs and more than half by the end of the subsequent six months.[26]

This equation, which clearly fits the estimation period well, tended to overpredict the price level in 1970. However, a substantial part of this error may be due to defects in the official recording of price rises in the C.P.I. The R.P.I. (retail price index) and the C.P.I. normally move closely together: in 1970, however, a substantial gap began to open up between them. Comparing rates of change on the same period a year before, the increase in the R.P.I. was 0·5, 0·8 and 1·5 per cent higher in the first three quarters respectively of 1970 than the increase in the C.P.I. To the extent that these discrepancies throw doubt on the value of the official C.P.I. figures, the 'true' overprediction of price changes given by the equation amounts to rather little. Nevertheless, it would not have been at all surprising if in the face of the vary rapid rise in wage costs prices had failed to adjust quickly enough.

NOTES

1 One thinks of the work of L. Dicks-Mireaux (*Oxford Economic Papers*, XIII) and latterly of Gillion (*National Institute Economic Review*, no. 46) in this regard.

2 J. K. Bowers, P. C. Cheshire and A. E. Webb, 'The Change in the Relationship between Unemployment and Earnings Increases: A Review of some Possible Explanations', *National Institute Economic Review*, no. 54 (November 1970).

3. It may seem surprising that the table does not show a fall in unit non-labour factor costs in the last period. That it does not is due to the fact that this item includes not only gross trading profits (which did in fact fall – gross, as well as per unit of output in this period) but also rent and self-employment incomes (which rose) as well as the surpluses of public corporations and enterprises. That the rise due to indirect taxes is so much larger in 1968–9 than in 1967–8 (it might have been expected to be about the same) is due to the literal accounting nature of the exercise. If S.E.T. is accounted for on an 'accrual' rather than on a payments basis, which is how it is treated in the national accounts, this discrepancy would be ironed out. Presumably, in practice, firms will tend to have based their prices on an accruals-based concept of S.E.T., so that variations in profit margins absorb some of the temporary rises and falls in recorded net indirect taxes.

4. O.E.C.D., *Inflation: The Present Problem* (Paris, Dec 1970).

5. The previous tendency for export prices to rise less than domestic prices had, however, never applied to the United Kingdom with quite the same force as to the generality of overseas industrial nations. See *National Institute Economic Review*, no. 43 (Feb 1968) p. 23.

6. See, for example, *National Institute Economic Review*, no. 47 (Feb 1969) pp. 27–9; no. 51 (Feb 1970) pp. 34–6; and in no. 54 (Nov 1970) the article by Bowers, Cheshire and Webb, 'The Change in the Relationship between Unemployment and Earnings Increases'.

7. This follows the investigation by Bowers, Cheshire and Webb, op. cit.,

which indicated that since 1966 and until 1969 vacancies continued to give a reasonable fit in equations of this type, where unemployment did not.

8. W. L. Smith 'On some Current Issues in Monetary Economics: An Interpretation', *Journal of Economic Literature*, II, 3 (Sept 1970).

9. R. M. Solow, *Price Expectations and the Behaviour of the Price Level* (Manchester U.P., 1969).

10. Michael Parkin, 'Incomes Policy: Some Further Results on the Determination of the Rate of Change of Money Wages', *Economica*, n.s., XXXVII, 148 (Nov 1970).

11. Seasonal and 'incomes policy' dummies failed to perform well and were omitted from the regressions quoted in Table 4. Central difference expressions of the rate of change were used.

12. An additional argument for doing this would be that it is now apparent that, relative to unemployment, vacancies suggest a much more buoyant labour market in 1967, 1968 and 1969, and some of the assessments of incomes policy used unemployment-related equations to check policy effectiveness. These equations would presumably have tended to give rather low predicted figures of the rate of wage and earnings increase in the absence of incomes policy, leading to unduly low estimates of policy effects. But, for what it is worth, the earnings/vacancies relationships quoted in Table 3 above do not show a significant effect when incomes policy 'dummies' are used, and the estimated effect, even taken at face value, is extremely small.

13. Gösta Edgren, Karl-Olaf Faxén and Clas-Erik Odhner, 'Wages, Growth, and the Distribution of Income', *Swedish Journal of Economics* (1969).

14. Cf. G. D. N. Worswick, 'Services and Inflation', *Manchester Statistical Society* (1962).

15. The estimates were obtained by subtracting from the value of expenditure at current market prices the net indirect taxation as given for each group in the Blue Book. The resultant current price estimates were then deflated by the constant (1963) price estimate to obtain the deflators. As the constant price estimates were only available at market prices, the procedure involves assuming that the average rates of net indirect taxation for each group in 1963 remained constant throughout.

16. This in turn implies that the relative apportionment of expenditure on different goods and services remains unchanged at the zero overall rate of price inflation.

17. *New Earnings Survey* Table 142.

18. 'Redistribution' is implicity defined here as a narrowing of differentials in percentage terms. Redistribution of this kind is, of course, quite compatible with a widening of differentials in absolute terms.

19. Comparison of income shares within the corporate sector might have been preferable, but 1970 data on this basis were not available. The annual data for 1959–69 show, however, that the trends and year-to-year movements in corporate income shares are very similar to those in total income shares shown in the table.

20. Deviations of the profits share from its trend were regressed on deviations from trend G.D.P. and the 1969 and 1970 observations were then

predicted from the equation. The results suggested the order of magnitude referred to in the text.

21. *National Institute Economic Review*, no. 51 (Feb 1970) p. 27.

22. Ibid.

23. The rate of growth of the sum of public authorities' current spending, investment and exports is forecast to be 2·7 per cent again this year, and next year 3·1 per cent.

24. This refers to the forecast for the economy given in chap. ii of the *National Institute Economic Review*, no. 55 (Feb 1971)–Eds.

25. The adjustment for indirect tax content is arrived at essentially by assuming that all net indirect taxes are 'fully passed on'. This assumption is modified in the case of S.E.T.

26. See *National Institute Economic Review*, no. 52 (May 1970) pp. 17–18.

2. Inflation and the Southampton Model

IVOR PEARCE*

My brief as I understand it is to demonstrate in twenty minutes how inflationary forces are generated and transmitted in the Southampton Model. Unfortunately this is a brief which it is much easier to accept than it is to speak to. The reason for this is that it is not possible simply to isolate one or two equations of our model and say that these alone measure the forces which determine price changes. As in the real world we are attempting to simulate, to explain inflation it is necessary to explain everything.

The philosophy which underlies the specification of the Southampton Model demands that each equation should represent some decision taken with a definite end in view by someone or some group of persons on the basis of evidence which they have before them. We are trying to get away from a method of prediction which relies upon more or less complicated methods of extrapolation and move towards a model designed to identify first the data which economic units look at when they take decisions and second the weight which they attach to each element of that data.

If we wished to put to our model the question 'What causes inflation?' it would be natural to look first at the set of equations which reflect price-fixing decisions. There are two parts to this, first the determination of ex-works prices by manufacturers and second the choice of distributors' profit margins. Central to the model we have equations which relate ex-works price changes to unplanned stock changes (or length of order books), profitability and a capacity index. It seems sensible to suppose that a manufacturer will raise prices when demand is high (when stocks fall below the planned level), and more so when production is approaching full capacity; or he may raise prices when

* Ivor Pearce is Professor of Economics at the University of Southampton.

profitability is low. This is the kind of hypothesis we have been trying to test and there is some evidence that over our sample period profitability and capacity together 'explain' a fair proportion of observed price changes. Obviously it is a crucial question whether a producer faced with excess demand (falling stocks) will raise prices or increase production. Those who favour the demand management approach to economic control are now being forced to recognise that increased production does not *necessarily* induce increased aggregate demand any more than cheaper money necessarily induces more investment. High unemployment combined with large wage increases would naturally follow if producers, worried by inflation, chose to meet increased demand by higher prices rather than greater production. So far, however, the evidence we have suggests that this has not been the case and that producers have increased output in response to demand. On the other hand our sample data does not extend to the most recent years and it may well be that the picture has very much changed in the last eighteen months or so.

Evidently, there is an important question to be settled which cannot be settled by looking at data on price formation alone. The formation of production plans is just as important an element in an inflationary situation as price policy. Thus in the Southampton Model we have a set of supply equations, by industry, which attempt to identify and measure the forces which determine manufacturers' output decisions. We imagine that pricing and output plans are made simultaneously on the basis of the same evidence, namely the state of demand, profitability and capacity. Closely allied to these equations and equally relevant to the problem of inflation we have also functions determining investment in fixed equipment, the arguments being a capacity usage index and a variable defining changes in the 'normal' ratio of output to capital.

Results so far indicate that (again over the sample period) producers react to events in what we have come to believe is the traditional way. Price tends to be adjusted to recover a normal profit whilst production is designed to maintain an 'ordinary' level of stocks. Price changes are best explained by profitability changes whilst output changes tend to be determined by demand. These conclusions are consistent with the idea that the level of employment can be easily regulated by controlling aggregate demand and that inflation remaining once employment is so regulated must be cost-induced. Against this, however, I emphasise once again that our sample period does not go beyond 1966 and casual empiricism suggests that something new may have happened recently. It seems likely that beliefs about inflation are beginning to play some part in investment and production decisions so as to reduce both production and investment. Increased demand might then simply mean increased prices. This is a hypothesis we are proposing to test.

We come now to the second part of market price determination, namely decisions regarding distributors' profit margins. Distribution is of course a kind of production, but the amount of distribution service produced is not well measured by the value of commodities distributed. It is difficult to distinguish the demand for the goods distributed from the demand for the service distribution. We cannot readily observe an increased pressure of demand for distribution services, nor is there much evidence that changes in distributors' margins are generated by demand changes. Even so it is clear that variations in distributors' margins are an important element in price changes. Indeed in some industries it appears that changes in distributors' margins have generated price changes of up to 9 per cent. The best 'explanation' of distributors' margins we have found is sales variations. Our findings lend some support to the hypothesis that distributors have relatively fixed costs and that they fix margins so as to yield fixed total profits. Thus when sales increase, margins tend to fall relatively.

The general price level is of course made up of ex-works prices, margins, import prices and taxation. Naturally therefore the Southampton Model is arranged so that external effects, i.e. rising world prices or changes in tax policy, are incorporated. In part the object of the computing exercise is to find the best weights in which the various elements are to be combined. The price index so evolved then enters into other equations, e.g. the wage equations, wherever appropriate.

I now re-emphasise the point with which I began. In the Southampton Model price-fixing equations when determined do not enable us to predict the expected degree of inflation without reference to the rest of the model. They simply present us in turn with the problem of predicting the unplanned stock changes and profitability which are the arguments of the price-fixing equations. On the other hand the two arguments clearly represent respectively the 'demand-induced inflation' and the 'cost-induced inflation' of economic theory.

To predict 'unplanned stock changes' we use the identity:

> unplanned stock changes equals production plus imports less consumption less exports less planned stock changes.

Each element in this identity has to be separately predicted. We have import equations and consumption equations. Consumption calls for the prediction of aggregate spending which calls for prediction of the wage bill. It calls also for an estimate of intermediate demand which is generated by production plans through an input–output translator.

On the profitability side we have to consider both wages and prices of intermediate goods, as well as corporate taxation. The loops in the model are quite complex and it would be out of place to attempt to give more detail here. Something should be said, however, about wage determination since the Conference is likely to be very much concerned with this.

Pursuing the general philosophy of our model we see the wage-rate fixing process as a decision taken presumably on the basis of evidence. We attempt to relate wage-rate changes to changes in measurable facts, trying to identify those facts which are most likely to influence decision. The Phillips curve relates wage-rate changes to the level of unemployment. Is it likely that trade union leaders are much influenced in making wage claims or accepting settlements by the level of unemployment in their industry? No doubt they are concerned, but one would suppose that the idea of a trade-off between wages and employment would be quite foreign to their thinking. Naturally both employers and unions use every argument they can devise, whether good or bad, but we are interested only in those arguments which carry weight.

Union leaders will make large claims when they can see high profitability in their industry, and when other unions have recently won large increases. They will demand large increases also when prices have been rising rapidly. And these are arguments which it is not easy to resist. Employers on the other hand will accede to large demands when profitability is high and when losses due to strikes are likely to be high, that is, when the ratio of capital to output in the industry is high. Furthermore employers will more readily grant wage increases when they believe that they can pass on those increases in higher prices, that is, when demand is high and when there is a belief that the Government of the day will not allow aggregate demand to fall. To us it seems possible to incorporate measures of all of these influences into a wage-fixing equation which will more accurately represent the wage-bargaining process than the Phillips curve. Indeed the Phillips curve seems a good example of a statistical relation which may or may not exist but which, even if it did, could not really reflect a decision process. If it exists it may simply show that certain conditions associated with large increases in wage rates are frequently associated also with low unemployment. The relation is some kind of reduced form, an observed relation which tells us little about cause and effect. Thus we can never be quite sure why it works when it does or why it does not work when it doesn't.

3. Inflation and the London Business School Model

R. J. BALL*

We have been attempting to make forecasts for the British economy since the end of 1966. This was just after the severe measures of July when, amongst other things, a wage freeze was imposed. Since then, for short-term forecasting purposes we have had a model which has been like Hamlet without the Prince of Denmark. The one thing that we have not had in the system is a wage-rate equation.

Before we started forecasting in 1966, we had an equation explaining movements in wage rates which was rather similar to many that others had estimated. After it was dropped out, we have forecast wage rates by a combination of a series of things that Michael Artis has described; that is to say, we have tried to assess the likely development of wage rates from information about existing claims and our own judgement of the economic climate. Our procedure has been to take the forecast of the wage rate, arrived at in this way, and to translate it into a forecast of average earnings which became a function of the wage rate and the pressure of demand.

In estimating the pressure of demand we have not made any use of the unemployment statistics. We have been particularly concerned at various stages about what the unemployment figures were really telling us about the pressure of demand, and we have had considerable difficulty in forecasting the level of unemployment itself. It appeared to us that in 1966 there was some shift in the relationship in unemployment and output movements – a relationship which we have never really satisfactorily re-established since. As a result, instead of unemployment we have tended to use other proxy measures of the pressure of demand and in particular simply the ratios of either

* R. J. Ball is Professor of Economics at the London Graduate School of Business.

G.D.P. or industrial production to their trend values. We could of course have looked at more sophisticated demand measures, making some use of vacancy statistics for example. The difficulty about this is that in a simultaneous system the individual components of the measures have themselves to be explained. This in turn tends to bring you back to some simple relationship with output. Some very interesting work has been done on which measures of the pressure of demand correlate most closely with variables like wage-rate changes. However, the general point remains: if, for example, the capacity output was developed from a production function approach, the elements of the production function themselves have to be explained. Moreover, a great deal of slippage enters into the system. It does not follow that because measure A actually correlates better than measure B that better predictions will be obtained in the end if measures A and B are outputs of the system.

Since 1966 we have followed much the same pattern in so far as wage rates have been made exogenous and subsequently related to earnings. The relationship we have in the model is not fundamentally different from what we started with. The price sector of the system is discussed below. It might be worth pointing out, however, that in fact we have two models – L.B.S. 2 which is the basic short-term forecasting model which is discussed in this paper, and a much larger version, L.B.S. 3, which is designed for more detailed policy and simulation work. In L.B.S. 3 we are doing something along the lines presented by Ivor Pearce. In L.B.S. 3 there are ten consumption categories and ten consumer prices to explain. Consumer prices are derived from wholesale prices which in turn are obtained by combining appropriate industrial prices. In this system industrial prices are generated for fourteen industry groups. Such a system requires us of course to make use of input–output information to tie up the industrial with the wholesale prices. However, this system has not yet been used for forecasting so I shall not discuss it any further in detail.

There are at present eight prices in L.B.S. 2, a model which now runs to about a hundred equations and identities. These are the G.D.P. deflator, the price of final expenditure, the price of total consumer expenditure, the price of non-durable expenditure, the price of durables, the price of imports of goods and services, the price of exports, of goods and services and the price of new housing. Leaving on one side the foreign trade prices, the general approach is to pivot on a forecast of the price of final expenditure which is derived from a mark-up equation similar to the one described by Michael Artis and used by the National Institute. The main difference is that we have attempted explicitly to introduce a proxy for standard cost. We have tried several measures of this, but one of the simplest, which seems to work quite well, is to take a four-quarter moving average of unit labour costs. One test of the reasonableness of this measure may be derived from comparing the coefficients of actual unit labour costs and of a variable consisting of the difference between actual and standard costs proxied in this way. The coefficients turn out to be statistically indistinguishable, which implies that the proxy for standard cost could well stand on its own. Other factors such as expenditure tax rates and import costs enter into this equation in a familiar manner. The lags implied by this relationship are relatively short, in so far as all the effects of the change of unit labour costs come through in the space of twelve months, but they are not distributed in the way the National Institute's are. We have become rather worried in practice over the last three years about distributed lag equations which fit well but fall to pieces in our hands when we actually come to make predictions over successive periods. I am quite sure that you are all familiar with the problem of seeing a 99·99 per cent fit with a large number of lagged endogenous variables disappear in effect when we actually come to ask ourselves what is going to happen in eighteen months' time. We have become very wary about this and have therefore tried as much as we can to avoid these simple lag structures.

From the final expenditure price we then derive the price of total consumption. The relationship between the two is not tight. There is some cyclical movement which is partially removed by introducing the ratio of the final expenditure price to its trend value as an additional variable. Serial correlation, however, remains high, which is a characteristic of nearly all our price equations. The price of durables is in turn related to the price of total consumption and some attempt to allow for tax-rate changes which is, however, not statistically significant at present. Non-durable goods price is obtained by identity. To complete our estimate of the G.D.P. deflator from its identity, we require prices for exports and imports. Our export price equation is similar to the one discussed by Michael Artis. We also introduced a world price which is certainly important because one knows that export prices on the whole have tended to rise less rapidly than domestic prices, in previous periods at any rate. Clearly, the interpretation is that the world price acts as a competitive constraint which limits the actual rise in export prices relative to domestic prices. Import prices were treated as exogenous up to about the end of 1968 when we became rather dissatisfied with the procedure on the whole. Import prices show some cyclical variation and have tended to respond to some extent to movements in world trade. When world trade has been growing relatively rapidly, import prices have tended to rise relatively rapidly and vice versa. This relationship has not been doing too well recently and we have been tending to underestimate rises in import prices. I suspect that we should have some world price measure similar to that introduced in the export price equation to pick up the faster overall rate of world inflation. It may be noted that both export and import prices equations contain dummy variables to allow for the change in the exchange rate in 1967. It is interesting to note that these say that the impact effect of devaluation was to raise export prices by about 8·4 per cent and import prices by about 9·7 per cent. This is interesting in view of the low value that this puts on the shift in terms of trade as an impact result of devaluation.

I have already referred to the considerable degree of serial correlation in these relationships. I referred earlier to other work on price relationships for L.B.S. 3 and it is quite remarkable the way in which serial correlation is widespread throughout these relationships. We have tried all sorts of ways to remove it with alternative variable and lag specifications but have been notably unsuccessful. The most sensible thing to do at this stage is simply to make more efficient estimates after an appropriate serial correlation transformation. The equations as currently estimated are given in an annex to this note.

It might well be asked why we have not put more research into the movement of wage rates rather than leaving them exogenous as we have done. The answer to this is really twofold: firstly, as we and the National Institute have repeatedly emphasised, you can have very substantial errors in your forecast of wage rates without this having very large effects on your forecast of the real economy. The difference between a 5 per cent wage-rate increase and an 8 per cent wage-rate increase on an annual basis with regard to forecast of consumers' expenditure in real terms is not very great. Within the range that wage rates have moved prior to the end of 1969 the game did not seem to be worth the candle. The second is that, in terms of the feedback into the system in so far as prices feed through to determine profits and investment and foreign trade competitiveness, the lags that we have in these relationships are really quite long. Consequently, errors in forecasting other components of the real G.D.P. may also not be greatly affected by errors in wage-rate forecasting. Where forecasts of the real G.D.P. are wrong they are usually wrong for other reasons. However, this does not absolve us from the need to do further research, although one of the difficulties of managing a large economic system is that resources cannot often be intensively applied to very particular problems such as this. The question then arises as to what likely hypotheses there are that might explain the recent inflationary phenomenon.

One notes that this afternoon there will be extensive discussion on the whole issue as to whether the Phillips curve has broken down, whether we have misinterpreted it or whether in fact it never existed in the long run anyway. A number of issues have come out of the work of Phelps, Lucas, Rapping *et al.* which relate to these questions. Our feeling from an operating point of view is that the relationship has certainly broken down in its traditional form so that some rehabilitation is needed. My own favourite candidate as part of the rehabilitation process is what I have called the frustration hypothesis. Broadly speaking, this implies that wage-earners do seek to realise some real wage objectives, the frustration of which eventually causes the Phillips curve to shift. Recent discussion of this problem has of course been focussed on price expectations and the argument has been that it is expectations about prices which shift the Phillips curve. Recent testing of the expectations hypothesis seems to show that the coefficient on the price expectation is less than unity, but the problem of measuring expectations in this context raises serious problems as to how this result is to be interpreted.

There will no doubt be a variety of *ad hoc* explanations put forward in the course of today as to the origins of the current inflation. It is perhaps worth a last reflection that whatever these ideas attempt to explain in the context of the U.K. economy, they may well fail to account for the fact that inflation has been proceeding on a world-wide scale. Germans, Frenchmen, Irishmen and Englishmen may all have their *ad hoc* explanations for what is going on in their own countries, but it is highly likely that these explanations vary from country to country and do not provide any unifying theme. It is this factor among others that inevitably makes one suspicious about the various *ad hoc* explanations that can be offered. In this context one cannot be terribly optimistic that some simple regression analysis is going to clear this matter up very quickly.

ANNEX
LONDON BUSINESS SCHOOL FORECASTING MODEL

PRICE EQUATIONS

Dependent variables — *Independent variables*

(1) $$PGDP = (FE/GDP)PFE - (MGS/GDP)PMGS - (FCA/GDP)TX - (SET^*/GDP)$$

(2) $$PFE = \underset{(0{\cdot}0207)}{0{\cdot}1228} + \underset{(0{\cdot}0814)}{1{\cdot}3487}ULC + \underset{(0{\cdot}1414)}{0{\cdot}6986}(PMGS(MGS/FE)) + 1{\cdot}1313(TX(FCA/FE)) - 1{\cdot}4441\left(ULC - \tfrac{1}{4}\sum_{i=0}^{3} ULC\right) - \underset{(0{\cdot}0029)}{0{\cdot}0020}Q1 - \underset{(0{\cdot}0029)}{0{\cdot}0016}Q2 - \underset{(0{\cdot}0030)}{0{\cdot}0007}Q3$$

$\bar{R}^2 = 0{\cdot}9969$ D.W. $= 0{\cdot}7$ S.E. $= 0{\cdot}0068$

$$(3)\ PTC = \underset{(0{\cdot}006)}{1{\cdot}006PFE} - \underset{(0{\cdot}0362)}{0{\cdot}1133(PFE/PFET)} - \underset{(0{\cdot}002)}{0{\cdot}004Q1} - \underset{(0{\cdot}002)}{0{\cdot}001Q2} + \underset{(0{\cdot}002)}{0{\cdot}001Q3} + \underset{(0{\cdot}0362)}{0{\cdot}1069}$$

$\bar{R}^2 = 0{\cdot}998$ D.W. $= 0{\cdot}8$ S.E. $= 0{\cdot}005$

$$(4)\ PND = ((TC*PTC)-(CD*PD))/CND$$

$$(5)\ PD = \underset{(0{\cdot}067)}{0{\cdot}320} - \underset{(0{\cdot}0066)}{0{\cdot}0087Q1} - \underset{(0{\cdot}0070)}{0{\cdot}0097Q2} - \underset{(0{\cdot}0066)}{0{\cdot}0124Q3} + \underset{(0{\cdot}1225)}{0{\cdot}5656PTC} + \underset{(0{\cdot}0659)}{0{\cdot}0856TX}$$

$\bar{R}^2 = 0{\cdot}96$ D.W. $= 0{\cdot}7$ S.E. $= 0{\cdot}1$

$$(6)\ PXGS = \underset{(0{\cdot}0871)}{0{\cdot}2427} + \underset{(0{\cdot}1190)}{0{\cdot}3257PTW} + \underset{(0{\cdot}0387)}{0{\cdot}4363PGDP} + 0{\cdot}084D9V - \underset{(0{\cdot}0034)}{0{\cdot}0027Q1} - \underset{(0{\cdot}0034)}{0{\cdot}0045Q2} + \underset{(0{\cdot}0035)}{0{\cdot}0003Q3}$$

$\bar{R}^2 = 0{\cdot}99$ D.W. $= 1{\cdot}5$ S.E. $= 0{\cdot}008$

$$(7)\ PMGS = \underset{(0{\cdot}0186)}{0{\cdot}8460} + \underset{(0{\cdot}0008)}{0{\cdot}0012T} + \underset{(0{\cdot}000324)}{0{\cdot}000945(TW/PTW)} + \underset{(0{\cdot}0093)}{0{\cdot}0972D9V} - \underset{(0{\cdot}0054)}{0{\cdot}0008Q1} - \underset{(0{\cdot}0058)}{0{\cdot}0169Q2} - \underset{(0{\cdot}0054)}{0{\cdot}0080Q3}$$

$\bar{R}^2 = 0{\cdot}98$ D.W. $= 1{\cdot}2$ S.E. $= 0{\cdot}0125$

$$(8)\ PMGSA = PMGS\dagger$$

$$(9)\ PNH = \underset{(0{\cdot}04)}{-1{\cdot}34} + \underset{(0{\cdot}000125)}{0{\cdot}000189\left(\tfrac{1}{4}\left(\sum_{i=1}^{4} AB/PNH\right)\right)} + \underset{(0{\cdot}0606)}{2.318PGDP} + \underset{(0{\cdot}0080)}{0{\cdot}0101Q1} + \underset{(0{\cdot}0078)}{0{\cdot}0121Q2} + \underset{(0{\cdot}0078)}{0{\cdot}0019Q3}$$

$\bar{R}^2 = 0{\cdot}99$ D.W. $= 1{\cdot}2$ S.E. $= 0{\cdot}018$

† defined as exogenous.

(10) $PFET = 0{\cdot}7102 + 0{\cdot}009T$
$(0{\cdot}0103)\ (0{\cdot}0002)$

$\bar{R}^2 = 0{\cdot}97$ D.W. $= 0{\cdot}09$ S.E. $= 0{\cdot}002$

(11) $FCA = -517{\cdot}2 + 0{\cdot}2552TC + 2{\cdot}32T$
$(149{\cdot}9)\ (0{\cdot}0345)\quad (0{\cdot}91)$

$\bar{R}^2 = 0{\cdot}97$ D.W. $= 1{\cdot}7$ S.E. $= 0{\cdot}98$

DEFINITION OF VARIABLES

(S.A. signifies seasonally adjusted variable)

Endogenous

(1) *GDP* S.A. Gross domestic product (average of expenditure and output estimates) (£m., 1963)

(2) *CND* S.A. Non-durable consumption (£m., 1963).

(3) *DC* S.A. Durable consumption (£m., 1963).

(4) *MGS* S.A. Imports of goods and services (£m., 1963) (excluding payments for U.S. military aircraft).

(5) *FCA* S.A. Factor cost adjustment (£m., 1963).

(6) *PGDP* Implicit price deflator for *GDP* (1963 = 1).

(7) *PFE* Implicit price deflator for *FE* (1963 = 1).

(8) *PTC* Implicit price deflator for total consumption (1963 = 1).

(9) *PND* Implicit price deflator for *CND* (1963 = 1).

(10) *PD* Implicit price deflator for *CD* (1963 = 1).

(11) *PXGS* Implicit price deflator for *XGS* (1963 = 1).

(12) *PMGS* Implicit price deflator for *MGS* (1963 = 1).

(13) *PMGSA* S.A. Implicit price deflator for *MGS* (seasonally adjusted) (1963 = 1).

(14) *AB* Advances on mortgages by building societies (£m., current).

(15) *PNH* Index of unit values of new dwellings mortgaged by building societies (1963 = 100).

(16)	*ULC*	S.A.	Labour cost per unit of final expenditure.
(17)	*PFET*	S.A.	Trend value of *PFE*.
(18)	*FE*	S.A.	Final expenditure (£m., 1963).
(19)	*TC*	S.A.	Total consumers' expenditure (£m., 1963).

Exogenous

(1)	*Q1*		Seasonal dummies.
(2)	*Q2*		
(3)	*Q3*		
(4)	*T*		Time trend, starting 5401 (1, 2, 3, . . .).
(5)	*TW*	S.A.	World trade in exports ($ billion, 1963).
(6)	*PTW*		Implicit price deflator for *TW* (1963 = 1)
(7)	*TX*		Expenditure tax rate (1963 = 1).
(8)	*SET**	S.A.	Recorded payments of Selective Employment Tax (£m., current).
(9)	*D9V*		Dummy variable for devaluation. Value of 0·5 in 1967(IV), +1 in 1968(I) inwards, zero elsewhere.

4. A Study of Wages and Prices in the U.K. 1949-1968

J. D. SARGAN*

INTRODUCTION

This paper reports recent econometric work on the movements of wages and prices in the U.K. using the model first introduced by Sargan [7]. It also draws freely on work done by Vernon for his Ph.D. [8]. For the recent estimates a Chow test has been applied to each equation to test for differences in the coefficients in income policy-on/policy-off periods following the precedent of Lipsey–Parkin [4], but the differences have not proved to be significant.

THE SARGAN–KUH MODEL

Empirically the form of the equation below arose by noting that if the lagged real wage is introduced as a variable into a standard Phillips wage equation it is statistically significant. This is enough to reject models which exclude this variable. Two economic explanations suggest themselves. One is that this represents the demand of trade unions for a rising real wage rate, and their ability to press for higher wages when the real wage rate for any reason has fallen below its trend line. An alternative explanation suggests that the usual measure of unemployment is not a valid measure of the excess supply of labour, and that an equation of the form below can be derived by considering the interaction of the demand and supply of labour, assuming that both are responsive to the real wage rate. This type of explanation was put forward by Kuh [2] and is related to contributions contained in Phelps [6].

* J. D. Sargan is Professor of Economics at the London School of Economics and Political Science.

With the productivity variable in both wage and price equations, the results obtained are given below:

$$\log(w_t/w_{t-1}) = \underset{(2\cdot66)}{0\cdot2818} - \underset{(2\cdot51)}{0\cdot0699}\log(w_{t-1}/p_{t-1})$$
$$+ \underset{(2\cdot35)}{0\cdot0507}\log(Y_{t-1}/h_{t-1})$$
$$- \underset{(1\cdot64)}{0\cdot00768}\log U_{t-1} - \underset{(1\cdot63)}{0\cdot00329}\log(p_{t-1}/p_{t-4}$$
$$+ \underset{(1\cdot88)}{0\cdot0553}Q_{1t} + \underset{(0\cdot65)}{0\cdot00202}Q_{2t} - \underset{(0\cdot46)}{0\cdot00134}Q_{3t} \quad (1\text{A})$$

$$R = 0\cdot439 \quad \text{D.W.} = 1\cdot73 \quad \text{S.E.} = 0\cdot0089$$

$$\log(p_t/p_{t-1}) = \underset{(2\cdot21)}{2\cdot2816} + \underset{(4\cdot63)}{0\cdot1132}\log(pm_{t-1}/w_{t-1})$$
$$- \underset{(5\cdot32)}{0\cdot6389}(\log p_{t-1}/w_{t-1})$$
$$+ \underset{(2\cdot05)}{0\cdot4424}\log(Y_{t-1}/h_{t-1})$$
$$- \underset{(0\cdot94)}{0\cdot0504}\log(T_{t-1}) + \underset{(0\cdot57)}{(0\cdot0025)}d_t - \underset{(3\cdot51)}{0\cdot0040}t$$
$$- \underset{(0\cdot07)}{0\cdot00008}D_t + \underset{(0\cdot28)}{0\cdot00945}Q_{1t}$$
$$+ \underset{(1\cdot17)}{0\cdot00529}Q_{2t} + \underset{(1\cdot02)}{0\cdot00412}Q_{3t} \quad (2\text{A})$$

$$R = 0\cdot688 \quad \text{D.W.} = 2\cdot20 \quad \text{S.E.} = 0\cdot0120$$

The data is quarterly from 1949(IV) to 1968(IV). The variables are:

w_t = official wage-rate index
p_t = official retail price index
pm_t = official import price index
Y_t = real G.N.P.
h_t = total man-hours = number of men × average weekly hours
U_t = percentage unemployment
Q_{it} = seasonal dummy for ith quarter
T_t = indirect taxes – subsidies/value of consumption at factor cost

d_t = dummy = 1 policy-on
= 0 policy-off
D_t = trend dummy defined by $D_t - D_{t-1} = d_t$
R = uncorrected multiple correlation
D.W. = Durbin–Watson statistic
S.E. = standard deviation of equation error.
t-ratios occur in brackets below each coefficient.

In the discussion below, the 5 per cent confidence interval is used to judge significance.

DISCUSSION OF EQUATION (1A)

The coefficient of lagged real wages is significant and correctly signed. The coefficient of productivity is of the correct sign and significantly different from zero, but not significantly different from minus the coefficient of real wages. (This implies that real wages fully incorporate changes in productivity.) The coefficient of unemployment is not significant but correctly signed. On the other hand the coefficient of the price change variable is not significant, and its negative sign is not what would be expected on *a priori* grounds. The equation can then be interpreted either as the unions bargaining for a real wage rate which increases at the same rate as real labour productivity, or on a Kuh interpretation, as the tendency for money wage rates to be proportional to the value of the marginal product of labour (given a Cobb–Douglas production function). Thus the estimates support an equation of the Sargan–Kuh type, and give no support for a Phillips curve with expected price change variable. On the other hand the implied lag on the adjustment of wages is of the order of three and a half years, and this is certainly larger than has been found before with previous studies for earlier time periods.

DISCUSSION OF EQUATION (2A)

The equation used differs from that used in my previous paper by including a distributed lag, rather similar to that of Nield [5]. However, it is not clear that this is preferable on statistical grounds to the form I used previously which had only a short lag on the price of imports, no lag on the wage rate and an autoregressive error. However, the implied lag is short (four and a half months) and the other coefficients are of the expected sign and size except for the productivity variable. I have experimented with real G.N.P. per worker, and with the introduction of various capacity variables, without being able to remove this significant wrong-signed coefficient. Recent work has used a Wharton-type index and non-linear transformations of such indices. Work by Vernon used real G.N.P. deflated by trends, a Wharton-type index, and an index of excess demand for labour based on a Dow–Dicks-Mireaux index. In no case was the coefficient significant or such as to suggest an important impact of such variables on the rate of change of prices.

ALTERNATIVE FORMS OF EQUATION

In the wage equation the productivity variable can be replaced by a linear trend. The resulting estimated equation is:

$$\log\,(w_t/w_{t-1}) = \underset{(2\cdot13)}{0\cdot04343} - \underset{(2\cdot82)}{0\cdot1309}\log(w_{t1}/p_{t1}) + \underset{(2\cdot66)}{0\cdot00054t}$$

$$- \underset{(1\cdot69)}{0\cdot00777}\log U_{t-1} - \underset{(1\cdot39)}{0\cdot00279}\log(p_{t-1}/p_{t-4})$$

$$+ \underset{(2\cdot13)}{0\cdot00629}Q_{1t} + \underset{(0\cdot93)}{0\cdot00288}Q_{2t} - \underset{(0\cdot34)}{0\cdot00099}Q_{3t} \quad (1\text{B})$$

$$R = 0\cdot456 \quad \text{D.W.} = 1\cdot71 \quad \text{S.E.} = 0\cdot0088$$

There is a slight improvement in the equation error variance. The average lag of the adjustment of wages is now less than two years. The implied trend in real wage rates is 1·6 per cent per annum. If both the trend and productivity variables are included in the same equation, neither coefficient is statistically significant, although both have positive signs.

In the case of the price equation the major problem is the sign of the coefficient of the productivity variable, whose logarithm can be closely approximated by two linear trends, one corresponding to a rate of increase of 1·4 per cent per annum until the end of 1958, followed by a second trend corresponding to a rate of increase of 3·2 per cent per annum. It is possible to demonstrate that it is only the trends in the productivity variable which determine its sign in equation (2A) by introducing into this equation a new variable which is zero up to the end of 1958, and then increases at a rate of one unit per quarter. The equation is then estimated by:

$$\begin{aligned}\log(p_t/p_{t-1}) = {} & \underset{(0\cdot18)}{0\cdot2119} + \underset{(4\cdot59)}{0\cdot1023}\log(pm_{t-1}/w_{t-1}) \\ & - \underset{(5\cdot99)}{0\cdot6826}\log(p_{t-1}/w_{t-1}) \\ & + \underset{(0\cdot16)}{0\cdot0365}\log(Y_{t-1}/h_{t+1}) - \underset{(0\cdot12)}{0\cdot00543}\log T_{t-1} \\ & - \underset{(3\cdot00)}{0\cdot0031}t + \underset{(2\cdot34)}{0\cdot0019}D_{2t} + \underset{(2\cdot64)}{0\cdot01040}Q_{1t} \\ & + \underset{(2\cdot06)}{0\cdot00903}Q_{2t} + \underset{(1\cdot68)}{0\cdot00657}Q_{3t} \qquad (2\text{B})\end{aligned}$$

$$R = 0\cdot717 \quad \text{D.W.} = 2\cdot18 \quad \text{S.E.} = 0\cdot0115$$

$$\begin{aligned}D_{2t} &= 0 \text{ from } 1949(\text{IV}) \text{ to } 1958(\text{IV}) \\ &= t - 1958(\text{IV}) \text{ from } 1959(\text{I}) \text{ to } 1968(\text{IV})\end{aligned}$$

The introduction of D_{2t} makes the productivity variable non-significant, but has little effect on the other coefficients. (2B) is still unsatisfactory in the absence of any explanation for the change in trend in the equation. Further work is in progress exploring the use of different tax variables, the use of the yield on ordinary shares as a substitute for planned profit rate, and the use of average earnings as a substitute for wage rates (although earlier work by Sargan [7] and Vernon [8] showed that prices are better explained by wage rates than by average earnings).

THE EFFECT OF INCOMES POLICY

Following Lipsey and Parkin it was decided to test whether there was a significant difference between quarters when an incomes policy was or was not in force by making a covariance analysis (Chow test). For all recent versions of the equations, separate equations have been estimated for policy-on/policy-off

TABLE 1. DEPENDENT VARIABLE $= \log (w_t/w_{t-1})$

Independent variable	Coefficient estimates for Policy off	Coefficient estimates for Policy on	Difference in coefficient	t-ratio for difference
Constant	0·5559	0·0805	−0·4734	1·03
$\log (w_{t-1}/p_{t-1})$	−0·1218	0·0130	0·1348	1·49
$\log (Y_{t-1}/h_{t-1})$	0·1071	0·0118	−0·0955	0·97
$\log U_{t-1}$	−0·01060	−0·0526	0·00534	0·54
$\log (p_{t-1}/p_{t-4})$	−0·01236	−0·00074	0·01162	0·12
Q_{1t}	0·00747	0·00747	0·00209	0·34
Q_{2t}	0·00170	0·00447	0·00277	0·43
Q_{3t}	−0·00387	0·00271	0·00658	1·10

Sum of squared residuals with separate equations = 0·004942.
Sum of squared residuals with the same equations = 0·005483.
$F_{8,61}$ = 0·836 (5 per cent confidence limit = 2·10).

TABLE 2. DEPENDENT VARIABLE $= \log (p_t/p_{t-1})$

Independent variables	Coefficient estimates for Policy off	Coefficient estimates for Policy on	Difference in coefficients	t-ratio for difference
Constant	0·4992	−1·1721	−1·6713	0·53
$\log (pm_{t-1}/w_{t-1})$	0·0737	0·0388	−0·0349	0·40
$\log (p_{t-1}/w_{t-1})$	−0·7141	−0·7078	0·0063	0·02
$\log (Y_{t-1}/h_{t-1})$	0·0788	−0·1929	−0·2717	0·47
$\log (T_{t-1})$	−0·0214	0·0652	0·0866	0·49
t	−0·0039	−0·0026	0·0013	0·54
D_{2t}	0·0020	0·0020	−0·0000	0·01
Q_{1t}	0·00772	0·01454	0·00682	0·81
Q_{2t}	0·00933	0·01229	0·00296	0·29
Q_{3t}	0·00286	0·01283	0·00997	1·16

Sum of squared residuals for separate equations = 0·00829.
Sum of squared residuals for same equation = 0·00891.
$F_{10,57}$ = 0·43 (5 per cent confidence limit = 2·03).

periods using the Lipsey–Parkin definition of these periods and the sums of squares of errors have been obtained for comparison with those from a single equation estimated for the whole sample period. In no case has the resulting F-ratio proved to be significant; indeed it has always been less than one, showing that the differences between policy-on/policy-off coefficients are less than expected. As an example of these results, Table 1 gives the results for separate estimates of equation (1A), the last column being obtained by dividing the difference in coefficients by an estimate of its standard error.

Although the actual coefficients estimated for the policy-on periods are all close to zero, the differences in the coefficient as between policy-on and policy-off periods are not statistically significant.

In Table 2 similar estimates are present for equation (2B).

A DISAGGREGATED MODEL OF WAGE DETERMINATION

It is clear that the aggregate wage determination equation does not throw light upon the determination of wages at the industry level, and that a study of this may much improve the understanding of changes in the general wage-rate index. The following sections are drawn from econometric work carried out by Keith Vernon using a different sample period, 1956(I) to 1967(III), and in some cases different variables from the work above.

Very few empirical studies of wage-rate determination have been undertaken at the industry level for the post-war period in the United Kingdom, and this is rather surprising since one would consider that industrial analysis would be the thing to do considering the hazards outlined by Lipsey [3] in drawing policy implications from an aggregate Phillips curve. It seems sensible to estimate wage-change equations for different industries and to note whether regression coefficients of variables that are appropriate to aggregate work coincide with those for an aggregate equation. In addition wage determination at the disaggregated level enables us to investigate several hypotheses that are not meaningfully described at the macro-level and in particular the phenomenon that workers in one industry will pay attention to overall wage movements and recent wage changes in other industries when filing their wage claims.

Principal hypothesis to be tested

The hypotheses to be tested with reference to industrial wage changes may be divided into two categories: (i) those hypotheses that can be readily translated into aggregate terms; and (ii) those that may only be investigated at some level of disaggregation.

The former include unemployment where the hypothesis in economy-wide terms becomes the aggregate Phillips curve, and the latter includes the phenomenon of where the employees in an industry will look to guidelines given by wage increases in other industries when they put in for a pay increase. This is described in more detail below.

The first variables investigated are the industry and overall unemployment levels, U_j and U respectively, to represent the excess demand for labour, since at this stage it was uncertain whether the overall climate of the labour market or localised industry demand was important.

In a preliminary analysis only a single price variable was included and this was the real wage adjustment term W/C, introduced by Sargan [7], though in the full analysis annual changes in consumer prices were included.

The next variable included in this analysis is the industrial wage rate lagged, deflated by the lagged aggregate wage rate. This represents an attempt to formalise a hypothesis suggested by Sargan [7] in his Colston paper but not tested there. Sargan hypothesised that a union, when it puts in for a wage claim, will have an eye on wage bargains struck earlier in the annual sequence of wage settlements. The union will compare the wage of its members with some 'normal' level of wage rates which may be approximated by the aggregate wage rate. If the union's wage compares unfavourably with this normal wage level then it will push for higher wage increases and per contra, if it compares favourably with the 'normal' wage level, then pressure on employers for wage increases will not be great. One thus expects the variable to appear in a regression equation with a negative coefficient.

The 'comparison' effect is a very attractive hypothesis and one that cannot be tested in an aggregate model. The difficulty is that the hypothesis is couched in terms of unions. Nevertheless all we have is industrial wage-rate data and it seemed profitable to test the hypothesis on this.

In addition to the so called 'comparison effect' two similar variables were introduced. The 'comparison effect' is couched solely in terms of comparisons of wage levels. Now might not one union compare not only its wage level with the wage level in other unions but also its wage change with other wage changes obtained by other unions that precede them in the annual wage round? The hypothesis is incorporated by introducing aggregate wage changes lagged one and two quarters.

Of course it is more likely that employees in an industry or union will follow a lead given by another specific industry or union.

The subscript j denotes the industry and the variable $\overline{W}$ represents the aggregate weekly wage rate.

The question now is to determine the industry which employees in another will follow in the annual wage round.

The path followed here is to correlate each industry's annual wage change W_{it}/W_{it-4} with the annual wage change of all other industries lagged one quarter and to select the industry whose lagged annual wage change had the highest simple correlation coefficient with the current annual wage change of the industry under investigation.

The rationale for believing that such comparisons will be made is found in Dunlop [1]. Dunlop believed that workers in different industries who come into contact for such reasons as that one industry supplies raw materials to the other will constitute a wage contour, and the promixity will cause the workers of one industry to have information of increases in the other and they will bargain for comparable increases.

The results of correlating W_{it}/W_{it-4} for eighteen different industries with W_{jt-i}/W_{jt-5} yielded some interesting results and in each case the industry j is given with those whose lagged wage changes it has the highest simple correlation r.

Industry i	*Industry j*	*r*
Agriculture, forestry, fisheries	Food, drink and tobacco	0·71
Leather goods	Transport and communication	0·55
Bricks and pottery	Transport and communication	0·68
Timber	Professional and scientific services	0·71
Other manufacturing	Construction	0·55
Gas, electricity and water	Bricks and pottery	0·65
Transport and communication	Professional and scientific services	0·71
Distributive trades	Textiles	0·58

Professional and scientific services	Mining and quarrying	0·71
Miscellaneous services	Professional and scientific services	0·58
Construction	Timber	0·58
Clothing and footwear	Paper and printing	0·73
Paper and printing	Professional and scientific services	0·81
Mining and quarrying	Professional and scientific services	0·53
Chemicals and allied industries	Construction	0·58
Textiles	Transport and communication	0·84
Food, drink and tobacco	Professional and scientific services	0·79
All metals combined	Mining and quarrying	0·81

In all cases the simple correlation coefficient is high and professional and scientific services appears to be the 'industry' to which other industries will frequently look when they want a yardstick for comparison. Increases in the professional and scientific services are on occasion highly publicised, particularly those in the civil service and in education, and in this respect will be looked on as benchmarks for other industries.

Transport and communication wage increases are also important here. Workers in many other industries, particularly clothing and textiles, are likely to come into contact with workers in the transport industry and information of a wage increase in the latter is likely to be passed on. Most of the other industries in the above table may be looked at in this manner or, in Dunlop's terminology, as 'wage contours'.

All these results indicate that as well as aggregate wage changes we should include past wage changes of other specific industries in our industrial wage-change equations.

We have described in some detail the principal economic hypothesis incorporated. However, several subsidiary hypotheses are investigated principally with regard to periods of wage restraint.

Subsidiary hypothesis

The simple time trend t is introduced to allow for increasing trade union pressure forcing wage changes up over time. Seasonal dummies S_{rt} are included since on the hypothesis of an annual wage round in each industry the seasonal element in industrial wage changes may be expected to be large, though it is doubtful whether this would be captured using annual wage changes.

The six dummy variables F_{qt} are reckoned to allow for periods of Government-prescribed pay pauses and wage freezes and to test the efficiency of such restraint. These political dummies take the value one when a wage restraint was thought to be operative and zero otherwise.

F_1 represents the period of restraint under Macmillan's Chancellorship (all 1956)

F_2 represents the Selwyn Lloyd pay pause (1961(III)–1962(II))

F_3 represents the incomes restraint under Maudling (1962(III) 1964(III))

F_4 represents the Labour Government's attempt at a prices and incomes policy (1965(I)–1966(II))

F_5 represents the Labour Government's absolute wage freeze (1966(III)–1966(IV))

F_6 represents the Labour Government's period of severe restraint (1967(I)–1967(II))

In addition to these 'freeze' variables three variables D_1 were introduced to see whether there was an undue increase in wages immediately after the period of restraint ended:

$D_1 = 1$ (1957(I))
$D_2 =$ (1964(IV) 1)
$D_3 = 1$ (1967(III))

The equation estimated by ordinary least squares for eighteen industries for the period 1956(I)–1967(III) may be written:

$$\begin{aligned}\log W_{it}/W_{it-4} = {} & \beta_0+\beta_1 t+\sum_{r=2}^{4}\beta_{rs}S_{rt}+\sum_{q=1}^{6}\beta_{Fq}F_{qt}+\sum_{r=1}^{3}\beta_{Dr}D_{rt}\\ & +\beta_2\log\tfrac{1}{4}\sum_{r=0}^{3}U_{t-r}+\beta_3\log\tfrac{1}{4}\sum_{r=0}^{3}U_{it-r}\\ & +\beta_4\log c_t/c_{t-4}+\beta_5\log w_{it-4}/c_{t-1}\\ & +\beta_6\log w_{it-4}/\bar{w}_{t-1}+\beta_7\log\bar{w}_{t-1}/\bar{w}_{t-2}\\ & +\beta_8\log\bar{w}_{t-2}/\bar{w}_{t-3}+\beta_9\log w_{jt-1}/w_{jt-5}\\ & +\beta_{10}\tfrac{1}{4}\Sigma(PX/Eh)+\beta_{11}\log w_{it-4}\end{aligned}$$

The results are presented in detail in Tables 3 and 4.

TABLE 3

Industry	β_0	β_1	β_{2S}	β_{3S}	β_{4S}	β_{F1}	β_{F2}	β_{F3}
Agriculture, forestry, fisheries	0·15416	0·00237 (0·00166)	−0·0065 (0·0041)	−0·0153 (0·0052)	−0·0140 (0·0048)	0·0152 (0·0081)	−0·0146 (0·0090)	−0·0183 (0·0121)
Leather goods	0·0649	0·0020 (0·0020)	−0·0022 (0·0052)	0·0070 (0·0055)	−0·0009 (0·0051)	−0·0048 (0·0120)	−0·0460 (0·0120)	−0·0663 (0·0198)
Bricks and pottery	0·6655	0·0058 (0·0015)	0·0032 (0·0043)	0·0014 (0·0039)	0·0012 (0·0036)	0·0169 (0·0077)	−0·0012 (0·0077)	−0·0051 (0·0105)
Timber	0·2484	0·0014 (0·0016)	0·0003 (0·0043)	0·0050 (0·0047)	0·0010 (0·0045)	0·0083 (0·0124)	0·0083 (0·0095)	0·0046 (0·0126)
Other manufacturing	0·1127	+0·0048 (0·0021)	−0·0003 (0·0054)	−0·0022 (0·0058)	−0·0066 (0·0056)	0·0250 (0·0121)	−0·0177 (0·0121)	−0·0089 (0·0166)
Gas, electricity, water	0·3695	0·0076 (0·0026)	−0·0076 (0·0064)	0·0028 (0·0068)	−0·0025 (0·0067)	−0·0003 (0·0150)	−0·0301 (0·0162)	−0·0205 (0·0195)
Transport and communication	0·5215	0·0036 (0·0014)	−0·0045 (0·0038)	−0·0055 (0·0041)	−0·0067 (0·0040)	−0·0039 (0·0097)	−0·0136 (0·0088)	−0·0079 (0·0113)
Distributive trades	0·0609	0·0040 (0·0017)	−0·0041 (0·0039)	−0·0013 (0·0042)	−0·0003 (0·0041)	−0·0002 (0·0096)	0·0158 (0·0115)	0·0092 (0·0123)
Professional and scientific services	0·5169	0·0032 (0·0015)	0·0045 (0·0047)	0·0023 (0·0049)	0·0042 (0·0047)	0·0072 (0·0129)	0·0073 (0·0100)	0·0112 (0·0135)
Miscellaneous services	0·5430	0·0048 (0·0017)	−0·0046 (0·0045)	−0·0055 (0·0048)	−0·0042 (0·0046)	0·0033 (0·0117)	−0·0054 (0·0111)	−0·0051 (0·0132)

TABLE 3 (*cont.*)

Industry	β_{F4}	β_{F5}	β_{F6}	β_{D1}	β_{D2}	β_{D3}	β_2	β_3
Agriculture, forestry, fisheries	−0·0188 (0·0153)	−0·0415 (0·0216)	−0·0551 (0·0213)	−0·0099 (0·0109)	−0·0361 (0·0152)	−0·0479 (0·0255)	0·0604 (0·0274)	−0·0595 (0·0384)
Leather goods	−0·0617 (0·0263)	−0·1028 (0·0340)	−0·1242 (0·0337)	−0·0072 (0·0147)	−0·0749 (0·0238)	−0·1270 (0·0420)	0·0529 (0·0421)	−0·0005 (0·0300)
Bricks and pottery	−0·0225 (0·0153)	−0·0536 (0·0211)	−0·0466 (0·0217)	−0·0036 (0·0105)	−0·0145 (0·0138)	−0·0559 (0·0235)	0·0741 (0·0412)	0·0500 (0·0334)
Timber	−0·0141 (0·0161)	−0·0189 (0·0230)	−0·0227 (0·0257)	−0·0039 (0·0154)	−0·0113 (0·0164)	−0·0133 (0·0293)	0·0591 (0·0347)	−0·0423 (0·0268)
Other manufacturing	−0·0314 (0·0209)	−0·0798 (0·0313)	−0·0942 (0·0356)	−0·0016 (0·0165)	−0·0023 (0·0211)	−0·0689 (0·0409)	0·0334 (0·0595)	0·0023 (0·0537)
Gas, electricity water	0·0382 (0·0262)	−0·0035 (0·0371)	0·0056 (0·0400)	−0·0122 (0·0207)	0·0268 (0·0236)	−0·0027 (0·0431)	0·0220 (0·0804)	−0·0236 (0·1036)
Transport and communication	−0·0061 (0·0139)	−0·0254 (0·0199)	−0·0225 (0·0206)	−0·0065 (0·0139)	−0·0053 (0·0137)	−0·0199 (0·0241)	−0·0316 (0·0462)	0·1018 (0·0663)
Distributive trades	0·0013 (0·0206)	−0·0255 (0·0289)	−0·0087 (0·0298)	−0·0152 (0·0111)	0·0130 (0·0176)	−0·0066 (0·0334)	−0·0109 (0·0433)	−0·0078 (0·0574)
Professional and scientific services	0·0156 (0·0178)	−0·0276 (0·0259)	−0·0035 (0·0257)	0·0057 (0·0131)	0·0163 (0·0170)	0·0223 (0·0286)	−0·0389 (0·0346)	0·0329 (0·0513)
Miscellaneous services	−0·0093 (0·0172)	−0·0208 (0·0241)	−0·0007 (0·0254)	−0·0102 (0·0156)	−0·0045 (0·0167)	−0·0298 (0·0285)	−0·0612 (0·0414)	0·1148 (0·0710)

TABLE 3 (*cont.*)

Industry	β_4	β_5	β_6	β_7	β_8	β_9	D.W.	R^2	k
Agriculture, forestry, fisheries	0·4615 (0·2861)	−0·1881 (0·3311)	−0·6629 (0·3182)	0·0265 (0·3476)	−0·5443 (0·3104)	0·2962 (0·1714)	2·0	0·88	−0·22
Leather goods	0·7646 (0·3916)	−0·1263 (0·4185)	−0·8133 (0·4439)	0·3344 (0·4809)	−0·4806 (0·4056)	−0·2023 (0·2358)	1·7	0·89	0·16
Bricks and pottery	0·5315 (0·2789)	−0·8560 (0·2963)	0·1388 (0·3067)	−0·1626 (0·3354)	0·2521 (0·2781)	0·3331 (0·1529)	1·8	0·86	0·10
Timber	0·7080 (0·3577)	−0·3645 (0·3574)	−0·7371 (0·4136)	−0·3199 (0·4357)	−0·1895 (0·3475)	0·0025 (0·1540)	1·5	0·88	0·22
Other manufacturing	1·1688 (0·4368)	−0·7602 (0·4603)	0·0266 (0·4586)	0·3408 (0·5219)	−0·1822 (0·4382)	0·1756 (0·1244)	2·1	0·83	−0·09
Gas, electricity, water	1·2420 (0·5202)	−1·5904 (0·5734)	0·7121 (0·5316)	0·7276 (0·6216)	0·1411 (0·5216)	0·3892 (0·3251)	1·7	0·88	0·14
Transport and communication	−0·1874 (0·2913)	−0·5737 (0·3119)	−0·2960 (0·3753)	0·2410 (0·4087)	0·3029 (0·3095)	0·0040 (0·1264)	2·13	0·88	−0·07
Distributive trades	−0·0280 (0·3260)	−0·7812 (0·3380)	−0·3470 (0·3634)	0·0023 (0·4245)	0·2672 (0·3475)	0·2151 (0·2047)	1·6	0·87	0·18
Professional and scientific services	0·3400 (0·3441)	−0·7259 (0·3540)	−0·0669 (0·4128)	0·2223 (0·4274)	0·5491 (0·3493)	0·1268 (0·0943)	1·8	0·91	0·09
Miscellaneous services	0·5283 (0·3762)	−1·0774 (0·3849)	−0·6363 (0·3818)	0·1482 (0·4533)	0·2480 (0·3718)	0·1055 (0·1561)	2·1	0·88	0·05

TABLE 4

Industry	β_0	β_1	β_{2S}	β_{3S}	β_{4S}	β_{F1}	β_{F2}	β_{F3}
Mining and quarrying	4·9113	0·0162 (0·0057)	0·0023 (0·0052)	0·0019 (0·0054)	−0·0005 (0·0055)	−0·0530 (0·0196)	−0·0183 (0·0092)	0·0044 (0·0113)
Chemicals and allied industries	0·0872	−0·0008 (0·0034)	0·0005 (0·0047)	0·0005 (0·0051)	−0·0016 (0·0049)	0·0056 (0·0134)	−0·0011 (0·0091)	−0·0088 (0·0099)
All metals combined	5·0507	0·0079 (0·0028)	−0·0062 (0·0038)	−0·0063 (0·0039)	−0·0038 (0·0039)	−0·0249 (0·0175)	−0·0074 (0·0077)	−0·0172 (0·0066)
Textiles	3·3675	0·0054 (0·0024)	−0·0000 (0·0023)	−0·0011 (0·0024)	−0·0013 (0·0023)	−0·0143 (0·0070)	−0·0057 (0·0047)	0·0087 (0·0044)
Clothing and footwear	3·8590	0·0078 (0·0044)	0·0049 (0·0048)	0·0040 (0·0052)	0·0030 (0·0050)	−0·0361 (0·0142)	−0·0280 (0·0071)	−0·0304 (0·0091)
Paper and printing	−1·1115	−0·00003 (0·0034)	−0·0043 (0·0048)	−0·0019 (0·0048)	−0·0039 (0·0051)	0·0187 (0·0264)	0·0012 (0·0095)	0·0027 (0·0088)
Construction	4·0989	−0·0067 (0·0029)	0·00035 (0·0045)	−0·0021 (0·0046)	−0·0072 (0·0050)	−0·0026 (0·0132)	0·0067 (0·0069)	0·0051 (0·0112)
Food, drink and tobacco	1·8030	0·0043 (0·0030)	−0·0019 (0·0028)	−0·0021 (0·0031)	−0·0053 (0·0030)	−0·0128 (0·0135)	−0·0003 (0·0053)	0·0070 (0·0077)

Table 4 *(cont.)*

Industry	β_{F4}	β_{F5}	β_{F6}	β_{D1}	β_{D2}	β_{D3}	β_2	β_3
Mining and quarrying	–0·0067	0·0046	–0·0076	–0·0304	0·0118	–0·0416	0·0796	–0·0870
	(0·0145)	(0·0219)	(0·0212)	(0·0189)	(0·0164)	(0·0240)	(0·0418)	(0·0434)
Chemicals and allied industries	–0·0194	–0·0559	–0·0708	–0·0120	–0·0108	–0·1018	–0·0071	0·0535
	(0·0110)	(0·0197)	(0·0210)	(0·0129)	(0·0152)	(0·0264)	(0·0633)	(0·0586)
All metals combined	0·0047	0·0217	0·0208	–0·0281	–0·0222	0·0380	–0·0331	0·0323
	(0·0098)	(0·0154)	(0·0162)	(0·0125)	(0·112)	(0·0203)	(0·0257)	(0·0198)
Textiles	–0·0043	0·0047	0·0079	–0·0087	0·0093	0·0182	–0·0497	0·0095
	(0·0056)	(0·0089)	(0·0080)	(0·0069)	(0·0068)	(0·0104)	(0·0150)	(0·0063)
Clothing and footwear	0·0039	0·0109	–0·0051	–0·0235	–0·0147	–0·0093	0·0346	0·0008
	(0·0127)	(0·0219)	(0·0228)	(0·0157)	(0·0132)	(0·0225)	(0·0426)	(0·0121)
Paper and printing	0·0086	–0·0144	–0·0214	0·0059	–0·0087	–0·0406	–0·0140	–0·0072
	(0·0113)	(0·0208)	(0·0202)	(0·0198)	(0·0135)	(0·0227)	(0·0426)	(0·0353)
Construction	–0·0270	–0·0531	–0·0861	–0·0193	0·0198	–0·0613	0·0479	0·0323
	(0·0116)	(0·0175)	(0·0188)	(0·0142)	(0·0156)	(0·0227)	(0·0257)	(0·0206)
Food, drink and tobacco	–0·0039	–0·0175)	–0·0162	–0·0152	0·0109	–0·0074	–0·0440	0·0356
	(0·0070)	(0·0124)	(0·0128)	(0·0114)	(0·0099)	(0·0163)	(0·0435)	(0·382)

TABLE 4 (*cont.*)

Industry	β_4	β_5	β_6	β_7	β_8	β_9	β_{10}	β_{11}	D.W.	R^2	k
Mining and quarrying	0·3072 (0·4354)	−0·4785 (0·5418)	0·5437 (0·4834)	0·3691 (0·4223)	0·3127 (0·5320)	0·3191 (0·1810)	−1·1051 (0·5058)	−0·2002 (0·1200)	2·0	0·91	−0·01
Chemicals and allied industries	0·9029 (0·3591)	−1·3438 (0·4577)	0·0387 (0·4251)	0·0820 (0·3770)	0·3802 (0·4812)	0·0584 (0·1101)	0·1608 (0·3299)	0·3163 (0.1028)	1·7	0·86	0·16
All metals combined	−0·2261 (0·2483)	−0·1340 (0·3232)	0·1730 (0·3854)	0·6995 (0·3547)	0·6112 (0·3836)	0·1822 (0·0919)	−0·9808 (0·3511)	0·0422 (0·0824)	1·9	0·92	0·03
Textiles	−0·1221 (0·1417)	0·1462 (0·1834)	−0·3531 (·02900)	0·2307 (0·2264)	0·0875 (0·2407)	0·3191 (0·1230)	−0·6217 (0·1861)	−0·0258 (0·0377)	2·5	0·94	−0·24
Clothing and footwear	0·2580 (0·4410)	−0·1661 (0·4044)	−0·3041 (0·5527)	−0·6765 (0·4961)	−0·0352 (0·5089)	0·3442 (0·1538)	−0·7683 (0·3501)	0·0290 (0·2188)	1·9	0·92	0·05
Paper and printing	0·1524 (0·3132)	−0·5006 (0·3804)	−0·7754 (0·4888)	−0·1952 (0·3876)	−0·1588 (0·4956)	0·0855 (0·1679)	0·3500 (0·3590)	−0·0568 (0·1088)	1·6	0·93	0·19
Construction	0·2008 (0·3294)	0·3642 (0·3975)	−0·9491 (0·4630)	0·0428 (0·3654)	−0·8500 (0·4682)	0·1452 (0·1291)	−0·5389 (0·3442)	0·7790 (0·1720)	2·4	0·90	−0·20
Food, drink and tobacco	0·0927 (0·1875)	−0·2311 (0·2439)	−0·3874 (0·2587)	0·1681 (0·2366)	0·1838 (0·2985)	0·0437 (0·1001)	−0·2791 (0·2752)	−0·0252 (0·0655)	2·3	0·91	−0·18

RESULTS OF THE REGRESSIONS

In all cases the proportion of variation in annual industrial wage changes that is explained is high at about 0·9 and serial correlation in the residuals is rarely present, which is remarkable considering we are using annual changes.

The coefficients of the freeze dummies crop up with the correct negative sign in 70 cases out of 108, though the standard error of the coefficients is often large. Industries that appear to have been particularly affected by successive periods of wage restraint are leather goods, bricks and pottery, other manufacturing, chemicals and allied industries and construction. This perhaps reflects the weakness of trade unions in these sectors.

With regard to the introduction of total and industrial unemployment in the individual equations no consistent pattern emerges. The coefficients of total unemployment β_2 have the correct sign in nine out of eighteen cases and the coefficients of industrial unemployment β_3 have the correct sign in eight out of eighteen cases. Often the coefficients of aggregate and industrial unemployment tend to be equal in size and opposite in sign.

However, industrial unemployment and total unemployment are highly correlated and ideally we should introduce each measure into an equation separately.

The coefficients of annual price change β_4 seem sensible and in only three cases occur with the incorrect negative sign; in general they range in size from 0·2 to 1·0

Likewise the coefficients of the real wage variable β_5 generally occur with the correct negative sign and range in size from about 0·5 to 1·0 which seems a reasonable range for adjustment coefficients when annual changes are considered.

The coefficients β_6 represent a comparison effect when industry wages are compared to some overall wage level. We expect a negative coefficient and in twelve cases out of eighteen the correct sign is obtained with coefficients varying in size from $-0{\cdot}3$ to $-1{\cdot}0$.

The parameters β_7 and β_8 represent the consideration of recent changes in the overall wage rate on the current wage-rate change, and in ten cases out of eighteen each pair of coefficients is of the expected positive sign. In the remaining eight cases there is generally one positive coefficient.

The last of the so-called comparison coefficients β_9 shows the effect of introducing an industrial wage-change variable previously determined by simple correlation coefficients. The coefficients β_9 are of the correct positive sign in all but one case. Thus the hypothesis that an industry will compare its wage changes with recent changes in particular industries is tangible.

KUH'S VALUE PRODUCTIVITY HYPOTHESIS

The coefficients β_{10} and β_{11} in Table 4 indicate an attempt to incorporate the average value productivity of labour and lagged wage rates into eight industry wage-determination equations. Average value productivity is measured by the wholesale price index for the output of the industry multiplied by the index of industrial production and deflated by man-hours.

This introduction of Kuh's [2] hypothesis at the industry level is disappointing. Only in the case of construction do value productivity and lagged wage rates occur with coefficients of the correct opposite sign and approximate equality in magnitude. Elsewhere either the coefficient of lagged wages is negative and significant and the coefficient of value productivity meaningless, or the coefficient of value productivity is positive and significant and the coefficient of the lagged wage rate unimportant.

CONCLUSION

The annual change in wage rates in various industrial groupings can be explained reasonably well by variables representing periods of wage restraint, price change and real wage terms and measures representing wage comparisons with other industrial groups and with some overall wage level.

The results regarding the introduction of unemployment in aggregate or industrial form are not clear-cut and the two measures introduced together probably give rise to multicollinearity.

An attempt to test the Kuh hypothesis on eight industries resulted in failure, though this is perhaps due to the poor proxies of value productivity used.

REFERENCES

[1] DUNLOP, J. T., *The Theory of Wage Determination* (New York, St Martin's Press, 1957).

[2] KUH, E., 'A Productivity Theory of Wage Levels: An Alternative to the Phillips Curve', *Review of Economic Studies*, XXXIV (1967) 333–60.

[3] LIPSEY, R. G., 'The Relation between Unemployment and the Rate of Change of Money Wage Rates in the U.K. 1862–1957', *Economics*, XXVII (1960) 1–31.

[4] LIPSEY, R. G. and PARKIN, J. M., 'Incomes Policy: A Reappraisal', *Economics*, XXXVII (1970) 115–38.

[5] NIELD, R., *Pricing and Employment in the Trade Cycle* (Cambridge U.P., 1963).

[6] PHELPS, E. S., *Micro-economic Foundations of Employment and Inflation Theory* (New York, McGraw-Hill, 1970).

[7] SARGAN, J. D., 'Wages and Prices in the United Kingdom', in *Econometric Analysis for National Economic Planning*, ed. P. E. Hart, G. Mills and J. K. Whitaker (London, Butterworths, 1964).

[8] VERNON, K., 'An Econometric Study of Wage and Price Inflation in the U.K. for the Post-War Period' (unpublished Ph.D. thesis, University of London, 1969).

PART TWO

The Phillips Curve and Incomes Policy

5. The Phillips Curve, Expectations and Incomes Policy

DAVID LAIDLER*†

I

The 'Phillips curve' made its first explicit appearance in the literature only thirteen years ago and has ever since played a central role in the analysis of inflationary situations.[1] Even though the basic concept is extremely familiar, it is worth discussing it briefly at the outset, for such a discussion will make it much easier to set out the way in which recent work on the role of price expectations in inflationary situations and on incomes policies fits in with the basic analysis.

Fig. 1 depicts a 'Phillips curve'. On the vertical axis is measured the percentage rate of change of money wages per unit of time ($\dot{W}$), and on the horizontal axis the percentage of the labour force unemployed (U). The curve itself depicts a smooth negative relationship between two variables and cuts the horizontal axis at a positive level of unemployment. Now there are three questions (at least) to be asked about the relationship depicted in Fig. 1. What economic theory predicts that it should exist? Does empirical evidence confirm that it does exist? Finally, what does the existence of such a relationship imply for the design of economic policy in the face of inflation?

A textbook of scientific method would suggest that these questions should be answered in the order they are posed above. However, the world is not so tidy, and in early work on the relationship it was the last two questions that received most

* David Laidler is Professor of Economics at the University of Manchester.

† I am grateful to Michael Parkin for his help at all stages of the preparation of this essay, and to George Zis for drawing my attention to a number of errors in the first draft. Remaining errors and omissions are, of course, my own property.

attention. In his original paper, Phillips (1958) paid only slight attention to questions of theory and concentrated on presenting a formidable body of evidence that, at least as far as the United Kingdom was concerned, a relationship such as that depicted in Fig. 1 did exist and indeed had existed unchanged since 1861.

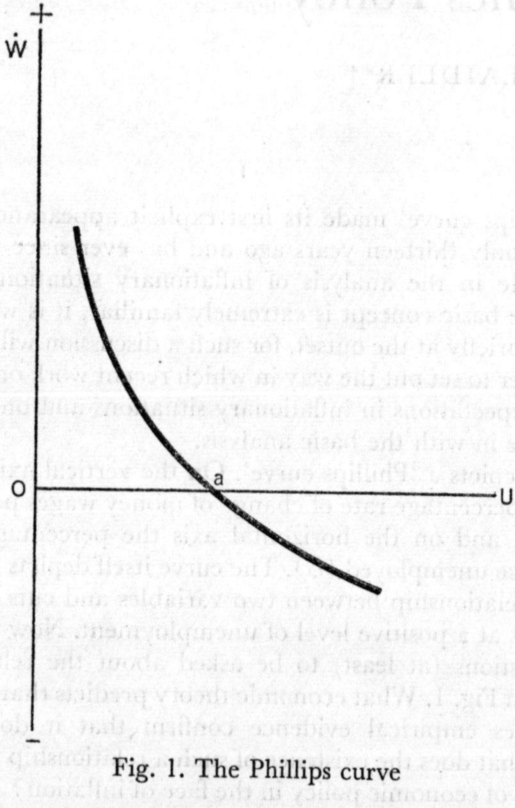

Fig. 1. The Phillips curve

The methods that Phillips used to estimate the form and slope of the relationship were unorthodox, but details of those methods need not in any case concern us here. The important thing to note is that in estimating his curve he applied those methods only to data drawn from before the First World War. He then showed that post-First World War data lay along the very same curve with the post-Second World War data apparently lying closest of all.[2]

Such stability as this in a relationship between two variables over such a long time period is rare indeed in empirical economics, and taken by itself is sufficient to explain a great deal about the rapidity with which economists accepted the Phillips curve. However, there are two other attractive features to the analysis. First, there is the matter of its policy implications. Up till the late 1950s the basic problem for macro-economic policy was thought of as being the simultaneous attainment of price stability and a high level of employment. Though early post-war pessimism about attaining high employment was not justified by events, price stability proved much more elusive.[3] The Phillips curve provided a ready-made explanation for the 'failure' of policy. It suggested that high employment and price stability were incompatible, and that the British economy could only have more of one at the expense of less of the other. To the positive question 'How can one have price stability and high employment?' the Phillips curve seemed to give the answer 'One can't'. It also suggested that it would be more to the point to ask the normative question 'Which combination of unemployment and inflation of those attainable is the most desirable?' Given that economists had been unable to answer the positive question, it is not surprising that they were (and are) attracted by a concept that suggested they were asking the wrong question in the first place.[4]

The final, but not necessarily the least important, attraction of simple Phillips curve analysis lies in the theoretical justification advanced for it. As it stands, Fig. 1 merely portrays a relationship between two variables; it is clearly impossible to carry out any analysis of that relationship unless one has an explanation of why it exists. Lipsey (1960) provided such an explanation. He argued that wages tend to fall in conditions of excess supply of labour and to rise in conditions of excess demand, and he also argued that unemployment varies systematically and inversely with the level of excess demand for labour.[5] Clearly, when labour is in excess supply, that excess supply will manifest itself in unemployed people seeking jobs. However, Lipsey also noted that a national labour market is far from frictionless: even when overall the supply of labour equals the demand for labour there will exist positive 'frictional' unemployment. Since supply and demand being in balance results in a steady wage rate'

Lipsey argued that this frictional unemployment was indicated by point *a* in Fig. 1, where the Phillips curve cuts the horizontal axis. He then argued further that he would expect the pressure of positive excess demand for labour to result in frictional unemployment falling below *a* because jobs become easier to find as the job vacancy rate increases along with the demand for labour.

Excess demand for labour can be produced either by shifts in the supply curve of labour or the demand curve, and is quite independent of the sources of those shifts. Thus Lipsey's theoretical explanation of the Phillips curve makes that analysis neutral as between 'demand pull' and 'cost push' theories of the inflationary process. One economist may regard inflation as being completely the result of bad monetary policy, and another can argue that it is solely the consequence of the activity of monopolistic trade unions, but either position leaves room for its proponent to accept the Phillips curve analysis as elaborated by Lipsey. In short, the Phillips curve and its policy implications seemed to provide an insight into the nature of the inflationary process about whose importance economists on all sides of debates about the likely causes and appropriate cures for inflation could agree.[6]

II

The simple theory of the Phillips curve described above, and its apparent policy implications, were absorbed with remarkable speed into the generally accepted corpus of macro-economics, and though the early and mid-1960s generated a large enough literature on the topic, in my judgement at least, nothing of basic importance was added by this literature to the fundamental contributions of Phillips and Lipsey.[7]

It was not until the late 1960s that two circumstances were to produce both new academic interest in the Phillips curve and genuine intellectual advance in our understanding of it. In Britain, the attempt by the late Government to influence the rate of inflation by way of a prices and incomes policy, whether or not it was prompted by a conscious effort to by-pass the inflation–unemployment trade-off implicit in the Phillips curve, was certainly amenable to interpretation and analysis as such. Incomes policy seems an important subject for study and the

Phillips curve a natural tool to use in the course of that study.[8] In the United States an important role in the resurgence of interest in monetary economics was played by the analysis, both positive and normative, of the relationships between expectations about the rate of inflation and the behaviour over time of the velocity of circulation of money. The variable proved particularly powerful in dealing with data drawn from inflationary situations. It was again a natural, not to say fruitful, extension of the analysis of price expectations to look at their role in the determination of the rate of money wage inflation.[9]

Now in empirically analysing recent British experience, Parkin (1970) has shown that it is helpful to deal simultaneously with the effects of incomes policy and inflationary expectations; both seem to have played a role in generating the relevant data so that the effects of both have had to be allowed for when the data are analysed. However, the two phenomena are analytically distinct, and it will be convenient initially to treat them separately here.

There is, as I noted earlier, an element of ambiguity in Lipsey's analysis of the labour market behaviour that produces the Phillips curve.[10] It starts from two propositions: that the supply and demand for labour determine the equilibrium wage level, and that the rate of change of the wage level in disequilibrium will depend upon the extent of the disequilibrium as measured by the excess demand for labour. Now the Phillips curve is an hypothesis about the behaviour of *money* wages while orthodox supply and demand analysis of the labour market is about the behaviour of *real* wages, and the two concepts are only interchangeable in conditions of price-level stability. If the excess demand for labour is inversely related to the level of unemployment and positively related to the rate of change of the *real* wage, then we may predict that there will exist a stable inverse relationship between the rate of change of *real* wages and the level of unemployment. However, this relationship is not the Phillips curve; to get from it to the Phillips curve we must introduce the expected rate of price inflation into our model.

We need the expected rate of inflation and not its actual current rate because individual wage bargains are struck at discrete intervals and, for any particular bargain, it is not the current price level that matters in determining the real wage that is being aimed at but the level of prices that is expected to rule over the period for which the bargain is being struck. Thus the rate at which the money wage rate will change between any two bargains will be influenced by how price expectations have changed between the times at which the two bargains are struck, and not *directly* by how the price level itself has changed

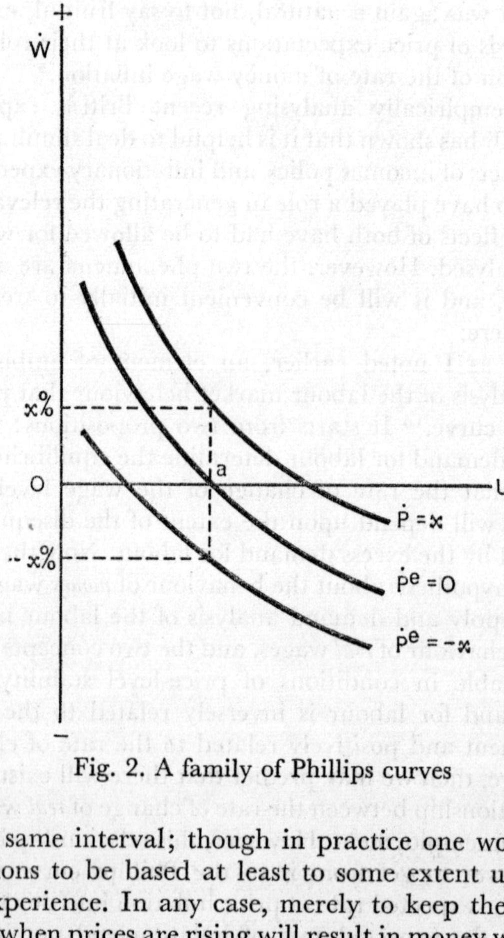

Fig. 2. A family of Phillips curves

over the same interval; though in practice one would expect expectations to be based at least to some extent upon actual recent experience. In any case, merely to keep the real wage constant when prices are rising will result in money wages rising at the expected rate of price inflation, and attempts to increase real wages will result in money wages rising faster than the expected rate of price inflation.

Once we insist that the supply of and demand for labour determine the real wage, and once we note that wage bargains get struck at discrete intervals so that it is expected and not current prices that enter into the determination of the relevant real wage, we find that, in terms of Fig. 1, there is a different Phillips curve for every expected rate of price inflation ($\dot{p}^e$). Representatives of a family of such curves are drawn in Fig. 2, and they have the characteristic implied by the above analysis that each level of unemployment corresponds to a unique rate of change of the *real* wage rate.

Now the foregoing argument implies much more than that there exists a variable, changes in whose value can shift the Phillips curve. Causation does not run only one way from the expected rate of price inflation to the rate of wage inflation. This becomes clear the moment one considers the way in which these variables are likely to interact over time, and, as we shall now see, the nature of their interaction is such as to lead to the conclusion that the trade-off between wage inflation and the level of unemployment implied by the Phillips curve is mainly a short-run phenomenon. Indeed, the strict logic of the argument that follows implies that the trade-off is *solely* a short-run phenomenon – that the 'long-run' Phillips curve is vertical – but this latter proposition, though it is the most contentious one in current academic debates about the role of price expectations in the Phillips curve, is not in my judgement fundamental to any of the implications of the analysis for anti-inflationary policy. The fact that the trade-off becomes steeper with the passage of time is what is important from this point of view, and everyone involved in these debates seems to agree that it does so.

Why this should be the case is best seen by way of an example. Let Fig. 3 depict the situation in an economy in which there is price stability – and expected price stability – and in which U_0 yields a rate of wage inflation $\dot{W}_0$ which is just compensated for by rising labour productivity. Now if the authorities in this economy were to decide that U_0 was too high a level of unemployment, that U_1 was preferable, they could initially achieve this level of unemployment by policies which would also lead to a rate of wage inflation of $\dot{W}_1$. However, with no change in productivity growth, prices would begin to rise at a rate equal to $\dot{W}_1 - \dot{W}_0$. Now so long as people form their expectations about inflation on the basis of current and past behaviour of prices, the price inflation thus induced would begin to become anticipated. It would continue at the same rate so long as the authorities pursued policies to maintain wage inflation at a rate of $\dot{W}_1$, and the longer it continued at that rate the closer to the

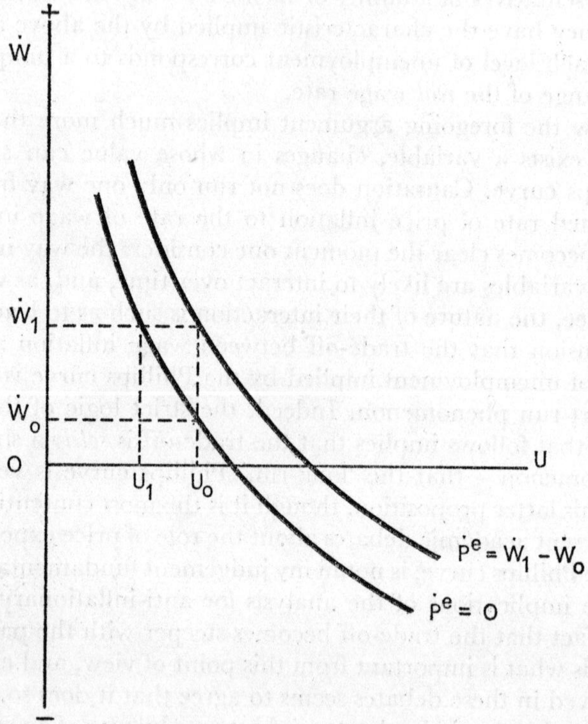

Fig. 3. Short- and long-run response of unemployment to the rate of wage inflation

actual rate of inflation would the expected rate move. Thus, the closer to its ultimate location (at $\dot{p}^e = \dot{W}_1 - \dot{W}_0$) would the short-run Phillips curve shift and the closer to U_0 would the level of unemployment compatible with the rate of wage inflation $\dot{W}_1$ become.

There have been a number of empirical investigations of the kind of wage–price spiral implied in the above example, and there seems to be abundant evidence that wage inflation which proceeds sufficiently fast to involve price inflation does lead the public to form expectations about price inflation that shift the traditional (what I am now calling the 'short-run') Phillips curve upwards. In the long run the trade-off between inflation and unemployment vanishes completely only if actual inflation becomes perfectly anticipated, and there does seem to be doubt as to whether the mechanism involved works quite as perfectly in practice as it does in the foregoing fairly abstract piece of economic analysis; nevertheless there is no disagreement that the trade-off becomes considerably less acute as time passes and people permit current inflation to influence their expectations.[11] This is an extremely important discovery from the point of view of the design of anti-inflationary policy, as we shall now see.

The Phillips curve as originally conceived presented policy-makers with a simple trade-off indeed: more unemployment for less inflation. The introduction of expectations into the analysis complicates the trade-off. Again an example is the best way to see this. Suppose the 'long-run' Phillips curve is such as is depicted in Fig. 4, and I have drawn it with a slope to emphasise the independence of what I have to say of extreme assumptions about perfect learning mechanisms being embodied in the model, and suppose we begin at point *X* on that curve with a given rate of inflation and a given level of unemployment. Suppose the Government of the day finds point *X* uncongenial and prefers point *Y*; how is it to get there? There are many routes, but a comparison of two of them will suffice to illustrate the nature of the policy trade-off involved in choosing a route.

First, suppose the Government attempts to attain at once the rate of inflation compatible with *Y*. This would involve taking policy steps to contract the excess demand for labour to such an extent that initially the economy would move to Y^1 on the short-run Phillips curve that passes through *X*. Clearly the actual rate of inflation would then be below that expected on the short-run Phillips curve passing through *X* and, as expectations were revised downwards, this short-run Phillips curve would shift to the left until point *Y* was reached.

Alternatively the authorities could choose to move immediately to the level of unemployment compatible with ultimate equilibrium at *Y*. This would involve shifting the economy to point *Y*[11] on the short-run Phillips curve. Again, the actual inflation rate would fall below the expected one, and again the constant revision of expectations in the light of experience would eventually result in the economy reaching *Y*. However, inasmuch as people learn about the likely future rate of inflation from current experience, the bigger is the discrepancy between

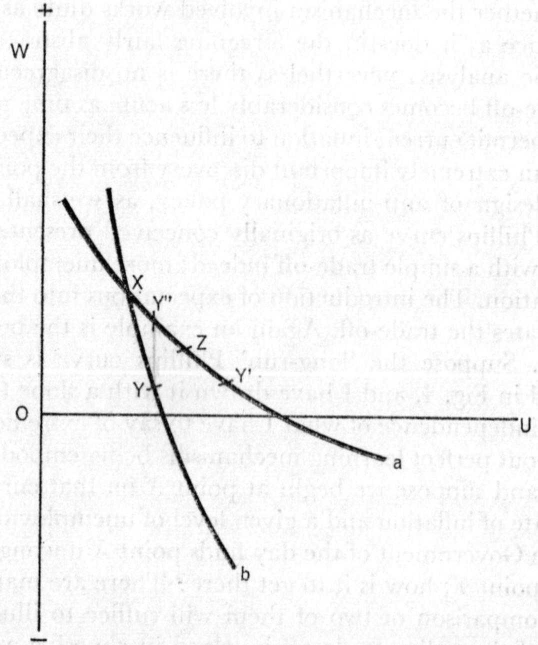

Fig. 4. Long- and short-run Phillips curves
a. Short-run curve
b. Long-run curve

experience and expectations, the faster are expectations likely to be revised. This is a well-tested proposition and in the present context it implies that the first route from *X* to *Y* considered will be a more rapid one than the second.

Now the decision to start the foregoing analytic example from a point of equilibrium on the long-run Phillips curve was a matter of expositional convenience only. In Britain at the moment, both the rate of inflation and the level of unemployment are high by standards of recent history. Phillips's original analysis suggested that a level of unemployment of just under $2\frac{1}{2}$ per cent combined with productivity growth in the region of 2–3 per cent per annum would lead to virtual price stability! This fact suggests that the current British situation is best represented by a point on a short-run Phillips curve to the right of the long-run one, a point such as Z. Indeed, if inflation expectations are still catching up with experience the point Z, far from being static, might actually be moving upwards. However, this does not mean that the foregoing analysis is irrelevant. If the basic mechanism sketched out above is a good model of the effects of inflation in the labour market, it is still true that we may expect to reduce the rate of inflation only slowly if we maintain unemployment at its present level, and that if we seek a rapid end to inflation this must involve a higher level of unemployment than we have at present.

This comparison of routes whereby inflation may be ended is of course merely illustrative of a general proposition about the trade-offs implied by the introduction of inflation expectations into the Phillips curve, and that proposition is as follows. The more rapidly is the rate of inflation reduced, the higher will be the average level of unemployment while it is being reduced. One can bring inflation to a halt quickly by having more unemployment for a relatively short time, or slowly by having less unemployment for a longer time. This is the qualitative nature of the policy trade-off. I do not think we can yet say anything very precise about its quantitative nature other than to note that the experience of both Britain and the United States over the last few years suggests that, if unemployment rates are to be kept from rising any higher than they are at present, then the timetable for significantly reducing the rate of inflation must be conceived of in terms of years rather than months.

Indeed we need not confine ourselves to the evidence of the last few years on this matter. The analysis we have been discussing leads to the conclusion that any attempt to reduce the current rate of inflation below its expected rate will lead to an increase in the unemployment rate which, though 'transitory', may nevertheless endure for an uncomfortably lengthy period. There is no reason to suppose that this conclusion applied only to situations in which the relevant inflation rates are positive, and once this is grasped, the events of the later 1920s and 1930s in Britain and those of the 1930s in the United States may also be regarded as evidence of the consequences of rapid reductions in the rate of inflation relative to its expected level. One might also note that when viewed in this broader perspective, modern theories of the Phillips curve come to look like more general versions of Keynes's hypothesis about the downward rigidity of money wages. They predict, after all, that the rate of change of money wages is rigid downwards relative to the expected rate of price inflation, and a special case of this is a downward rigidity in the level of money wages when the expected rate of inflation is zero.

Now the analysis of the last few paragraphs assumes that price-level expectations are only influenced by data generated within a 'wage–price spiral', and that the workings of the labour market are not interfered with so as to alter the manner in which wages respond to market forces. Some form of incomes policy is frequently put forward as a means of breaking into the mechanism described above in such a way as to enable the economy to by-pass the sacrifices of output inherent in the unemployment generated by reducing the rate of inflation by conventional methods.[12]

There are two distinct ways in which incomes policy might break into this spiral. It might influence the way in which real wages respond to shifts in the supply of and demand for labour, or it may influence expectations about inflation independently of the current behaviour of prices. As we shall see in a moment, incomes policy as practised in the past seems to have been effective in interfering with the supply and demand mechanism in the labour market – not always with the results anticipated – but I must confess to having doubts about according any unique role to incomes policy as a means of influencing expectations; since I know of no study either published or unpublished on this particular issue, however, these doubts are not as firmly based as they might be.

There is no question that it would be highly desirable to have a tool with which expectations about inflation could be damped independently of a fall in the actual rate of inflation. In terms of Fig. 4 such a tool would shift the 'short-run' Phillips curve downwards and to the left independently of the wage–price mechanism described above and hence enable the rate of inflation to be reduced at a lower cost in unemployment than otherwise.

This shift of the short-run Phillips curve would not, in and of itself, reduce the rate of inflation of course. There is nothing in the foregoing analysis to suggest that changing expectations alone will have any influence on the rate of inflation; it simply suggests that if expectations about inflation can be changed independently of the influence of information transmitted by market forces, then a given rate of inflation will be attainable at a lower cost in transitory unemployment than otherwise. The Phillips curve analysis is, as I noted at the outset, silent and neutral on the appropriate policies with which to achieve a given rate of inflation.

Even so, a policy with the ability to change expectations would be a useful part of any anti-inflationary package, and incomes policy is often portrayed as being peculiarly suited to that role. However, I cannot see why. The key to breaking the expectations link in the wage–price spiral involves convincing those involved in wage bargaining that past evidence on price increases is not a reliable indicator of what is going to happen in the future. If the Government announces its intention to influence the future rate of inflation by way of an incomes policy, this will change expectations if incomes policy is expected to work. Equally, however, an announced intention to reduce the rate of inflation by reducing the rate of growth of the money supply will influence expectations if the policy proposal is credible. What is important is that the Government's willingness and ability to reduce the rate of inflation should be believed in and not the means by which this end is to be achieved. Since there is no reason to suppose that the public has more faith in the anti-inflationary powers of incomes policy than in those of more traditional policy tools, there is no reason why the recognition of the importance of the role played by expectations in the inflationary process should imply that incomes policies are peculiarly effective anti-inflationary devices.

There is another side to the case for using incomes policy to affect expectations, however, though it seems no better grounded. It can be argued that by actually imposing restraints on prices and incomes for a period, the actual rate of inflation will be reduced, the expected rate of inflation reduced, and the spiral broken. However, to have anything more than a temporary effect, such a policy would have to convince the public that the course of prices while it was in force was a good indicator of the likely course of prices when the policy was removed.

As I have already noted, there is a good deal of evidence to support the view that price expectations are on the whole largely based on past experience, but it is probably a mistake to apply this evidence to the very special circumstances of the transition from a period of prices and incomes control to one in which these controls are relaxed. It is at least a plausible hypothesis that this is the very time at which the public would regard past experience as a particularly bad guide to the future. If this hypothesis is true, incomes policy can, at best, interrupt the wage–price spiral for only so long as it is imposed. If the act of imposing the policy leads to a downward revision of expectations about inflation, then the act of removing it is as likely to lead to those expectations being revised upwards again – unless of course the end of incomes policy is accompanied by the introduction of other anti-inflationary mesuraes that the public expect to hold down the rate of change of prices. In that case, though, it is the public's belief in the efficiency of the new policies, rather than the legacy of an incomes policy, that holds down expectations of inflation. One cannot help but wonder if the so called 'wage–price explosion' that followed the relaxation of incomes policy by the late Government may not be explained by its failure to replace that policy with some other credible (and visible) any-inflationary measures.

Be that as it may, if incomes policy has no special virtue as a means of influencing expectations about the rate of change of prices, this does not imply that it is a generally ineffective anti-inflation weapon. Casual analysis might suggest, and indeed the view was quite widely held among economists until recently, that incomes policy would hold back the rate of wage inflation that might be experienced at any particular level of excess demand for labour; this because the imposition of incomes policy somehow involved introducing extra friction that forces tending to make money wages rise would have to overcome.

Incomes policy could be thought of as shifting the Phillips curve (presumably long-run and short-run, though the distinction was not current at the time that this view of incomes policy was at its most popular) and lessening the seriousness of the inflation–unemployment trade-off implied by it.

Early attempts to investigate the degree to which incomes policies had shifted the Phillips curve in post-war Britain suggested that they had had some success. There did seem to be evidence that some systematic shifting of the relationship had taken place upon the introduction of incomes policy.[13] However, this evidence rested on the assumption that the only effect of incomes policy was to shift the Phillips curve parallel to itself; Lipsey and Parkin (1970) found no difficulty at all in demonstrating that careful analysis of the theory underlying the curve did not in fact lead to the prediction that incomes policy would shift the curve parallel to itself. Rather they argued that an effective incomes policy would both shift and alter the slope of the relationship. Hence the evidence alluded to above was produced by misconceived tests and implied nothing at all about the effectiveness or otherwise of incomes policy.

Not only were Lipsey and Parkin able to show that incomes policy both shifted and altered the slope of the Phillips curve in principle, they were able to show (using statistical methods that have, admittedly, been much criticised) that it had apparently done so in practice, that the use of incomes policy seemed to have pivoted the curve until it became virtually horizontal, in the manner illustrated in Fig. 5. Their original work did not allow for the likely influence of inflationary expectations – surely the reason why their so-called 'policy off' results do not extrapolate well to present experience – but subsequent work by Parkin showed that to make explicit allowance for expectations did not in any way affect the conclusion that in the presence of incomes policy the rate of wage inflation is independent of the level of unemployment, and indeed of the level of excess demand for labour.

Now this suggests that incomes policy is a double-edged weapon. Applied at a low level of unemployment it decreases the rate of wage inflation, but applied at a high level it increases it. Moreover – with the single exception of the period 1947–50 in which price and wage controls were only part of a much larger array of restrictions imposed on market behaviour – Lipsey and Parkin found that incomes policy had been applied at times of relatively high unemployment so that it had, if anything, worsened rather than improved the situations with which it was supposed to deal.

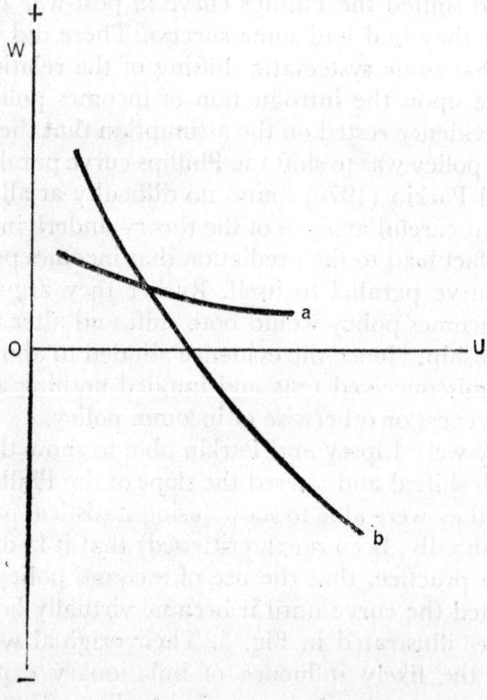

Fig. 5. The Lipsey–Parkin hypothesis about the effect of incomes policy on the Phillips curve

a. Incomes policy on Phillips curve.
b. Incomes policy off Phillips curve.

The interesting question about these results is what is it that determines the rate of wage inflation when it is not responding to the market forces of supply of and demand for labour. The answer advanced by Lipsey and Parkin, which has not been subjected to any independent testing and hence must not be regarded as anything more than a tentative hypothesis, is that, though enough of the national labour market is competitive to ensure that the market as a whole works approximately 'as if' it were competitive throughout in normal (policy off) times, there are important segments of the market, notably the public sector, where competitive theory is far from obviously applicable. Incomes policy affects the Phillips curve by disrupting the competitive sectors of the labour market. This leaves the other non-competitive sectors to set a 'norm' for wage increases that then tends to be widely adopted.[14]

This is not to say that non-competitive sectors of the labour market are unaffected by incomes policy, but since we have little idea about how they work in its absence there is no way of knowing whether or how they are in fact influenced. This is unfortunate because the implications of the Lipsey and Parkin results are clear enough. Either incomes policy is applied at periods of below-average unemployment or it will make matters worse rather than better. This conclusion can only be escaped if some way can be found of ensuring that wage increases in non-competitive sectors of the labour market are brought down to below what competitive forces would allow at times of above-average unemployment. Since we know so little about wage bargaining in non-competitive conditions, it is hard to see how such policies can be devised other than by a process of trial and error. Moreover, this presupposes that the trouble does stem from non-competitive sectors of the labour market in the first place: it is worth reiterating that this proposition is an as yet untested hypothesis.

One final *caveat* is in order before this discussion of incomes policy is brought to a close. Even if it did prove possible to devise an incomes policy that unambiguously could be seen to shift the Phillips curve downwards and to the left so that the rates of wage and price inflation could be reduced at a smaller cost in unemployment than in the absence of such policy, it would not follow that it was desirable to implement it. We regard unemployment as a 'cost' of reducing the rate of inflation mainly because unemployment involves loss of output. Output can be lost by misusing resources as well as by not using them. Fluctuations in relative wages in competitive labour markets are, in principle at least, the means whereby labour gets reallocated towards more productive uses. If incomes policy interferes with this mechanism, it is at least possible that it will produce, as a by-product, sufficient misallocation of the employed labour force as to impose losses that more than offset the gains that arise from having more of the labour force employed. In judging the effectiveness of incomes policy in reducing the costs of bringing down the rate of inflation, these potential allocative effects are just as important as the more obvious impact of the policy on the overall level of employment. However, since there seems to be no evidence that we know even how to use incomes policy in such a way as to reduce consistently the rate of inflation associated with a given level of unemployment, the lack of any work on the allocative effects of incomes policy does not perhaps represent such a serious gap in the literature as it otherwise might.

III

The conclusions that have been drawn in the foregoing discussion are easily summarised. The Phillips curve represents an hypothesis about the way in which the labour market behaves during inflationary situations. Neither in its original form nor in the more sophisticated versions that have been produced recently does it have anything to say about the causes of or cures for inflation. The Phillips hypothesis states that, if a lower rate of inflation is desired, then a higher rate of unemployment must be tolerated. Originally it appeared that the rate at which one variable was traded off against the other was independent of the time horizon over which policy was being designed, and of the past inflationary experience of the economy. More sophisticated analysis, both theoretical and empirical, has shown that the trade-off is more complex.

The amount of unemployment that will be associated with a given rate of inflation at any moment in time will be higher the more rapid has been inflation in the recent past, at least so long as past experience affects expectations about the future. Given that past experience has been of a higher rate of inflation, the longer a given rate of inflation is sustained the lower will be the level of unemployment associated with it. This is because expectations adjust to current experience and what we have termed the 'short-run' Phillips curve shifts so that unemployment and inflation rates approach equilibrium on a steep – in the ideal limiting case, vertical – 'long-run' Phillips curve. Thus the policy trade-off when seeking to reduce the rate of inflation is between a rapid reduction associated with a relatively short period of 'high' unemployment and a slow reduction associated with the existence of 'low' unemployment over a longer period.

It would undoubtedly be desirable to find a way around this trade-off if possible, and one method of softening it would be to influence expectations independently of the market information that normally goes into their formation. It would appear that incomes policy is neither better nor worse conceived to break into the wage–price spiral in this way than any other policy. An announced intention of bringing down the rate of inflation can persuade the public to discount past experience in forming expectations so long as it believed that the announcement will be followed by effective action. There is no reason to suppose that an announced intention to use incomes policy will be any more credible than an announced intention to use any other policy tool. Moreover, we know so little about the factors determining expectations that we cannot rule out as implausible the possibility that the removal of even a successful policy of incomes restraint might not itself lead to an increase in inflationary expectations, and a worsening of the terms of the inflation–unemployment trade-off.

Incomes policy can influence the inflationary spiral at another point by breaking the excess demand for labour/rate of change of (real) wages link in the causative chain. However, available evidence suggests that this has only been done once in the post-war period in such a way as to lower the rate of inflation; in all the other instances incomes policy seems to have increased the rate of inflation above what it otherwise would have been. We have no well-tested explanation of why the policy has worked this way, and hence can have little confidence in our ability to design an incomes policy that will not have a similar effect on the future. Moreover, nothing is known about the effects of such policies on the allocative efficiency of the labour market.

All in all, I would conclude that we know so little about how to design a successful incomes policy that it would probably be better to forget about it altogether, face up to the difficult policy choice inherent in modern versions of the Phillips curve, and, recognising that the time horizon for noticeably reducing the rate of inflation without further significant increases in unemployment in a matter of years and not months, set about designing a long-term strategy for dealing with the problem using more conventional tools of monetary and fiscal policy. Given the current state of the balance of payments, and given that Britain is far from being the only country facing inflation, it may even be the case that a policy of reducing the rate of inflation only very slowly can be carried through without exchange-rate depreciation. If it cannot, then the policy choice becomes more complicated still. To discuss this issue in any detail would take me far beyond the scope of this paper; for this reason, and not because prepared policy towards the exchange rate is an important element in the control of inflation, I shall not pursue this aspect of the problem any further.

NOTES

1. In Phillips (1958). Note, however, that the relationship was implicit in the model used in Phillips (1954).

2. Cf. Phillips (1958): Fig. 1 (1861–1913), Fig. 9 (1913–48), Fig. 10 (1949–57).

3. Hutchinson (1968), particularly chap. 1, provides a ready source of quotation from the pronouncements of economists on this problem in the immediate post-war period.

4. It has often been remarked that the Radcliffe Committee were unfortunate in that the period over which their report (1959) was prepared saw a revival of interest and faith in traditional monetary policy among academic economists so that the report was out of fashion by the time it appeared. It is also true that the idea of trade-offs between policy goals came to the forefront over the same period and the Radcliffe Report was totally uninfluenced by this concept. I suspect that this omission contributed just as much to the cool reception of the Report among academic economists as did its failure to note the 'monetarist revolution'.

5. The reader will note that there is an ambiguity about the term 'wages' here. The Phillips curve has to do with money wages and orthodox analysis of the supply and demand for labour with real wages. As we shall see below, it was precisely this ambiguity, and the desire to clarify it, that led economists to introduce expectations about inflation into the analysis of the Phillips curve. However, in 1961, the problem apparently went unremarked. We may, in retrospect, regard Lipsey as having produced a theory of the Phillips curve for the special case in which the expected rate of inflation is zero.

6. This argument presupposes that the 'cost push/demand pull' distinc-

tion is synonymous with the distinction between demand-side and supply-side disturbances. Matters are not quite so clear-cut, for as Michael Parkin has pointed out to me, the term 'cost push', when applied to wage inflation has sometimes been used to characterise circumstances in which wages rise independently of the concurrent existence of excess demand for labour. As we shall see below, expectations of inflation shared by both demanders and suppliers of labour can cause money wages to increase without there ever arising any excess demand for labour. Thus, recent Phillips curve analysis incorporating expectations about inflation can comprehend this other 'cost push' concept in a manner that earlier analysis could not.

7. A good deal of the 1960s literature had to do with the fact that, for the United States, a simple two-variable Phillips curve was far from stable over a long period. A glance at Fig. 1 of Samuelson and Solow (1960) will confirm the extent of this problem. The United States experience need not concern us here, but two aspects of British work ought to be noted.

First, Hines showed (1964) that the rate of change of trade union membership as a proportion of the labour force was a statistically significant variable, additional to the unemployment rate, indeed virtually swamping the unemployment rate, in explaining the rate of change of money wages. He argued that this variable was a proxy for union aggressiveness and that his result was evidence for the existence of 'cost push' inflationary pressures. However, he failed to explain why this aggressiveness did not operate through shifts in the supply curve of labour and hence have its influence taken account of, along with the many other factors that presumably influence the excess demand for labour, in the unemployment rate. Thus Hines's statistical relationship is difficult (if not impossible) to interpret in terms of Lipsey's rationalisation of the Phillips curve. At the same time Hines did not present clear alternative specification of labour market behaviour, so it is hard to know whether the interpretation he offers of the apparent importance of the rate of change of unionisation is reasonable.

Second, the point at which the Phillips curve cuts the horizontal axis (if we ignore inflationary expectations) is supposed to measure 'frictional' unemployment. Phillips' original curve implies a frictional unemployment rate of between 6 and 7 per cent. Lipsey argued that frictional unemployment was likely to be particularly high when there were large inter-regional discrepancies in the excess demand for labour – even though these cancelled out in the aggregate. This is because it is more difficult for the unemployed to move inter-regionally than intra-regionally to find work. This argument of Lipsey's thus suggests that the Phillips curve would tend to shift leftwards as inter-regional discrepancies in unemployment rates become smaller, and vice versa. Work by Archibald (1969) has tended to confirm this hypothesis and has potentially interesting implications for regional policy.

8. Principal contributions here are Smith (1968), Lipsey and Parkin (1970) and Parkin (1970).

9. Though the idea of an expected rate of inflation goes back at least as far as Irving Fisher (1896), it made its first explicit appearance in modern monetary economics in the work of Friedman (1956), Cagan (1956) and Bailey (1966). It was introduced into the Phillips curve literature by Phelps

(1967), who has also used the concept in work on monetary problems (1965), and Friedman (1968). The only study of which I am aware that uses the concept when dealing solely or even mainly with U.K. data on wage inflation is Parkin (1970). Cagan (1969) does, however, present some preliminary results for Britain.

10. Cf. note 5 above. This is not to say that the analysis that follows is free of ambiguities. To a demander of labour, the real wage is given by the ratio of the money wage rate to some index of the price of his output, while to a supplier it is given by the ratio of the money wage rate to some index of the price of the bundle of goods he typically consumes. In a closed economy in which relative prices were not changing, these two different price indices would necessarily move together, but not otherwise. I know of no work on this particular point, and hence cannot judge the extent to which the following analysis might be vitiated by ignoring the problems raised by it.

11. On this matter, see, for example, work by Cagan (1969) and Solow (1969) for the U.S., and, as already noted, Cagan (1969) and Parkin (1970) for the U.K. Of these, only Cagan's results might imply that the Phillips curve becomes vertical in the long run, though this writer has severe doubts about the methods by which Solow produced results implying that it did not (cf. Laidler, 1970).

12. Much in what follows hinges on what is meant by 'incomes policy'. I take it to mean direct intervention to control prices and money incomes, either by legal restraints or moral suasion, and would not term the mere setting of a target rate of growth of prices and money incomes an 'incomes policy'. Thus it is the choice of policy instruments that defines an incomes policy, not the choice of policy targets.

13. Smith (1968) is a typical example of such studies, which hinge on the inclusion in regression equations of an intercept shift dummy variable for 'incomes policy' on periods. This method is an adequate device for investigating shifts in functional relationships only if there is good *a priori* reason to suppose that the shift being investigated would be a parallel one if it occurred.

14. This explanation is set out by Lipsey and Parkin (1970) pp. 120–2. There is less emphasis there on the public-private sector division, and on the distinction between competitive and non-competitive segments of the labour market, than there is in my interpretation of the Lipsey–Parkin hypothesis. I am indebted to Michael Parkin for clarifying the original analysis along these lines.

REFERENCES

ARCHIBALD, G. C., 'The Phillips Curve and the Distribution of Unemployment', *American Economic Review, Papers and Proceedings*, LIX (May 1969).

BAILEY, M. J., 'The Welfare Cost of Inflationary Finance', *Journal of Political Economy*, LXIV (1966), 93–110.

CAGAN, P., 'The Monetary Dynamics of Hyperinflation', in Milton Friedman (ed.), *Studies in the Quantity Theory of Money* (Univ. of Chicago Press, 1956).

——, 'Theories of Mild Continuing Inflation: A Critique and Extension', in Stephen W. Rousseas (ed.), *Proceedings of a Symposium on Inflation: Its Causes, Consequences and Control* (Wilton, Conn.: The Calvin K. Kazanjian Economics Foundation Inc., 1969).

FISHER, I., 'Appreciation and Interest', Publications of the American Economic Association, 3rd ser., XI (Aug. 1896) 331–442.

FRIEDMAN, M., 'The Quantity Theory of Money: A Restatement', in Friedman (ed.), *Studies in the Quantity Theory of Money* (Univ. of Chicago Press, 1956).

——, 'The Role of Monetary Policy', *American Economic Review*, LVIII (Mar 1968) 1–17.

HINES, A. G., 'Trade Unions and Wage Inflation in the United Kingdom 1893–1961', *Review of Economic Studies*, XXXI (1964) 221–52.

HUTCHINSON, T. W., *Economics and Economic Policy in Britain 1946–1966* (London, Allen & Unwin, 1968).

LAIDLER, D., 'Recent Developments in Monetary Theory: Discussion Paper', in D. Croome and H. G. Johnson (eds), *Money in Britain 1959–1969* (Oxford Univ. Press, 1970).

LIPSEY, R. G., 'The Relation between Unemployment and the Rate of Change of Money Wage Rates in the United Kingdom, 1862–1957', *Economica*, n.s., XXVII (Feb 1960) 1–31.

——, and PARKIN, J. M., 'Incomes Policy: A Reappraisal', *Economica*, n.s., XXXVI (May 1970) 115–38.

PARKIN, J. M., 'Incomes Policy: Some Further Results on the Determination of the Rate of Change of Money Wages', *Economica*, n.s., XXXVII (Nov 1970) 368–401.

PHELPS, E., 'Anticipated Inflation and Economic Welfare', *Journal of Political Economy*, LXXIII (Feb 1965) 1–17.

——, 'Phillips Curves, Expectations of Inflation and Optimal Unemployment over Time', *Economica*, n.s., XXXIV (Aug 1967) 254–81.

PHILLIPS, A. W., 'Stabilization in a Closed Economy', *Economic Journal*, LXIV (June 1954) 290–323.

——, 'The Relation between Unemployment and the Rate of

Change of Money Wage Rates in the United Kingdom', *Economica*, n.s., xxv (Nov 1958) 283–99.

Radcliffe Committee (Committee on the Working of the Monetary System), *Report* (London, H.M.S.O., 1959).

Samuelson, P. A., and Solow, R. M., 'Analytical Aspects of Anti-Inflationary Policy', *American Economic Review*, L (May 1960) 177–94.

Smith, D. L., 'Incomes Policy', chap. iii of R. E. Caves and Associates, *Britain's Economic Prospects* (Washington: Brookings Institution; London: Allen & Unwin, 1968).

Solow, R. M., 'Recent Controversies on the Theory of Inflation: An Eclectic View', in Stephen W. Rousseas (ed.), *Proceedings of a Symposium on Inflation: Its Causes, Consequences and Control* (Wilton, Conn.: The Calvin K. Kazanjian Economics Foundation Inc., 1969).

6. The Phillips Curve: Incomes Policy and Trade Union Effects

LESLIE GODFREY*

In a recent paper Lipsey and Parkin [15] studied the effects of incomes policies in post-war Britain. They estimated a two-equation model and used their point estimates of the structural coefficients and the associated regression residuals to support some arguments which have disturbing implications for policy-makers wishing to reduce inflation. On the basis of their estimated model, Lipsey and Parkin came to the conclusion that not only had wage and price restraints usually been ineffective, but that sometimes they had actually had the perverse effect of increasing the rate of inflation above the value it would otherwise have assumed. If Lipsey and Parkin are correct, then incomes policies must be judged to be rather unsatisfactory tools for the control of wages and prices. However, their conclusions are derived from the estimated equations, and so stand or fall on the acceptability of the model's specification and estimation. It is argued that a further minor assumption is needed for the original derivation to be accepted, and comments are also made upon some implications of the choice of variables. However, our main criticism of [15] is that the estimating and testing procedures are unacceptable, and that the results obtained should not be used to support economic arguments. The estimation method applied by Lipsey and Parkin is biased and inconsistent, and so cannot be expected to bring us somewhere near to knowing the true values of the structural coefficients. It follows that it is hardly likely that the estimated model will be useful for the analysis of incomes policies. An alternative method of estimation is therefore proposed, and some results obtained by re-estimating the model are presented. Some preliminary work on the influence of trade unions on the Phillips relation is also outlined.

* Leslie Godfrey is Lecturer in Economics at the University of Exeter.

1. THE DERIVATION AND SPECIFICATION OF THE STRUCTURAL EQUATIONS

The model specified in [15] was

$$\dot{p} = a_1 + a_2\dot{w}_{-\mathrm{r}} + a_3\dot{m}_{-\mathrm{s}} + a_4\dot{q}_{-\mathrm{t}} \tag{1}$$

$$\dot{w} = a_5 + a_6[\psi(U)]_{-\mathrm{u}} + a_7\dot{p}_{-\mathrm{v}} + a_8 S_{-\mathrm{w}} \tag{2}$$

where $\dot{p}$ = the proportionate rate of change of an index of prices; $\dot{w}$ = the proportionate rate of change of wages or earnings; $\dot{m}$ = the proportionate rate of change of import prices; $\dot{q}$ = the proportionate rate of change of output per head; $\psi(U)$ = some function of the percentage of the labour force unemployed; and S = some measure of the aggressiveness of trade unions, r, s, t, u, v and w are lags in quarters.

Lipsey and Parkin argued that in order to study the effects of hypothetical policy changes, the equations (1) and (2) should be derived from a well-specified model. We are of the opinion that the derivation of the price equation needs a further assumption. On certain rather restrictive assumptions, the following price equation was obtained (equation (5) of [15]):[1]

$$\dot{p} = \left\{\frac{(1+\mu)}{(1-\beta)}\frac{W_{-\mathrm{r}}L_{-\mathrm{t}}}{P}\right\}\dot{w}_{-\mathrm{r}} + \left\{\frac{(1+\mu)}{(1-\beta)}\frac{M_{-\mathrm{s}}T}{P}\right\}\dot{m}_{-\mathrm{s}} - \left\{\frac{(1+\mu)}{(1-\beta)}\frac{W_{-\mathrm{r}}L_{-\mathrm{t}}}{P}\right\}\dot{q}_{-\mathrm{t}} \tag{3}$$

which was rewritten as

$$\dot{p} = a_1\dot{w}_{-\mathrm{r}} + a_2\dot{m}_{-\mathrm{s}} + a_3\dot{q}_{-\mathrm{t}} \tag{4}$$

It was then argued that (4) corresponded to (1) with the intercept set to zero and with the prior restriction that the coefficient of $\dot{w}_{-\mathrm{r}}$ should be minus the coefficient of $\dot{q}_{-\mathrm{t}}$. However, for this argument to hold, the expressions enclosed in { } in (3) should be fixed numbers, otherwise the problem of fluctuating coefficients has to be faced. The additional assumption needed to ensure that (4) provides acceptable coefficients is that the expected shares of labour and imports in the total value of output be constant. It was assumed in [15] that $\Pi = \beta P$ and that $CD = \mu(WL + MT)$. It is clear that the share of profits in the total value of output is the constant β. If we do assume that the expected shares of labour and imports are constant, then, since the share of unmeasured inputs is the combined share of labour and imports multiplied by μ, the share of unmeasured inputs is also a constant. We therefore require that all factor shares be constant. This can be thought of as requiring that the production relationship in the minds of the entrepreneurs be of the generalised Cobb–Douglas form, since this production function yields constant-factor shares under conditions of perfect competition and profit maximisation.

We now consider the choice of variables in [15] and discuss an aspect of this problem related to the investigation of the impact of unions on wages. The rate of change of the percentage of the labour force unionised ($\dot{N}$) is included in the Lipsey–Parkin regressions as a measure of trade union aggressiveness, as first suggested by Hines [11]. Hines found that $\dot{N}$ was the most important determinant of changes in money wage rates in the post-war period up to 1961, but Lipsey and Parkin found that this variable was insignificant during their policy-off periods, which to a great extent overlap with the post-war sample period of [11]. This disagreement is obviously disturbing. However, it is very difficult to compare the two sets of results and to attempt to explain the differences, since Lipsey and Parkin selected an index of weekly wage rates as the wage variable and Hines used an index of hourly wage rates. The influence of trade unions must therefore remain something of an open question, especially in view of the fact that the quarterly series of $\dot{N}$ values used in [15] had to be constructed by interpolation. This is most unfortunate, given the current interest in the economic role of the unions.

2. THE ESTIMATION OF THE LIPSEY–PARKIN MODEL

If the derivation of (1) given by Lipsey and Parkin is to be accepted, then it follows that (1) should be estimated subject to the restrictions outlined above and the usual asymptotic χ^2 test applied to evaluate the consistency of the *a priori* restrictions with the sample information. Lipsey and Parkin in fact used unrestricted ordinary least squares (OLS). The cost of using unrestricted OLS, rather than restricted estimation, has at least two aspects: firstly, the opportunity to test the theoretical formulation of the model is lost; secondly, restricted estimation is more efficient, provided that the constraints imposed are valid. But a more obvious cost of the Lipsey–Parkin procedure is that OLS estimators are biased and inconsistent in a simultaneous equation model. The lags present on the variables of the right-hand sides of equations (1) and (2) might lead one to believe that OLS would yield consistent estimators, provided the equation errors were serially independent. But it is to be recalled that in the equations actually estimated by Lipsey and Parkin only one of these variables had a non-zero lag and this was the import price variable; so that the regressors of the wage and price equations cannot be regarded as predetermined and OLS estimators are indeed inconsistent. We therefore have no statistical justification for expecting the resulting point estimates to tell us anything useful about the true values of the parameters of the model.

The authors justified their use of OLS on the grounds that the variables other than $\dot{w}$ and $\dot{p}$ could not be regarded as predetermined (with the exception of $\dot{m}$), therefore the usual estimation methods, e.g. two-stage least squares, were not feasible. This position is, of course, related to that of Liu [16], and without the specification of the rest of the model containing the wage–price subset, the very identifiability of the equations of this subset must be open to question. In fact, according to the authors, the model of [15] consists of two equations in five endogenous variables, and so at least three more equations will be needed to complete the system. Even if the equations can be estimated at all, OLS estimators have nothing to recommend them statistically. The theory of the classical linear regression model is inapplicable and the test procedures of [15] are invalid. If it is assumed that the Durbin–Watson (DW) statistics calculated from the OLS residuals mean something, then they provide more evidence against the choice of OLS as the estimating technique. The DW statistics reported in [15] often show evidence of strong positive autocorrelation, and so the t-ratios given in the original paper may be extremely misleading and seriously overstate the significance of the estimated coefficients.

3. AN ALTERNATIVE METHOD OF ESTIMATION

The method outlined in this section is designed not only to take account of endogenous regressors and first-order autoregressive errors, but also to incorporate any prior restrictions which may be available. Sargan [19] has considered the case of estimating a structural equation with autoregressive errors when no restrictions are used. The model is then

$$\mathbf{y} = X\mathbf{b} + \mathbf{u} \tag{5}$$

$$u_t = \rho u_{t-1} + e_t, \; | \rho | < 1 \tag{6}$$

$$R\mathbf{b} = \mathbf{r}. \tag{7}$$

The e_t are assumed to be independently normally distributed with mean zero and variance σ^2, and (7) represents the linear between parameter constraints. The number of regressors is p, the number of observations is T ($T > p$), and there are m constraints ($m < p$). A subscript 1 will be used to denote a lagged value of the relevant matrix or vector, but subscripts on coefficient vectors will denote the relevant iteration value of the corresponding estimate.

Let there be a matrix of instruments Z, so that

$$\text{plim}\,(Z'\mathbf{e}/T) = \mathbf{o}$$
$$\text{and plim}\,(Z'X/T) = \bar{M}_{zx}, \text{ a non-zero matrix.}$$

The number of instrumental variables, and therefore the rank of Z, is k ($k > p + 1$). Define the projection matrix Q by

$$Q = Z(Z'Z)^{-1}Z',$$

so that premultiplication by Q projects vectors into the k-dimensional space spanned by the columns of Z. Given a value of ρ, the systematic parts of the autoregressive transforms of the regressand and the regressors are

$$Q\mathbf{y} - \rho Q\mathbf{y}_1 = \mathbf{y}^*$$

and

$$QX - \rho QX_1 = X^* \quad \text{(say)}.$$

Let Sargan's autoregressive instrumental variable (AIV) estimator be denoted by $\tilde{\mathbf{b}}$, and the restricted autoregressive instrumental variable (RAIV) estimator be denoted by $\hat{\mathbf{b}}$. The theory of AIV estimators and computational procedures are to be found in [19]. The RAIV estimators are obtained by minimising

$$[(\mathbf{y} - \rho\mathbf{y}_1) - (X - \rho X_1)\mathbf{b}]'Q[(\mathbf{y} - \rho\mathbf{y}_1) - (X - \rho X_1)\mathbf{b}]$$

subject to $R\mathbf{b} = \mathbf{r}$.

Define the Lagrangian ϕ by

$$\phi = [(\mathbf{y} - \rho\mathbf{y}_1) - (X - \rho X_1)\mathbf{b}]'Q[(\mathbf{y} - \rho\mathbf{y}_1) - (X - \rho X_1)\mathbf{b}] - 2(\mathbf{b}'R' - \mathbf{r}')\boldsymbol{\lambda} \quad (8)$$

where $\boldsymbol{\lambda}$ is a $m \times 1$ vector of multipliers. We seek to minimise ϕ with respect to $\mathbf{b}$, $\boldsymbol{\lambda}$ and ρ.

An iterative solution is necessary and an Orcutt-type procedure is sketched which the author has found to work well in practice. Suppose we take an initial value of ρ, e.g. $\rho_0 = 0$, and determine the associated $\mathbf{y}^*$ and X^* values. The function to be minimised is then

$$\phi = (\mathbf{y}^* - X^*\mathbf{b})'(\mathbf{y}^* - X^*\mathbf{b}) - 2(\mathbf{b}'R' - \mathbf{r}')\boldsymbol{\lambda}.$$

For a minimum with respect to $\mathbf{b}$, we have

$$0 = -X^{*\prime}\mathbf{y}^* + (X^{*\prime}X^*)\hat{\mathbf{b}} - R'\hat{\boldsymbol{\lambda}} \quad (9)$$

($\hat{\mathbf{b}}$ in (9) is of course the iteration value conditional on ρ_0, and not the final value).

Thus,
$$\hat{\mathbf{b}} = (X^{*\prime}X^*)^{-1}X^{*\prime}\mathbf{y}^* + (X^{*\prime}X^*)^{-1}R'\hat{\boldsymbol{\lambda}}$$
$$= \tilde{\mathbf{b}} + (X^{*\prime}X^*)^{-1}R'\hat{\boldsymbol{\lambda}}. \quad (10)$$

Multiplying both sides of (10) by R and applying $R\hat{\mathbf{b}} = \mathbf{r}$, yields

$$\mathbf{r} = R\tilde{\mathbf{b}} + [R(X^{*\prime}X^*)^{-1}R']\hat{\boldsymbol{\lambda}}, \text{ or}$$
$$\hat{\boldsymbol{\lambda}} = [R(X^{*\prime}X^*)^{-1}R']^{-1}(\mathbf{r} - R\tilde{\mathbf{b}}). \quad (11)$$

Combining (10) and (11) we obtain

$$\hat{\mathbf{b}} = \tilde{\mathbf{b}} + (X^{*\prime}X^*)^{-1}R'[R(X^{*\prime}X^*)^{-1}R']^{-1}(\mathbf{r} - R\tilde{\mathbf{b}}). \quad (12)$$

So, given ρ_0, (12) provides $\hat{\mathbf{b}}_0$ ($\tilde{\mathbf{b}}_0$ also being calculated conditionally upon the ρ_0 value). To continue the iterative method, a new value of ρ is needed, and this is derived from the Euler-necessary condition for a minimum with respect to ρ. If we define

$$\hat{\mathbf{u}} = \mathbf{y} - X\hat{\mathbf{b}}$$

then

$$\hat{\rho} = (\hat{\mathbf{u}}_1{}'Q\hat{\mathbf{u}})/(\hat{\mathbf{u}}_1 Q \hat{\mathbf{u}}_1). \qquad (13)$$

Having obtained $\hat{\mathbf{b}}_0$, the next iteration value of ρ, i.e. ρ_1, can be calculated from (13); we then find $\tilde{\mathbf{b}}_1$ and subsequently $\hat{\mathbf{b}}_1$ from (12). The whole process then continues until convergence is achieved.

We next turn to the asymptotic variance matrix of the RAIV estimators, i.e. AV($\hat{\mathbf{b}}$). The corresponding matrix for the AIV estimators is to be found in Sargan's paper ([19] p. 29). We introduce the following notation: $\Delta\hat{\mathbf{b}} = \hat{\mathbf{b}} - \mathbf{b}$; $\Delta\tilde{\mathbf{b}} = \tilde{\mathbf{b}} - \mathbf{b}$; $H = (I - (X^{*\prime}X^*)^{-1}R'[(X^{*\prime}X^*)^{-1}R']^{-1}R)$; $\bar{H} = \text{plim} H$. A little manipulation yields

$$\Delta\hat{\mathbf{b}} = H\Delta\tilde{\mathbf{b}}$$

so that

$$\text{AV}(\hat{\mathbf{b}}) = \bar{H}\text{AV}(\tilde{\mathbf{b}})\bar{H}'. \qquad (14)$$

The computational costs of the AIV and RAIV methods are not negligible, and so the model specification is well worth testing. Sargan has proposed a test of the specification represented by (5) and (6);[2] so a useful first step is to obtain AIV estimates and then to apply this test. If the model passes the test, then we proceed to test the consistency of the *a priori* restrictions of (7) with the sample information by calculating

$$(R\tilde{\mathbf{b}} - \mathbf{r})'[R\text{AV}(\tilde{\mathbf{b}})R']^{-1}(R\tilde{\mathbf{b}} - \mathbf{r}),$$

which is asymptotically distributed as χ^2_m on the null hypothesis that the restrictions are correct. If the sample value of the test statistic is less than some preset significance level, then the more efficient RAIV estimates should be obtained.

Finally, we show how the Lipsey–Parkin price equation fits into the framework of this section. The restrictions to be imposed upon (1) are $a_1 = 0$ and $a_2 = -a_4$, so we have

$$\mathbf{b}' = (a_1\, a_2\, a_3\, a_4)$$

$$R = \begin{bmatrix} 1 & 0 & 0 & 0 \\ 0 & 1 & 0 & 1 \end{bmatrix}$$

and

$$\mathbf{r}' = (0 \quad 0).$$

There only remains the matter of the choice of the instrumental variables. In order to estimate equations (7) and (8) of [15], at least six instruments must be used. The dummy variable **1**, $\dot{m}_{-1}$ and $\dot{m}_{-2}$ are obvious candidates, and lagged endogenous variables can be included in Z since these are also uncorrelated in the probability limit with the e_t. If one wanted to use some of the predetermined variables explicitly mentioned by Lipsey and Parkin, e.g. government expenditures and exports, then series could be constructed by interpolation in exactly the same way as they constructed the quarterly series for the Hines trade union variable.

4. THE RE-ESTIMATION OF THE LIPSEY–PARKIN MODEL

Two sets of results are reported in this section. The first set of results is intended to demonstrate that estimates obtained by the AIV method, which is designed to take account of autoregressive errors and endogenous regressors, are quite different from the Lipsey–Parkin estimates obtained by the statistically unsatisfactory OLS method. The second set of results represents an attempt to investigate the influence of incomes policies on the structural coefficients of the model.

Lipsey and Parkin ([15] p. 28) give the following estimated equations as R^2 maximising for the whole period, i.e. 1948(3)–1968(2) (standard errors are given in parentheses):

$$\dot{p} = \underset{(0{\cdot}548)}{1{\cdot}374} + \underset{(0{\cdot}102)}{0{\cdot}562}\dot{w} + \underset{(0{\cdot}019)}{0{\cdot}085}\dot{m}_{-1} - \underset{(0{\cdot}042)}{0{\cdot}145}\dot{q} \qquad (15)$$

$$R^2 = 0{\cdot}697 \qquad \text{DW} = 0{\cdot}946.$$

$$\dot{w} = \underset{(0{\cdot}973)}{4{\cdot}147} - \underset{(0{\cdot}503)}{0{\cdot}891}U + \underset{(0{\cdot}084)}{0{\cdot}482}\dot{p} + \underset{(1{\cdot}590)}{3{\cdot}315}\dot{N} \qquad (16)$$

$$R^2 = 0{\cdot}616 \qquad \text{DW} = 0{\cdot}742.$$

These equations were re-estimated by the AIV method, and the following results obtained:[3]

$$\dot{p} = \underset{(3{\cdot}070)}{0{\cdot}903} + \underset{(0{\cdot}531)}{0{\cdot}731}\dot{w} + \underset{(0{\cdot}048)}{0{\cdot}052}\dot{m}_{-1} - \underset{(0{\cdot}244)}{0{\cdot}230}\dot{q} \qquad (17)$$

$$\hat{\rho} = \underset{(0{\cdot}119)}{0{\cdot}528} \qquad s^2 = 1{\cdot}444 \qquad \chi^2 = 1{\cdot}438 \text{ (1 d.f.)}.$$

$$\dot{w} = 2{\cdot}957 - 0{\cdot}674U + 0{\cdot}728\dot{p} - 1{\cdot}193\dot{N} \quad (18)$$
$$(3{\cdot}397) \quad (1{\cdot}556) \quad (0{\cdot}336) \quad (7{\cdot}616)$$
$$\hat{\rho} = 0{\cdot}641 \quad s^2 = 1{\cdot}044 \quad \chi^2 = 0{\cdot}137 \text{ (1 d.f.)}.$$
$$(0{\cdot}096)$$

The instruments used for the price equation were $\mathbf{1}$, $\dot{m}_{-1}$, $\dot{m}_{-2}$, $\dot{q}_{-1}$, $\dot{w}_{-1}$ and $\dot{p}_{-1}$, and the instruments for the wage equation were $\mathbf{1}$, $\dot{m}_{-1}$, $\dot{N}_{-1}$, U_{-1}, $\dot{w}_{-1}$ and $\dot{p}_{-1}$.

The χ^2 statistics act as tests of the consistency of the assumed forms of the structural equations and equation error processes with the sample data. The sample values are insignificant and so the model specification can be accepted.

The $\hat{\rho}$ values are the estimates of the autoregressive parameters of the first-order schemes, and are both highly significant, suggesting marked serial correlation of the equation errors.

It may be useful to compare the results of the two different methods by considering the point estimates and the *t*-ratios.

(a) Price equation: point estimates

Vbl.	$\mathbf{1}$	$\dot{w}$	$\dot{m}_{-1}$	$\dot{q}$
OLS	1·374	0·562	0·085	−0·145
AIV	0·903	0·731	0·052	−0·230

(b) Wage equation: point estimates

Vbl.	$\mathbf{1}$	U	$\dot{p}$	$\dot{N}$
OLS	4·147	−0·891	0·482	3·315
AIV	2·957	−0·674	0·728	−1·193

(c) Price equation: *t*-ratios

Vbl.	$\mathbf{1}$	$\dot{w}$	$\dot{m}_{-1}$	$\dot{q}$
OLS	2·51	5·53	4·60	3·48
AIV	0·29	1·38	1·08	0·94

(d) Wage equation: *t*-ratios

Vbl.	$\mathbf{1}$	U	$\dot{p}$	$\dot{q}$
OLS	4·26	1·77	5·76	2·09
AIV	0·87	0·43	2·17	0·16

There are clearly substantial differences in the two sets of estimates of the model. It is useful when considering these differences to talk of them in terms of percentage changes in the original Lipsey–Parkin estimates. As far as the economic variables of the price equation are concerned, the coefficient of $\dot{w}$ has increased by 30 per cent, and the coefficients of $\dot{m}_{-1}$ and $\dot{q}$ have decreased by 39 per cent and 59 per cent respectively. The coefficient of U in the wage equation decreases by 24 per cent, the increase in the coefficient on $\dot{p}$ is about 50 per cent and the $\dot{N}$ coefficient falls by over 100 per cent.[4]

The *t*-ratios derived from using AIV techniques are all much lower than the corresponding Lipsey–Parkin values, and indeed it is difficult to find a significant variable in the re-estimated price equation. The only significant variable in the wage equation is $\dot{p}$.

The price equation (17) passes the specification test, and so the next step is to apply the test of the acceptability of the *a priori* restrictions that the constant term should be zero and that the coefficient on $\dot{w}$ should be minus the coefficient on $\dot{q}$ (see [15] p. 117). The sample value of the test statistic mentioned in section 3 greatly exceeded the 5 per cent value for a χ^2 variate with two degrees of freedom, and so the theoretical constraints on the price equation were rejected in favour of the unrestricted form. RAIV estimates are, therefore, not presented.

In order to test the stability of the model, a dummy variable approach was adopted. Jump variables for the intercept and the slopes were included as additional regressors in the equations. Significant coefficients on the jump variables indicate structural changes due to the influence of incomes policies. This procedure is not entirely satisfactory, since it involves the assumption that each incomes policy has had the same effect on the parameters of the wage–price system. However, this assumption is implicit in the Lipsey–Parkin approach of fitting the equations to the policy-on and policy-off periods separately.

Lipsey and Parkin fitted the price equation to the 'policy-on', 'policy-off' and 'entire' periods, and then applied an F-test for the stability of this relationship. The result of their test was that there were significant variations in the regression coefficients. However, it will be recalled that it was strongly argued above that the test procedures used by Lipsey and Parkin were invalid. In fact, no significant jump variable could be found when the augmented price equation was estimated. We present an equation which provides weak evidence that the $\dot{m}_{-1}$ variable has less effect on $\dot{p}$ in policy-on periods. The estimated equation is

$$\begin{aligned} \dot{p} = \underset{(3\cdot856)}{1\cdot519} + \underset{(0\cdot666)}{0\cdot624\dot{w}} + \underset{(0\cdot068)}{0\cdot079\dot{m}_{-1}} - \underset{(0\cdot085)}{0\cdot117\dot{m}^*_{-1}} - \underset{(0\cdot284)}{0\cdot241\dot{q}} \quad (19) \\ \hat{\rho} = \underset{(0\cdot125)}{0\cdot560} \qquad s^2 = 1\cdot328 \qquad \chi^2 = 1\cdot316 \text{ (1 d.f.)} \end{aligned}$$

where $\dot{m}^*_{-1} = \dot{m}_{-1}$ in policy-on periods
$= 0$ in policy-off periods.

The sum of the coefficients of $\dot{m}_{-1}$ and $\dot{m}^*_{-1}$ is negative, but relatively trivial changes in the coefficients produce a small positive sum. This result would be in line with the findings of Lipsey and Parkin ([15] p. 134). It should also be noted that both the coefficient and *t*-ratio on $\dot{w}$ are smaller in the re-specified price equation than in (17).

The estimation of the wage equation again gave results very different from those of Lipsey and Parkin, who had found 'dramatic changes'. No significant jump variable could be detected, and most of the relevant *t*-ratios were below one. The following equation was obtained which gave some support to the Lipsey–Parkin argument that incomes policies created a relation between wage increases and union aggressiveness where none previously existed:

$$\begin{aligned} \dot{w} = \underset{(2\cdot213)}{3\cdot502} - \underset{(0\cdot837)}{0\cdot823U} + \underset{(0\cdot275)}{0\cdot677\dot{p}} - \underset{(7\cdot548)}{2\cdot493\dot{N}} + \underset{(22\cdot324)}{13\cdot215\dot{N}^*} \quad (20) \\ \hat{\rho} = \underset{(0\cdot818)}{0\cdot257} \qquad s^2 = 1\cdot291 \qquad \chi^2 = 0\cdot470 \text{ (1 d.f.)} \end{aligned}$$

where $\dot{N}^* = \dot{N}$ in policy-on periods
$= 0$ in policy-off periods.

This effect might be due to unions becoming more aggressive because they feel that incomes policy holds down wages, but allows prices and profits to rise. There are, however, two reasons for not overstating the importance of the implications of (20): firstly, the sum of the coefficients of $\dot{N}$ and $\dot{N}^*$ is not significantly different from zero; secondly, the $\dot{N}$ series was constructed by interpolation from annual data and so there are likely to be substantial errors of measurement.

The unemployment variable is insignificant in both of the

wage equations estimated in this paper, i.e. equations (18) and (20); so that it is not the case that incomes policies have been successful in breaking the relationship between $\dot{w}$ and U, but simply that no such relation seems to have existed since 1948.

It is important to note that when the model was re-estimated using a method designed to take account of endogenous regressors and autoregressive errors, there was only one significant t-ratio in the whole system, the t-ratio on $\dot{p}$ in the wage equation.[5] If we adopt the criterion of assessing models on the basis of the estimated coefficients being significant, then the Lipsey–Parkin model does not appear to be an adequate representation of the wage–price process.

Two criticisms may be made of the analysis above. The first criticism is that the assumption of only first-order autoregressive errors is restrictive because quarterly data are used and that higher-order schemes (in particular a fourth-order scheme) may be appropriate. This problem is fairly easy to handle, and all that is needed is a simple generalisation of the Sargan AIV estimator.

If θ stands for the lag operator, i.e. $\theta^r x_t = x_{t-r}$, then for the general case of up to sth-order autoregressive errors, we form

$$\rho(\theta) = 1 - r_1\theta - r_2\theta^2 \ldots - r_s\theta^s$$

and minimise

$$\phi^* = [\rho(\theta)(\mathbf{y} - X\mathbf{b})]' Z(Z'Z)^{-1}Z'[\rho(\theta)(\mathbf{y} - X\mathbf{b})]$$

with respect to the structural and autoregressive coefficients. (For further discussion of the method and computational procedures, see Godfrey [10].) The author has re-estimated both equations of the model allowing up to fifth-order processes. The main conclusions were the same for both sets of results: the null hypothesis of serial independence was rejected, only $\hat{r}_1$ was ever significant and it was always significant. The empirical evidence therefore supports the assumption of first-order autoregressive errors, and the AIV estimator used in section 4 is indeed appropriate.

The second criticism is that the method used to test for significant incomes-policy effects on the parameters of the model is inadequate. Given that all the results suggest a need to take account of autocorrelated errors, it is not possible to run separate fits to policy-on and policy-off periods because certain moment matrices which need to be inverted in the estimation procedure are singular for the 1956 sub-period. However, it is possible to extend the simple jump variable technique of section 4.

For example, consider the problem of investigating policy effects on the intercept of the wage equation. If INC is an incomes policy dummy variable taking the value unity in policy-on periods, then the method used above is to fit

$$\dot{w}_t = a_5 + a_5^*\mathrm{INC}_t + a_6 U_t + a_7 \dot{p}_t + a_8 \dot{N}_t + u_t \tag{21}$$

and to test for the significance of the estimate of a_5^*. It could be argued that the effect of an incomes policy depends not only upon the current situation, but also upon what has happened in the past. This line of argument suggests that we should employ relationships of the type

$$\dot{w}_t = a_5 + \sum_{i=0}^{\infty} a_i^*\mathrm{INC}_{t-i} + a_6 U_t + a_7 \dot{p}_t + a_8 \dot{N}_t + u_t. \tag{22}$$

If a geometric lag distribution is assumed, then (22) may be rewritten as

$$\dot{w}_t = a_5 + a_0^*\left[\frac{1-\pi}{1-\pi\theta}\right]\mathrm{INC}_t + a_6 U_t + a_7 \dot{p}_t + a_8 \dot{N}_t + u_t. \tag{23}$$

Multiplying both sides of (23) by $(1-\pi\theta)$ yields a relationship which can be estimated. There will be between parameter restrictions on this estimating equation, but it is more important to note that if the u_t are serially independent, then the final equation error

$$v_t = u_t - \pi u_{t-1}$$

will be first-order moving average. Autoregressive errors are much easier to deal with in estimation than moving average errors, and so it may be useful in applied work to approximate the moving average process by a fairly high-order autoregressive scheme as suggested by Durbin [6]. In general, such approximations will probably eliminate a great deal of the effects of serial correlation, but cannot be expected to provide very accurate estimates of the nuisance parameters characterising the autocorrelation.

The author did not in fact use such extensions of the jump variable method on the original Lipsey–Parkin model because of dissatisfaction with the economic specification of this model. In particular, it was felt that more attention should be paid to the influence of trade unions on the rate of change of money wages. Some tentative evidence on trade union effects is given below.

5. TRADE UNIONS AND WAGE DETERMINATION

Despite the extensive empirical work on the determination of the rate of change of money wage rates, there has been relatively little econometric analysis of the influence of trade unions. Although Dicks–Mireaux and Dow [5] had found that a subjective index of union pressure included in their analysis had a statistically significant coefficient, Hines [11] was the first investigator to study U.K. wage–price movements using a model explicitly relating wage changes to variables acting as instruments for trade union activity. The proxy variables used by Hines were the percentage of the labour force unionised (N) and the annual change in this percentage ($\dot{N}$) (Hines used annual data only and so did not have to use interpolation to construct a quarterly series on $\dot{N}$). Although Hines argued that trade unions did affect wage changes independently of the demand for labour on the basis of the success of the $\dot{N}$ variable, the standing of the point estimates and associated asymptotic standard errors of [11] has recently been questioned. Thomas and Stoney [22] have shown that when considered as a stochastic difference equation system, the estimated Hines model is dynamically explosive. They argue that this implies the inconsistency of two-stage least squares (2SLS) estimators, and state that Koopmans, Rubin and Leipnik [14] proved that 2SLS was consistent *only if* the model was dynamically stable; but as far as the author is aware the result established in [14] was that *if* the system was stable, then the Cowles Commission quasi-maximum likelihood estimators were consistent. Indeed their remarks on this matter are very much open to question in view of the results obtained by Sargan [20] which would seem to indicate the consistency of 2SLS in the general case when some of the model's characteristic roots are inside the unit circle, some are on the unit circle and some are outside the unit circle. However, the usual formulae for computing asymptotic standard errors are inappropriate, and t-tests should not be applied if the model is explosive. It is therefore very difficult to interpret Hines's original estimates and some economists may consider that the dynamic properties of the model suggest misspecification. Thomas and Stoney proposed an alternative definition of p, and demonstrated that the modified system was stable. Estimation of the wage equation of the modified model yielded rather higher coefficients on the unionisation variables and a rather lower price coefficient.

Despite the success of the reformulation suggested by Thomas and Stoney, it is difficult to believe that N and $\dot{N}$ are adequate proxies for union pushfulness during the period studied below, i.e. 1956(1) to 1969(3). Burrows and Hitiris [4] pointed out that for the period 1955–1967 (which substantially overlaps with this paper's sample period), the percentage of the labour force unionised fell between 39·76 per cent and 40—57 per cent. It seems most unlikely that these very small variations in union membership provide an acceptable instrument for changes in union militancy over the sample period. Burrows and Hitiris [4] suggested that a more useful proxy might be the proportion of working days lost through strike action, or some related variable. However, there is not a great deal of evidence on the role of strikes in wage determination, and even the qualitative nature of the strike effect is open to question. It may be useful to specify a simple model of wage-rate changes in a partially unionised labour market in order to examine the influence of strikes more closely. The following additional notation will be used: W = the general index of money wage rates; W_n = the index of non-union money wage rates; W_u = the index of union money wage rates; and $\bar{N}$ = the proportion of the labour force receiving union rates. Now, $\bar{N}$ will exceed N to the extent that non-union labour employed by unionised firms is paid at union rates, and employers pay union rates in order to forestall unionisation.

Assume $$\bar{N} = \psi N, \psi \geqslant 1. \tag{24}$$

N can reasonably be assumed to be constant in the light of the empirical evidence, and so $\bar{N}$ will also be assumed to be a constant (this is clearly less justified than the assumption on N).

In the absence of trade unions, the major determinants of the rate of change of money wage rates are likely to be the rate of inflation and the excess demand for labour represented by some function of the unemployment rate. The following wage equation is specified for the no-unions case:

$$\dot{w} = \dot{w}_n = a_0 + a_1 U^k + a_2 p + \epsilon \tag{25}$$

where ϵ is a disturbance term. Consider the Phillips relation of equation (25). First, the value of the point estimate of a_2 will have implications for the 'expectations hypothesis' (see Friedman [8] and Phelps [18]). The simplest version of this hypothesis suggests that the Phillips curve can be written as

$$\dot{w} = a_0' + a_1' U^k + p^e + \epsilon' \tag{26}$$

where p^e = the expected rate of inflation. The argument underlying the *a priori* restriction that the coefficient on p^e be unity is that when workers expect a certain rate of inflation they will demand correspondingly higher money wage rates in the future. In so far as it is valid to substitute p for p^e, the statistic $(1-\hat{\alpha}_2)/SE(\hat{\alpha}_2)$ can be used to test the consistency of the 'expectations hypothesis' with the sample data.

Second, earlier work using a simple scan technique had suggested a value of k equal to $-1{\cdot}5$, and this value was used, rather than an attempt to estimate k and the as simultaneously. Several other writers had used a value of unity for k, e.g. [2], [11], [15], and so results are also presented for an augmented linear Phillips relation.

Since about 40 per cent of the labour force of the U.K. is unionised, the no-unions model is inappropriate. If $\bar{N} \neq 0$, then the general wage index is given by

$$W = W_u \bar{N} + W_n(1 - \bar{N}). \tag{27}$$

Let $$W_u = W_n(1+\lambda) \tag{28}$$

so that λ is the union wage differential. Hence,

$$W = W_n(1 + \bar{N}\lambda). \tag{29}$$

Taking logs and differentiating with respect to time yields

$$\dot{w} = \dot{w}_n + \left[\frac{\bar{N}}{1+\bar{N}\lambda}\right] \cdot \frac{\partial \lambda}{\partial t} \tag{30}$$

Substituting for $\dot{w}_n$ from equation (25), we obtain

$$\dot{w} = a_0 + a_1 U^{-1.5} + a_2 \dot{p} + \left[\frac{\bar{N}}{1+\bar{N}\lambda}\right] \cdot \frac{\partial \lambda}{\partial t} + \epsilon. \qquad (31)$$

The approach adopted in this paper is to use a strikes variable as a proxy for the union differential (see Holt [12] and Ashenfelter, Johnson and Pencavel [2]). If the strikes variables used is denoted by S_t, then the final estimating equation will be taken as

$$\dot{w} = a_0 + a_1 U^{-1.5} + a_2 \dot{p} + a_3 S + a_4 \Delta S + \epsilon. \qquad (32)$$

As mentioned above, the qualitative nature of the relationship between λ, the union wage differential, and S, an appropriate strikes variable, is open to dispute, and we proceed to outline the arguments behind the opposing views.

Holt [12] suggested that strikes were likely to be *negatively* correlated with the union differential. In times of low unemployment, unions will probably be able to get larger absolute wage changes than they could in times of high unemployment, but this applies equally to non-unionised labour, and Holt argued that the ratio of the union wage rate to the non-union wage rate dropped in tight labour markets. This effect may be due to the individual's quit threat becoming more important to the employer than the union's strike threat as unemployment falls, and to the increasing advantage of collective bargaining over individual bargaining as unemployment increases. Moreover, a negative correlation between profits and unemployment is to be expected over the cycle, and so, if Holt's hypothesis is correct, just when the union differential is being eroded, the trade unions observe that employers are enjoying high profits which could be used to maintain or increase the differential. The employers may have other plans for the profits, and so there is the possibility of industrial dispute. Pencavel [17] regressed a strikes variable on a set of regressors which included unemployment and profits as a percentage of total compensation, using British data for 1950(1) to 1967(2). The results obtained in [17] support the opinion above that strike activity increases as the market gets tighter. The unemployment variable had a significant negative coefficient and the profits variable had a significant positive coefficient. Assuming that Holt's contention that tight labour markets lead to reduced union wage differentials is correct, then a *negative* correlation between the number of strikes and the union differential is to be expected.

However, it is possible to argue that one of the main determinants of the union differential is the militancy of union members, and that strike activity is positively related to rank-and-file union pressure on wages (see Ashenfelter and Johnson [1], and Ashenfelter, Johnson and Pencavel [2]). This alternative argument suggests a *positive* correlation between the number of strikes and the union differential. Further, if this argument, rather than Holt's view, is correct, then Pencavel's results clearly imply that there is a tendency for the union differential to increase as unemployment falls, i.e. that the power of trade unions is greatest in times of high excess demand for labour.

The author prefers the militancy argument concerning the sign of the strikes proxy's coefficient, and indeed there is some empirical evidence to support this preference. Ashenfelter, Johnson and Pencavel [2] specified a simultaneous equation model in which the rate of change of money wages was explained by the unemployment rate, the rate of inflation, the percentage rate of change of trade union membership and the number of industrial strikes per union member. A variety of simultaneous equation estimation techniques were applied to annual data relating to U.S. manufacturing industry over the period 1914–1963. It was always found that the estimated coefficients on the unionisation and strikes variables were highly significant and *positive*. The strike activity variable employed in [2] cannot be used in a quarterly wage–price model of the U.K. economy because of the absence of quarterly data on union membership. In this study, the number of stoppages in all industries other than mining was used as the strikes variable S_t.[6] It is quite possible that there are more appropriate measures of union pushfulness, and so the empirical work below should be regarded as preliminary experimentation.

Equation (32) will be considered as part of a four-equation model. The endogenous variables of this system are $\dot{w}$, $\dot{p}$, S and ΔS. Since $\Delta S = S - S_{-1}$, two stochastic equations explaining $\dot{p}$ and S are needed to complete the model. The unemployment rate, U_t, is assumed to be predetermined with respect to the wage–price–strike sub-system. No doubt in a much larger economy-wide model, U would be an endogenous variable, but it is assumed that such a model would be block-recursive with U explained in a higher-order block of structural relationships (see Fisher [7]). No attempt has been made to specify and estimate equations for $\dot{p}$ and S in this paper. However, some variant of the Lipsey–Parkin price equation could be used for $\dot{p}$, and the recent paper by Pencavel [17] provides a model of the determination of S. It is hoped to present estimates of various specifications of a complete model in forthcoming work.

Before equation (32) can be estimated, it is necessary to define operational counterparts to $\dot{w}$ and $\dot{p}$. The data employed to estimate (32) are quarterly, and varying definitions of percentage changes have been used in other quarterly studies, e.g. compare Lipsey and Parkin [15], Pencavel [17] and Solow [21]. This technical problem has been discussed by Black and Kelejian [3], who pointed out that the common practice of using overlapping four-quarter wage-rate changes rested on two assumptions. First, wage rates are fixed once a year, and second, one-quarter of the total number of wage adjustments take place each quarter. Gillion [9] demonstrated in his study of wage rates, earnings and wage-drift in the U.K. that the second assumption was inconsistent with his sample data. It was therefore decided to use quarter-to-quarter changes, i.e. $\dot{p} = (P - P_{-1})/P_{-1} \times 100$ per cent, and $\dot{w} = (W - W_{-1})/W_{-1} \times 100$ per cent.

Equation (32) was estimated using the method described in [10], and the estimates associated with the fourth-order autoregressive error case were

$$\underset{}{\dot{w}} = \underset{(0{\cdot}2384)}{0{\cdot}6762} + \underset{(0{\cdot}1934)}{0{\cdot}1589\dot{p}} - \underset{(0{\cdot}5628)}{0{\cdot}3536U^{-1{\cdot}5}} + \underset{(0{\cdot}0534)}{0{\cdot}1055\,(S/100)} - \underset{(0{\cdot}1761)}{0{\cdot}0736\,\Delta(S/100)} \qquad (33)$$

$$s^2 = 0{\cdot}2583 \qquad \chi^2 = 0{\cdot}6045 \qquad (3 \text{ d.f.})$$

$$\hat{r}_1 = \underset{(0{\cdot}2287)}{-0{\cdot}1168} \quad \hat{r}_2 = \underset{(0{\cdot}1336)}{-0{\cdot}0848} \quad \hat{r}_3 = \underset{(0{\cdot}2438)}{-0{\cdot}4289} \quad \hat{r}_4 = \underset{(0{\cdot}5438)}{-0{\cdot}1304}$$

When a linear Phillips curve was specified, the following set of estimates was obtained:

$$\dot{w} = \underset{(0{\cdot}2848)}{0{\cdot}3809} + \underset{(0{\cdot}1802)}{0{\cdot}1302\dot{p}} + \underset{(0{\cdot}1311)}{0{\cdot}0808U} \qquad (34)$$

$$+ \underset{(0\cdot0512)}{0\cdot1104}\,(S/100) - \underset{(0\cdot1658)}{0\cdot0539}\,\Delta(S/100)$$

$$s^2 = 0\cdot2596 \qquad \chi^2 = 0\cdot6690 \qquad (3 \text{ d.f.})$$

$$\hat{r}_1 = \underset{(0\cdot2203)}{-0\cdot1202} \quad \hat{r}_2 = \underset{(0\cdot1331)}{-0\cdot0892} \quad \hat{r}_3 = \underset{(0\cdot2493)}{-0\cdot4198} \quad \hat{r}_4 = \underset{(0\cdot5243)}{-0\cdot1664}$$

The results above do not appear to be sensitive to the choice of the unemployment variable. The s^2 estimate and the χ^2 specification test statistic are very similar in (33) and (34), and the χ^2 values are clearly insignificant.

The coefficient of the strikes variable, S_t, is highly significant and positive; so that the results of this paper are in line with those obtained by Ashenfelter, Johnson and Pencavel [2]. The estimated equations indicate that union militancy, as represented by the number of stoppages, is an important determinant of the rate of change of money wage rates.

Although the insignificance of the unemployment variable was not altogether unexpected, the insignificance of the $\dot{p}$ coefficient was disturbing. The small t-ratio on the price-change variable may be due to an inappropriate definition of $\dot{p}$, but the author feels that collinearity between the instrumental variables used is responsible for the high standard errors of (33) and (34). A list of instrumental variables employed in this study is given in Appendix B, and it will be seen that the 12-space of the instruments for (33) and (34) is that spanned by the variables **1**, U, U_{-1}, $U^{-1\cdot5}$, $U_{-1}^{-1\cdot5}$, S_{-1}, S_{-2}, S_{-3}, $\dot{w}_{-1}$, $\dot{w}_{-2}$, $\dot{p}_{-1}$ and $\dot{p}_{-2}$. It seems very likely that a high degree of multicollinearity will exist between these instruments, given the correlation between successive observations on typical economic variables. Re-estimation of the wage equation, using outside instruments to augment a selection of the instrumental variables used in this paper, might well yield much reduced standard errors and a significant coefficient on $\dot{p}$.[7] One possible procedure would be to take the first four or five principal components of the instruments employed above, and then to add variables constructed from series such as government expenditures, import prices and export prices.

Clearly, a great deal more needs to be done on the specification and estimation of wage-determination models emphasising the role of unions before any conclusions can be drawn. In particular, disaggregated studies should be carried out to investigate demonstration effects and inter-industry differences, and different strike proxies should be tried. However, despite the strictly experimental nature of the empirical work of this paper, it seems likely that union pushfulness was an important influence on the rate of change of wages over the period 1957(3) to 1969(3) (six quarters' observations were lost because of data transformations and the requirements of the estimation procedure). These explorations suggest that more detailed and systematic econometric analysis will produce worth-while results.

The estimates of the autoregressive parameters of (33) and (34) are not significant at the conventional 5 per cent level, but the estimate of r_3 is significant at the 10 per cent level. It is interesting to note that all the autoregressive coefficients are negative. Although the author generally prefers to use seasonally unadjusted data for the estimation of economic models, the pattern of autoregressive parameters does suggest that seasonal dummies might usefully be added to the regressors of (32). Equation (32) was, therefore, re-estimated with seasonal dummies included, but their estimated coefficients were all insignificant, and the other estimates were not greatly affected.

It may be useful to make some remarks on the practice of specifying wage–price models in terms of proportionate rates of change. It has been pointed out that several different definitions of $\dot{p}$ and $\dot{w}$ have been used in empirical work. Furthermore, differing definitions of the key variables can lead to very different conclusions from the estimates of the same theoretical model, e.g. Burrows and Hitiris [4] re-estimated the model of [15] using quarter-to-quarter changes and found no significant explanations. It is possible that if $\dot{p} = (\log P_{+1} - \log P_{-1})/2$ had been used above, then the conclusions concerning trade union effects would have been quite unlike those of this paper.

In fact, it is not necessary to define empirical counterparts to proportionate rates of change in order to estimate the Lipsey–Parkin price equation. Integrating equation (2) and substituting the lags used in [15], we obtain

$$\log P = a_0 + a_1 t + a_2 \log W + a_3 \log M_{-1} + a_4 \log Q \quad (35)$$

which can be estimated directly. It may therefore prove useful to estimate price equations with the price level, rather than the rate of inflation, as the variable of interest. It may also be worth while to follow the example of Klein and Ball [13] and to specify models in terms of absolute wages and prices.

6. CONCLUSIONS

This paper first considered the recent Lipsey–Parkin article [15] which was concerned with the impact of incomes policies. It was argued that the ordinary least squares estimates calculated by Lipsey and Parkin were of little value, and that the conclusions of their investigation were not well founded. The model was re-estimated using a method designed to take account of the simultaneous equation problem and autocorrelated errors. All current dated variables in the wage–price sub-system were treated as endogenous (see [15] p. 127). The *t*-ratio on $\dot{p}$ in the wage equation was the only significant one in the whole of the re-estimated model; so that there is no well-defined two-equation model, but simply a correlation between $\dot{w}$ and $\dot{p}$. The findings of the Lipsey–Parkin analysis concerning the existence of significant incomes policy effects on the model's coefficients received no support from our results.

The influence of trade unions on the Phillips relation was then considered. The Hines variable $\dot{N}$ was rejected as an adequate proxy for union pushfulness, on the grounds that the percentage of the labour force unionised has been almost constant since 1955. A simple model of wage-rate changes was outlined, and the role of strikes in this model was discussed. A prototype wage-determination equation, which included a strikes variable as a proxy for union pressure on wage rates, was estimated and the strikes variable had a highly significant positive coefficient. This work is to be regarded as strictly experimental, and more precise estimates of the structural coefficients could no doubt be obtained by employing a different set of instrumental variables. However, despite the reservations expressed above, the evidence of this paper clearly suggests that using strikes variables as instruments for union militancy is a fertile field for further study.

Appendix A

DEFINITIONS OF VARIABLES AND SOURCES OF DATA

P : Index of retail prices, 'all items' index. Quarterly figures are obtained by averaging monthly data (*Monthly Digest of Statistics*).

$\dot{p}$: $\dot{p} = (P - P_{-1})/P_{-1} \times 100$ per cent.

W : Index of weekly wage rates for 'all industries and services – male and female'. Quarterly figures are obtained by averaging monthly data (*Monthly Digest of Statistics*).

$\dot{w}$: $\dot{w} = (W - W_{-1})/W_{-1} \times 100$ per cent.

U : Percentage of registered labour force wholly unemployed as percentage of the number in civil employment in the United Kingdom.
(The author is grateful to the Statistics Department of the Department of Employment and Productivity for providing these data.)

S : The number of stoppages beginning in each quarter, excluding stoppages in coal-mining. Stoppages involving fewer than ten workers and those lasting less than one day are excluded, except when the aggregate number of working days lost exceeded 100. Reasons for excluding coal-mining are given in Pencavel [17, p. 243] (*Employment and Productivity Gazette*).

ΔS : $\Delta S = S - S_{-1}$.

Note: All data are seasonally unadjusted.

Appendix B

INSTRUMENTAL VARIABLES

The following instruments were used for estimating the equations of the work on incomes policy effects and the Lipsey–Parkin model (definitions as in [15] and section 4 above):

Equation (17): $\mathbf{1}$, $\dot{m}_{-1}$, $\dot{m}_{-2}$, $\dot{q}_{-1}$, $\dot{w}_{-1}$ and $\dot{p}_{-1}$.
Equation (18): $\mathbf{1}$, $\dot{m}_{-1}$, $\dot{N}_{-1}$, U_{-1}, $\dot{w}_{-1}$ and $\dot{p}_{-1}$.
Equation (19): $\mathbf{1}$, $\dot{m}_{-1}$, $\dot{m}_{-2}$, $\dot{q}_{-1}$, $\dot{m}^{*}_{-1}$, $\dot{w}_{-1}$ and $\dot{p}_{-1}$.
Equation (20): $\mathbf{1}$, $\dot{N}^{*}_{-1}$, U_{-1}, $\dot{N}_{-1}$, $\dot{q}_{-1}$, $\dot{m}_{-1}$ and $\dot{m}_{-2}$.

The following instruments were used for estimating the equations of the work on trade union effects on the Phillips curve (definitions as in Appendix A):

Equation (33): 1, S_{-3}, $U^{-1\cdot 5}$, S_{-1}, $\dot{w}_{-1}$, $\dot{p}_{-1}$, U, U_{-1}, $U_{-1}^{-1\cdot 5}$, ΔS_{-1}, $\dot{p}_{-2}$ and $\dot{w}_{-2}$.

Equation (34): As for (33).

NOTES

1. The notation is as follows: P = market price of final output; W = price per unit of labour; L = quantity of labour used per unit of output; M = price per unit of imported materials; T = quantity of imports per unit of output; C = price per unit of other inputs (called unmeasured inputs); D = quantity of unmeasured inputs per unit of output; and Π = profit per unit of output. μ and β are constants.

2. The formula for the test statistic is given on p. 29 of [19].

3. The model was originally estimated with seasonal dummies in each equation in order to test for seasonality. The seasonal dummies were insignificant in every case and so the relationships were re-estimated without them.

4. These percentage figures should be treated with some caution, given the standard errors on the coefficients.

5. It is possible that the large standard errors reported in this paper reflect either a high degree of collinearity in the relevant variables, or a lack of identification, rather than the irrelevance of the regressors specified by Lipsey and Parkin.

6. See Appendix A for data sources and definitions of variables.

7. The equations presented in the discussion of the Lipsey–Parkin model were in fact estimated using several different sets of instruments. The results were not very sensitive to the choice of instrumental variables, and those most favourable to Lipsey and Parkin were used.

REFERENCES

[1] Ashenfelter, O. C., and Johnson, G. E., 'Bargaining Theory, Trade Unions, and Industrial Strike Activity', *American Economic Review*, LIX (1969) 35–49.

[2] Ashenfelter, O. C., Johnson, G. E., and Pencavel, J. H., 'Trade Unions and the Rate of Change of Money Wages in United States Manufacturing Industry', mimeo (1970).

[3] Black, S. W., and Kelejian, H. H., 'A Macro Model of the U.S. Labor Market', *Econometrica*, XXXVIII (1970) 712–741.

[4] BURROWS, P., and HITIRIS, T., 'Incomes Policy: A Comment', mimeo (1970).
[5] DICKS-MIREAUX, L. A., and DOW, C. R., 'The Determinants of Wage Inflation: United Kingdom, 1946–1956', *Journal of the Royal Statistical Society*, series A, CXXII (1959) 145–74.
[6] DURBIN, J., 'Efficient Estimation of Parameters in Moving-Average Models', *Biometrika*, XLVI (1959) 306–16.
[7] FISHER, F. M., 'The Choice of Instrumental Variables in the Estimation of Economy-Wide Econometric Models', *International Economic Review*, VI (1965) 245–74.
[8] FRIEDMAN, M., 'The Role of Monetary Policy', *American Economic Review*, LVIII (1968) 1–17.
[9] GILLION, C., 'Wage-rates, Earnings, and Wage-drift', *National Institute Economic Review*, no. 46 (1968) 52–67.
[10] GODFREY, L. G., 'On the Estimation of Simultaneous Equation Models with Lagged Endogenous Variables and Autoregressive Errors', mimeo (1970).
[11] HINES, A. G., 'Trade Unions and Wage Inflation in the United Kingdom, 1893–1961', *Review of Economic Studies*, XXXI (1964) 221–52.
[12] HOLT, C. C., 'Job Search, Phillips' Wage Relation, and Union Influence: Theory and Evidence', in E. S. Phelps (ed.), *Microeconomic Foundations of Employment and Inflation Theory* (Norton, New York, 1970).
[13] KLEIN, L. R., and BALL, R. J., 'Some Econometrics of the Determination of Absolute Prices and Wages', *Economic Journal*, LXIX (1959) 465–82.
[14] KOOPMANS, T. C., RUBIN, G., and LEIPNIK, R. B., 'Measuring the Equation Systems of Dynamic Economics', in T. C. Koopmans (ed.), *Statistical Inference in Dynamic Economic Models* (Wiley, New York, 1950).
[15] LIPSEY, R. G., and PARKIN, J. M., 'Incomes Policy: A Reappraisal', *Economica*, XXXVII (1970), 115–38.
[16] LIU, T. C., 'Underidentification, Structural Estimation and Forecasting', *Econometrica*, XXVIII (1960), 855–65.
[17] PENCAVEL, J. H., 'An Investigation into Industrial Strike Activity in Britain', *Economica*, XXXVII (1970) 239–56.
[18] PHELPS, E. S., 'Money–Wage Dynamics and Labour Market Equilibrium', *Journal of Political Economy*, LXXVI (1968) 678–711.

[19] SARGAN, J. D., 'Wages and Prices in the United Kingdom: A Study in Econometric Methodology', *Colston Papers*, XVI (1964) (Butterworths Scientific Publications).

[20] SARGAN, J. D., 'The Consistency of Quasi-Maximum Likelihood Estimates of Explosive Stochastic Difference Equations', mimeo.

[21] SOLOW, R. M., *Price Expectations and the Behaviour of the Price Level* (Manchester U.P., 1969).

[22] THOMAS, R. L., and STONEY, P. J. M., 'A Note on the Dynamic Properties of the Hines Inflation Model', *Review of Economic Studies*, XXXVII (1970) 286–94.

7 The Micro-economics of the Phillips Curve

MAURICE PESTON*

What I want to do in this paper is to present (or represent) a large number of ideas that can form the basis of discussion. It is not my intention to present any substantive results. Indeed a reading of some of the literature convinces one that an attempt to reach definite conclusions in this field is neither possible nor desirable. What can be done usefully is to list many of the propositions that have been put forward, to show where they are incompatible with one another, and to indicate the difficulties involved in deciding between them. Even here the sheer size of the literature means that attention can be directed only to some typical proposition of a sample of economists. Thus, although a survey article or book is vitally needed, this is not it. A further problem is that much of what has been written in this field is in the form of *obiter dicta* in articles devoted to other matters. Perhaps these are not meant to be taken at their face value. None the less it still seemed to be fairer to give references than not.

The first two questions to be dealt with are, what Phillips curve? and what micro-economics? In other words, is it not possible that the whole title of this paper denotes a meaningless enterprise?

Concerning the Phillips curve itself it is apparent that we are dealing with a wide variety of similar but not identical phenomena. At the one extreme, the view could be taken that any relationship with the rate of change of money wages as the dependent variable is a Phillips curve;[1] at the other, attention may be restricted to the case in which percentage employment and its rate of change are the dependent variables and the form of the function is non-linear.[2] In the latter sense, the curve can hardly

* Maurice Peston is Professor of Economics at Queen Mary College, University of London.

be said to exist at all; in the former, it has an all-pervasiveness reminiscent of the Holy Ghost.

In this connection the following taxonomy may be relevant to a complete treatment of the subject were anyone strong enough to carry it out:

(*a*) Are we dealing with wage rates or earnings?[3]
(*b*) Are we dealing with weekly rates or hourly?
(*c*) Are prices an explanatory variable?
(*d*) Are expected prices an explanatory variable?
(*e*) Is union strength an explanatory variable?
(*f*) Are profits an explanatory variable?
(*g*) Is the rate of change of unemployment an explanatory variable?
(*h*) Are we using annual or quarterly data?
(*i*) Are all the variables current values or are lagged values included as well?
(*j*) Is the relationship linear or non-linear?
(*k*) Are we dealing with a relationship that depends on particular epochs such as in Phillips's original article, or on an external force such as in the Lipsey-Parkin article, or are we looking for a unified explanation covering the whole period for which evidence is available?

Concerning the general subject of Phillips curves more narrowly construed, my own view is that there is a relationship worth looking at and explaining, but I am not at all convinced that it is the simple permanent relationship that Phillips put forward rather tentatively, and that others have made so much of. Clearly, there have been periods in which the relationship did not hold in the U.K.[4] More to the point, the famed connection between the curve estimated for the early period, 1861–1913, and the points in the post-war period is surely more of a curiosity than a sign of the strength of some underlying structure. For such quantitative permanence to have persisted in the face of so much qualitative change in the economy requires much more explanation than anybody has put forward yet.[5]

Turning to the relationship between micro-economics and macro-economics, I have long ago pointed out both the dangers of so-called solutions to the aggregation problem and their irrelevance.[6] Aggregation theory has an especially curious role in the econometric literature in that typically the micro-foundations of macro-models are set out at length only to be ignored at will when the models themselves are dealt with.[7] As a matter of fact micro- and macro-theory are frequently directed towards different problems. In particular, the form in which data become available necessitates a macro-formulation for the purposes of empirical testing. It is also true that many problems appear in a macro-form, for example the phenomena of unemployment and inflation. Apart from that, if it is granted that all empirical science is imperfect and incomplete there is not even a logical necessity that macro- and micro-theory should be compatible with each other at any point of time. This is, of course, not to suggest that all macro-economic formulations are necessarily correct, or that disaggregation is bad. It is possible that the collapse of a macro-economic relationship can be accounted for in micro-economic terms, and it is equally possible that micro-economic arguments will provide the insights necessary for the construction of new macro-economic hypotheses. All this is broad-brush and commonsensical, having little to do with aggregation theory.

In considering certain micro-economic matters, therefore, I do so because the literature is full of them and because they are interesting for their own sake. It is also possible that disaggregation will ultimately provide a solution to present difficulties in this field. It is not my view, however, that what is wrong with the Phillips curve and the present day analysis of inflation derives from an undue emphasis on macro-economic matters.

A further point at this stage concerns the difference between the concepts 'disaggregation' and 'micro-economics'. I interpret the latter to be the economics of the individual decision unit, firm, household, etc., and the theory of the markets for each individual good and service defined to correspond to those decision units. A model may be considerably disaggregated without getting down to the micro-fine structure of the economy, and, indeed, much of what I am concerned with is disaggregation still into extremely broad economic categories rather than micro-economics interpreted literally.

I now get down to the real business in hand, and a suitable place to start is Lipsey's original work, if for no other reason than that Corry and Laidler find it especially praiseworthy on its treatment of the disaggregated labour market.[8] Lipsey is concerned to explain why a positive amount of unemployment is associated with zero-wage inflation, and attributes this to frictional unemployment. He starts with a single market and his argument is in two parts: (*a*) the relationship between excess demand and the change in wages; (*b*) the relationship between unemployment and excess demand. He then goes on to consider a number of markets and the effect of aggregating them.

Now, there are some obvious criticisms that can be made of this analysis. Firstly, at no point does Lipsey tell us what these individual labour markets are. Are they national economy markets for occupational categories? Are they regional markets? Are they markets classified according to the industries demanding the labour? Secondly, are these markets separable in the sense that demand and supply are functions solely of their own wage rates, or are they interdependent in that demand and supply are functions of other wage rates? In the latter case, the increased supply of labour in one market as a function of its wage rate is a decrease in another market. Thirdly, given that, what is meant by the labour force of an individual market, and unemployment in a particular market? An unemployed man can surely be available for work in several markets. Fourthly, are there any reasons to believe that the adjustment process will be the same in each of these markets, however defined? Fifthly, is it not the case that the aggregation that occurs in practice is not the same on both sides of the functional relationship between wages and unemployment? The index of wage rates is a base-weighted index, the weights of which are the wage bills of various industries, etc. The index of unemployment is based on the sum of the registered unemployed. (The fact that we define unemployment as the number of men unemployed is a curiosity of economics and derives from the social significance of the individual man being out of work. A more appropriate index of unemployment might well weight each man by his economic significance measured, say, by his wage rate. It follows that the aggregate relationship even if derived according to Lipsey's method is a little more complicated than he realises; and his result about the macro-function being above the micro- does not hold even on his own assumptions.

If we take a simple case of two markets, we have the following relationships:

$$\dot{W} = (E_1 W_1 \dot{W}_1 + E_2 W_2 \dot{W}_2)/(E_1 W_1 + E_2 W_2) \qquad (1)$$

$$\dot{W}_i = f\left(\frac{U_i}{E_i}\right) \qquad i = 1,2$$

where E_i = employment, U_i = unemployment, W_i = wage rate, in market *i*.

Take E_i and W_i as given, i.e. the index is base-weighted and we are considering only the period before the weights are adjusted. Consider now what happens as total unemployment is given, but its distribution changes between the two markets. Substituting (2) into (1) and taking the derivative with respect to U_1,

$$\frac{d\dot{W}}{dU_1} = \frac{1}{E_1 W_1 + E_2 W_2}\left[W_1 f'\left(\frac{U_1}{E_1}\right) - W_2 f'\left(\frac{U - U_1}{E_2}\right)\right] \qquad (3)$$

It is clear that this curve does not lie wholly above the micro-adjustment curve *f*, but its position depends on the weights W_i. If, for example, we consider the point where percentage employment is the same in the two markets, an increase in U_1 will raise $\dot{w}$ for a given U if W_2 is greater than W_1, but will lower it if the reverse is true.[9] If the updating of the index is taken into account, more possibilities still will enter into the picture. (The result extends to any number of markets.) Thus, while the Lipsey result would follow for some wage-rate indexes, it does not follow for the index that is actually used in the U.K.

I shall not pursue this aspect of the problem further except to note that none of the other contributors says much about the micro-markets from which the aggregate labour market is derived. Corry and Laidler refer to different jobs,[10] and Vanderkamp to 'various labour markets' and 'various subsectors of that market'.[11] Both emphasise frictional and structural unemployment. Moreover, the spirit if not the letter of the Corry–Laidler paper appears to agree with the view that the connection between the aggregate Phillips curve and any micro-structure is likely to be rather complex.[12]

There is another aspect of disaggregation into individual

markets that is now worth considering. We must ask again what it is that is determined in these markets. Almost all the literature takes a static view and assumes that it is a wage rate (or some such thing) that is determined there, so that in equilibrium there is a zero change in the dependent variable. Changes in the dependent variable are then part of an equilibrating process. If, however, the relevant model is formulated in dynamic terms, the time path of wages is what is determined in equilibrium, so that only some of the observed movement of wages is due to disequilibrium. (Presumably, the equilibrium movement is picked up in part by the constant term in the Phillips curve or by a time trend if one is introduced. Even if that is the case, there remains the problem of explaining the equilibrium path at various levels of aggregation. There is also the complication that short-term and long-term disequilibrium movements may be present simultaneously.) It is also true that wage adjustments in some markets will derive from the demand side, and in others from the supply side. Indeed, both sorts of movement may occur simultaneously or seriatim in the same market. It will also be the case that in some markets wages are geared to the aggregate index of wage rates and not directly to the conditions of equilibrium.[13] Markets will, therefore, be moving in and out of equilibrium for a variety of causes all the time. This reinforces Lerner's view concerning the origin of inflation, and also causes me to question Samuelson and Solow's purpose in advocating disaggregation.[14,15] The object of disaggregation is not to pursue partial equilibrium analysis, but to examine the detailed working of the general equilibrium system. The trouble is that almost all their examples are partial equilibrium ones, and they give us no indication of how we are to pursue a multi-market analysis of this problem. All that one can say is that it makes little sense to study the determinants of the dynamic behaviour of a particular money wage rate in isolation, and that the dynamics of an aggregate wage index is not the simple sum of these micro-dynamics.

Let us now consider the demand for and supply of labour more explicitly. Looking at the private sector firm first, it may be expected that the demand for labour is a function of the conditions under which labour can be obtained (i.e., broadly speaking, the wage rate), what can be done with it once it is obtained (i.e., broadly speaking, its marginal product), and what can be done with this product (i.e., broadly speaking, market demand). A more detailed and realistic analysis of an individual firm would, of course, involve a great deal more than this, but the traditional approach does provide a useful taxonomy and a good starting point for further complications.[16] What requires particular emphasis here is that the firm's decision about a particular wage–employment combination involves a commitment through time. It is quite possible, therefore, that the quantity of labour demanded is a function of expected price, expected wage, and expected output and sales. This means that a suitable formulation of the demand curve would include the rate of change of price, wages and output as independent variables. The faster are prices and output rising, and the slower wages are rising, the greater will be the demand for labour. At the macro-level we might have, therefore, the demand for labour as a function of the rate of change of money wages; other things being equal, the faster money wages rise, the lower the level of employment of labour that firms will wish to offer.

A similar argument may be introduced to suggest that the supply of labour involves a commitment through time and it too may therefore be expected to be a function of the rate of change of money wages and the rate of change of prices. Again at the macro-level it might be assumed that the quantity of employment that unions are willing to supply will increase, other things being equal, the faster that money wages rise.

Now, if it is true that an element of rate of change of money wages is correctly to be introduced into the demand and supply curves of labour, a problem of identification of the observed Phillips curve arises. Assume, in particular, that the demand curve for labour fluctuates much more as a function of other variables such as price changes than does the supply curve. The actual observations of percentage wage changes and employment will then reflect the slope of the supply curve more than the demand curve, i.e. we will observe a positive relation between money wage changes and employment or a negative one between money wage changes and unemployment. What is more, if a significant change occurs in the supply curve of labour and it becomes much more price-sensitive, the typical observations may then change and we will observe a negative relation between money wage changes and employment or at least a strong positive relationship may disappear.

This is, of course, only a tentative view of the matter and is not intended as a total rejection of the interpretation of the Phillips curve as part of an equilibrating mechanism relating excess demand to wage-rate changes. It is not impossible that a correct explanation of the observed phenomena will contain an element of both approaches. One merit of the more dynamic view of the subject is, however, its potential ability to account for recent events in the U.K., but obviously we do not yet possess sufficient information to test that or any other hypothesis for the time being.

The demand curve for labour that we have postulated is part of the general argument concerning cost inflation, namely, that if unions push up wages too rapidly, demand for labour will fall and unemployment will result.[17] The direction of causation is from wage changes to unemployment and the connection is a positive one. This is to be contrasted with a shift in the demand curve for labour resulting from an increase in a variable such as expected demand. In that case employment and the rate of increase in money wages may move together, as the result of a third variable, and there is no causation from one to the other.

On the supply side one line of analysis has been to argue that union strength and pushfulness is a function of the state of the labour market as indicated by employment. We would have, therefore, a cost-push positive linkage between employment and wage increases, the direction of causation being from the former to the latter. To complete the picture it is not impossible to believe that a union could argue as follows: if the Government creates unemployment we must demand an increase in wages to compensate us. We now have a negative relationship between employment and wage changes, with again the direction of causation from the former to the latter. In sum, not unexpectedly, discussion at the micro-level gives rise to a great many possibilities of interpretation of Phillips curves, especially in a dynamic context. It also suggests that concentration on unemployment instead of employment might have been somewhat misleading.

We have mentioned price changes on a number of occasions, and there seems little doubt that these will be an important part of the key to the puzzle when we eventually find it. There is no shortage of economists who have emphasised the role of price changes and price expectations in this field.

Eleven years ago Solow and Samuelson hypothesised 'Real income consciousness is a powerful force'.[18] More recently Friedman and Phelps have discussed the subject in more detail.[19] In their paper Lipsey and Parkin interpret the price change variable in their wage equation as 'a proxy for the *anticipated* rate of change of prices'.[20] In addition, reference must be made to Solow's attempt to deal with adaptive price expectations, which are also discussed by Parkin in his most recent contribution.[21] In connection with all this Rees remarks that a key assumption is '. . . rationality on the part of participants in the labour market. Rationality is equated for the most part with the absence of money illusion.'[22]

Now, no one would wish to argue that there will be no price effect in the labour market. It may be assumed that employers and unions will be concerned with expected prices and these may be reflected in the rate of change of current prices or a weighted average of recent price changes.[23] This does not, however, give rise necessarily to the view that the observed coefficient of the price change variable in a Phillips curve should be unity in the sense that behaviour is really about real wages except for some transitory components. Rees deals in his article with some of these matters, but there are one or two additional points to be made. One obvious question is that if real wages matter, why do not both sides negotiate in terms of constant prices and agree to add the change in price index to the negotiated wage?[24] A part of the answer to this is surely that both sides of the wage bargain are not interested in the price level in the same way. The firm demanding labour is concerned with predicting the price at which its product can be sold. What it would be interested in is, therefore, real profits. To fix a wage rate in real terms would place on it the considerable burden of correctly predicting its own price relative to the general level of prices. The employer may wish to negotiate in money terms in order to share some of this risk with the employee. Similarly, the union may be anxious to negotiate in money terms if it believes it can gain therefrom. A price agreement may be simply a contracted obligation that does not suit all workers. More to the point, if the union believes its bargaining power is sufficiently large, it may feel capable of 'beating' the employer in the wage bargain and getting more than an adjustment for the general level of prices, i.e. it may believe it can get a larger share of the whole cake comprising productivity, relativities and inflation by treating it as a whole than by attacking its separate parts. Negotiating in these terms also enables the union leader to disguise how far he is endeavouring to beat a norm defined in terms of price inflation plus the increase in average real output per man. None the less, it is not altogether clear why the unions are not more anxious to negotiate in real wage terms.

Incidentally, it is worth recalling that the union leader is part of a prisoner's dilemma in setting the wage bargain. He may recognise that as a result of wage negotiations an inflation may result which makes everybody worse off, but his members will be worse off still if he acts in a moderate, responsible way and nobody else does. Indeed, if nearly all unions behave responsibly the gains to irresponsible behaviour by the remainder will be maximised. Similarly on the employer side an anti-inflationary posture by one firm leading to a strike may add to the payoffs of an inflationary policy pursued by its competitors. The purpose of an incomes policy is to recognise this prisoner's dilemma, and to act in an all-embracing way. That is why both a price and wage policy must be pursued simultaneously and universally even if some allocative losses result. This does not mean that an incomes policy is feasible since it requires agreement on which relativities may fairly be changed and which increases in productivity may fairly be reflected in money wage increases. It is simply that a necessary condition of a successful incomes policy is that good social behaviour on the part of some unions should not be penalised by the anti-social behaviour of other factor owners, whether they be capitalists or workers.

Reverting to the question of why the relevant behaviour in the economy does not adjust completely to allow for experience of price inflation, Phelps has already indicated that we are dealing with a learning process that may be slow both in recognising and adjusting to the increase in prices so that the transitory stage of increased employment may comprise a long period of real time.[25] This is especially the case if expectations are not single-valued but comprise a band of possibilities. But even when people are fully adjusted to the new price situation their real behaviour need not necessarily revert to that of the initial situation. This is because the real situation itself has changed. Firstly, there is the tax cut or public expenditure increase which has generated the new situation; secondly, there is an income redistribution from fixed-income groups to others; thirdly, the number of employed people and the rate of utilisation of capital has risen. The result may be that at a higher rate of increase in prices money wages may not have to rise *pari passu* to fulfil the real income expectations of the relevant decision-makers. Thus a high degree of capacity utilisation may become available in exchange for some extra inflation for a sufficiently long time to warrant the metaphysical designation permanent.[26]

If the productivity of the economic system itself is an increasing function of the rate of price inflation over some range, the expectational equilibrium is not the same in real terms for all rates of price inflation. In Phelps's terms, for each 1 per cent inflation one adds less than 1 per cent to a zero inflation Phillips curve and therefore unemployment can be reduced to make up the difference in money wages and prices. Considering that decision-making takes place in conditions of uncertainty and that there is in the U.K. a considerable antipathy to economic change, it is not absurd to argue that there may be a sustainable inflationary equilibrium involving less unemployment than the sustainable constant price equilibrium.

Another point to bear in mind concerns the mix of taxation and expenditure. If, as is sometimes argued, people overvalue the disutility of taxation and undervalue the utility of public expenditure, a real trade-off becomes available as a result of varying the tax–expenditure mix. A reduction in public expenditure together with a larger, unbalanced-budget neutral tax cut may shift the Phillips curve in a downwards direction and reduce the non-inflationary level of unemployment. More generally the natural rate of unemployment may not be independent of the structure of taxation and benefits.[27]

This brings me to my last point which is the strange neglect of the public sector in the analysis of inflation and the Phillips curve. Something like one-quarter of the labour force of the U.K. is in the public sector and a great many of them generate services which are not sold on the open market. It follows that a great many of the micro-structures that have been put forward to justify macro-models of wage and price increases are, strictly speaking, wrong. An attempt could be made to save the analysis by treating public sector demand for labour as exogenous, or as a constant amount to be added to private sector demand, but presumably some public sector demand is sensitive to the money wage rate. It is possible that the public sector suffers from money illusion, i.e. its adjustment to price expectations may not be the same as the private sector. In addition, it may not regard itself as subject to a profit constraint in the same way as the private sector. More generally, in inflationary situations it may prefer to a greater extent than the private sector to let its vacancy rate rise or its quality of employment fall rather than bid up wages. Indeed, the analysis of wage increases in the public sector might best be analysed in terms of public finance. A wage increase met by a government department or by a nationalised industry that then fails to meet its financial target is equivalent to an increase in public expenditure and may best be analysed in those terms. If the nationalised industry sticks to its target and raises its prices we have the case of public expenditure financed by increased indirect taxes, the net effect of which may be, in terms of effective demand, deflationary.[28, 29]

To conclude, my purpose has been to point out the enormous range of micro-economic considerations that economists have brought to bear to account for the existence or non-existence of the Phillips curve. Some have taken the aggregation procedure more seriously than others, but few have bothered to examine the construction of the actual aggregates with which they deal. More frequently the micro-considerations have been brought into the picture to provide a persuasive underpinning for the macro-model. There have been many suggestions that future research should be on a more disaggregated basis, but I hope I have shown that this is much more difficult than appears at first sight. In particular, great care must be taken in using the concept of the individual labour market. There is no shortage of micro-theory so that we have a vast number of micro-reasons to explain why the Phillips curve may have disappeared or was never there in the first place. The trouble is that there are too many competing explanations, and too few tests fine enough to distinguish between them.[30]

NOTES

1. It would then follow that Hines's relationships between union pushfulness and the percentage change in money wages was a Phillips curve even though percentage unemployment is not an important explanatory variable. A. G. Hines, 'Trade Unions and Wage Inflation in the United Kingdom', *Review of Economic Studies*, XXXI (1964) 221–51.

2. It would then follow that almost the only Phillips curves were those of Phillips himself and Lipsey. W. A. Phillips, 'The Relation between Unemployment and the Rate of Change of Money Wage Rates in the United Kingdom, 1861–1957', *Economica*, XXV (1958) 283–99. R. G. Lipsey, 'The Relation between Unemployment and the Rate of Change of Money Wage Rates in the United Kingdom 1861–1957: A Further Study', *Economica*, XXVII (1960) 1–31. One might also include the policy-off curve in the paper by R. Lipsey and J. M. Parkin, 'Incomes Policy: A Reappraisal', *Economica*, XXXVII (1970) 115–38.

3. Lipsey, in particular, emphasises that wage rates are the relevant dependent variable. He remarks, '. . . it is argued that *wage-earnings*, which are the actual amounts earned allowing for bonuses, overtime, short time, etc., should be used instead. To argue in this way is to ignore the facts that an empirical relation has been discovered between wage *rates* and unemployment, that a theory of the dependence of *rates* on unemployment has been put forward, and that this theory has passed tests other than the ones reported here. It also ignores the fact that, although *a priori* reasoning can suggest many reasons why rates and earnings might not move together, they do in fact stay, over a very long period of time, remarkably close together, so that any theory which explains one will go a long way towards explaining the other.' R. G. Lipsey, 'Can There Be a Valid Theory of Wages?', *Adv. Sci.*, XIX (1962) 105–12.

While this appears to be an unexceptionable position, it must be remembered that the original Phillips explanation was in terms of '. . . money wages rates, which are the price of labour services' ibid., (p. 283). It is surely relevant to note, therefore, that in fact money wage rates are not the price of labour services, and to ask 'What is the price of labour services?' Such a question might direct the researcher towards earnings, and including national insurance and S.E.T. as measuring the demand price and earnings net of tax as measuring the supply price of labour. Apart from that, the use of the Phillips curve in a model or as part of a theory of inflation is likely to depend on relating the dependent variable to the process of price formation and productivity which in turn may be more closely connected with earnings than wage rates. As an example, Paish's attempt to answer the question 'How much unemployment to prevent inflation?', depends among other things on going from hourly wage rates to earnings in order to compare the latter with changes in annual output per head. See F. W. Paish, 'Rise and Fall of Incomes Policy', in *How the Economy Works and Other Essays* (Macmillan, 1970) pp. 179–231.

4. Apart from the recent experience of the U.K. there is also considerable

doubt concerning the explanatory power of U in the period 1920–57. Hines, op. cit., p. 244; Lipsey, 'The Relation . . .', pp. 25–30. The significance of Phillips's results is also criticised by Guy Routh in a rather neglected article, 'The Relation between Unemployment and the Rate of Change of Money Wage Rates: A Comment', *Economica*, XXVII (1959) 299–315. I have myself subtitled an unpublished paper 'The Strange Case of the Disappearing Phillips Curve' (1970). The relationship does not hold in the U.K. for the recent past and nobody knows why. Casual remarks about changing expectations are another way of indicating an inability to account for events.

5. In this connection it is worth emphasising how cautious both Phillips and Lipsey were in presenting their results, as the following quotations show: 'These conclusions are of course tentative. There is need for much more detailed research between unemployment, wage rates, prices and productivity' (Phillips, op. cit., p. 299). 'There are at least three very serious problems involved here: (i) The estimated value can be shifted a great deal by fitting curves of different types, by including additional variables and by excluding particular years. *Thus, although it might be held with a high degree of confidence that a significant and very interesting relation has been discovered, a very low degree of confidence might be attached at this stage to a particular estimate of the parameters.* (ii) The theory contained in Section II suggests that the fitted relation may not be a very good guide to the relation between $\dot{W}$ and U if U were to remain substantially unchanged for a long time. (iii) A satisfactory theoretical explanation (together with independent tests) would be needed of the high correlation between $\dot{W}$ and P. Until more is known about the casual links between $\dot{W}$ and P it is very dangerous to argue as if either of these variables were independent of the other' (Lipsey, op. cit., pp. 30–1).

6. M. H. Peston, 'A View of the Aggregation Problem', *Review of Economic Studies* (1959) 58–64.

7. Examples are legion. The following are mentioned because they are to hand. They are not noticeably different from many others that could be cited: L. R. Klein, *A Preface to Econometrics* (Prentice-Hall, 1962); A. A. Walters, *An Introduction to Econometrics* (Macmillan, 1968); T. Merritt Brown, *Specification and Use of Econometric Models* (Macmillan, 1970). Walters with characteristic honesty remarks, 'In spite of these [aggregation] difficulties, the simplicity of the production function approach to aggregate data has apparently been sufficient to overcome the scruples of most investigators' (op. cit., p. 310).

8. B. Corry and D. Laidler, 'The Phillips Relation: A Theoretical Explanation', *Economica*, XXXIV (1967) 189–97. 'It is perhaps surprising that only one writer should notice that there is a problem here; the fact that he faced up to it is a tribute to the quality of Lipsey's work. Phillips's original statement of the theory underlying his hypothesis is no more than an application of general notions about excess demand, and he did not appear to realize fully that unemployment is not a perfect measure for this concept' (op. cit., p. 193).

9. Following Lipsey I assume that the dot over the wage-rate variables indicates percentage change in the multi-market case (op. cit., p. 13, para.

2). Routh's article cited above is one of the very few that concerns itself with the basic statistical material or mentions the way in which an aggregate wage rate is constructed. Reference may also be made to E. Kuska's attempts to explain the cyclical loops around the fitted curve, in 'The Simple Analytics of the Phillips Curve', *Economica*, XXXIII (1966) 462–7.

10. Op. cit., p. 194.

11. J. Vanderkamp, 'The Phillips Relation: A Theoretical Explanation–A Comment', *Economica*, XXXV (1968) 180.

12. They say, for example, 'Since the root of the problem seems to be in the determination of the level of frictional unemployment, it would appear that it would be fruitful to concentrate future research on this phenomenon rather than on the broader matter of the general nature of the relationship between wage changes and unemployment which has so far attracted most research effort' (op. cit., p. 197).

13. This, incidentally, gives us a reversal of the usual aggregation problem. The disaggregated wage rate is a function of the aggregate index of wages. It is likely that the interpretation of a great many inflationary phenomena is assisted by considering this reverse direction of causation of both individual wages and prices.

14. 'The "Who started it first" debate is a complete waste of time because there is no original situation in which there was a "just" or "normal" distribution of the product between wages and profits. Any increase can be seen either as the disturbance which bears the full responsibility for the inflation, or as nothing but the correction of an inequity perpetrated in previous history – all depending on the point of view.' A. P. Lerner, 'Inflationary Depression and the Regulation of Administered Prices', from *The Relationship of Price to Economic Stability and Growth* (1958), reprinted in *Readings in Macroeconomics*, ed. M. G. Mueller (Holt, Rinehart & Winston, 1966) 361–71. 'Inflationary depression' is now called 'stagflation', I understand.

15. 'What appear at first to be subtle and reliable ways of distinguishing cost-induced from demand-induced inflation turn out to be far from airtight. In fact, we are driven to the belief that aggregate data, recording the *ex post* details of completed transactions, may in most circumstances be quite insufficient. It may be necessary first to disaggregate.' P. A. Samuelson and R. M. Solow, 'Analytical Aspects of Anti-Inflation Policy', *American Economic Review*, L (1960) 177–94.

It is worth noting that this was one of the first articles to take the two dangerous steps of drawing the Phillips curve as a smooth relationship without a scatter of points around it, and to replace the change in wages with the change of prices on the vertical axis. The relevant figure is entitled 'Modified Phillips Curve in the United States. This shows the Menu of Choice between different degrees of unemployment and price stability, as roughly estimated from the last twenty-five years of American Data.'

Its equal in foolhardiness is to be found in the *Financial Times* of 9 Feb 1971, where Metcalfe and Richardson portray the Lipsey–Parkin policy-on, policy-off curves as smooth straight lines, although they do admit that nobody has yet accepted these results literally for policy purposes.

16. It is important to mention here that the traditional theory of the firm treats pricing, output and factor purchase as part of the same general decision. The condition that marginal revenue equals marginal cost and the conditions that marginal revenue product equals the marginal cost to the firm of a factor are equivalent for profit maximising, each following from the other. They are not two conditions but one. A model of the firm, therefore, does not require both of them. It follows that if the macro-model is constructed by analogy to the micro-model it too must not treat as independent the pricing equation and the demand for labour equation. It may have one but not both. Alternatively, if it does have both, the objectives of the firm must be treated as a residual element determined within the model. See L. A. Dicks–Mireaux, 'The Interrelationship between Cost and Price Changes 1946–1959: A Study of Inflation in Post-war Britain', *Oxford Economic Papers*, XIII (1961) 267–92. A further point to be made here relates to aggregation. If we start with a price determination equation for the firm and a wage determination equation, it is suggested that we can aggregate both to get the aggregate price equation and the Phillips curve. If, however, the aggregation is done on the basis of the dependent variable (i.e. price in the first case and wage in the second), it must be recognised that the aggregation will be inconsistent if actual price and wage indices are used. The former is essentially an output current weighted index which means that these should be the weights of the wage index of the price equation. The latter is an employment or wage bill base-weighted index which means that these should be the weights of the price index in the wage equation. In other words, if the aggregation procedure is taken seriously, the price index and the wage index should differ between equations. A typical example of this difficulty occurs in Lipsey and Parkin, op. cit. A further analytical error in the derivation of their macro-equations is that their price equation treats labour costs as an independent variable which requires the use of an earnings measure for wages while their wage equation uses wage rates as a dependent variable. Also there is no reason to believe that the prices that are relevant to their price equation are the same ones relevant to their wage equation, since the demanders of labour sell many intermediate goods and also, in the case of some part of the public sector, do not sell goods at all whereas the suppliers of labour buy final goods. They appear to be aware of this, but argue that it does not affect their results (p. 124). In that case one wonders why they bothered with their micro-approach in the first place.

17. Note that we have adopted a dynamic formulation here as opposed to the static formulation, 'if unions push up wages above the equilibrium level, unemployment will result'. An explicit dynamic formulation is to be found in Kuska, op. cit., pp. 465–7.

18. Op. cit., p. 187.

19. M. Friedman, 'The Role of Monetary Policy', *American Economic Review*, LVIII (1968) 1–17. He argues 'Employees will start to reckon on rising prices of the things they buy and to demand higher nominal wages for the future' (p. 10). Also E. S. Phelps, 'Phillips Curves, Expectations of Inflation and Unemployment over Time', *Economica*, XXXIV (1967) 254–81; 'Money-Wage Dynamics and Labour Market Equilibrium', *Journal of*

Political Economy, LXXVI (1968) 678–711; 'The New Microeconomics in Inflation and Employment Theory', *American Economic Review*, LIV (1969) 147–58.

One interpretation of these views is that the Philips curve has the wrong variable. The correct relationship is between the acceleration of money wages and percentage unemployment. In other words, Phillips and others considered the wrong time derivative of money wages, the first instead of the second. For the moment at least it must be remarked that the evidence in favour of this new view is even more tenuous than that supporting the earlier one.

20. Op. cit., p. 117.

21. R. M. Solow, *Price Expectations and the Behaviour of the Price Level* (Manchester U.P., 1969). D. Laidler has an important comment on Solow's work in *Money in Britain 1959–1969*, ed. D. R. Croome and H. G. Johnson (Oxford U.P., 1970) 119–21. Also M. Parkin, 'Incomes Policy: Some Further Results on the Determination of the Rate of Change of Money Wages', *Economica*, XXXVII (1970) 386–401. The 'norm' of this paper and that of Lipsey–Parkin appears to be of money rather than real wage-rate changes.

22. A. Rees, 'The Phillips Curve as a Menu for Policy Choice', *Economica*, XXXVII (1970) 227–38.

23. It is worth noting that employees and employers are likely to look at prices differently, the former net of indirect taxes and the latter gross of indirect taxes. In addition, as I have remarked above, aggregation of prices in the demand equation need not be the same as aggregation of prices in the supply equation.

24. 'One of the principal avenues of adjustment open to the union is an escalator clause or sliding scale that ties wages to the retail price index. The limited popularity of such clauses in both the United States and Great Britain after a long period of moderate inflation suggests that the cost of frequent adjustment is regarded as high' (Rees, op. cit., p. 233).

Negotiations must take place on the frequency of adjustment or the minimum price change needed for adjustment as well as the current price index to be used. All of these could put a price element into the wage bargain.

25. One is surely too glib in going from the theoretical discussion of the effects of a small equiproportionate change in all input and output prices to the practical problem of distinguishing the pure inflation effect from the various changes in relative prices that are going on. None the less, the housewife can surely easily calculate whether this week's bundle of goods costs more than last week's and by how much. Relevant lags in the inflation process may, of course, be between husband and wife. The latter may take time to convince the former of the existence of higher prices and the need for more money; the former may not pass on the full effect of a wage increase immediately.

26. In the simplest terms, in the employment range 1·5 to 3 per cent and with a time margin from now to 1981, if the Phillips curve exists at all, there is surely a real trade-off available to the U.K. Government between inflation and the degree of capacity utilisation.

27. The 'natural rate of unemployment' as discussed by Friedman (op. cit., p. 8) seems to be determined by at least as many variables as the 'velocity of circulation' and is, perhaps, as much of a given as that is. It seems, on Friedman's own analysis, to be sufficiently variable and distant to make lower unemployment and more inflation seem quite feasible in U.K. terms.

28. This would surely also be true of a private monopoly with under-utilised monopoly power.

29. Lipsey and Parkin, referring to the norm, do suggest that the nationalised industries may interpret it differently from the remainder of the economy (op. cit., p. 121).

30. There are also, of course, too many policies. Economics especially as reflected in newspaper articles and letters seems to have become like a ready-to-wear shop recently. 'If you don't like this policy, sir, we have plenty more for you to try!'

8. The Determinants of the Rate of Change of Money Wage Rates and the Effectiveness of Incomes Policy

A. G. HINES*

Inflation is an important and immediately pressing problem. In the U.K., the current inflation (i.e. the current rate of rise of appropriately chosen indexes of the aggregate wage and price levels) is of a magnitude which exceeds that which was experienced during the Korean war. It is a major problem for policy-makers for it has, as yet, been unresponsive to incomes policies which consist in the maintenance of a level of unemployment which is higher than anything which has been experienced in the past thirty years. There is also considerable debate concerning its responsiveness to incomes policy by fiat and/or exhortation. The current inflation also poses problems for the professional economist. Many are adherents of the Phillips curve which postulates the existence of a strong negative relationship between the level of unemployment and the rate of change of money wage rates. They would therefore expect that the rate of rise of money wages and of prices should be negligible or at any rate be substantially lower for the level of unemployment which is currently being held. This remains the case even after allowance is made for the price increases and the subsequent wage increases which are inevitably associated with devaluation. Moreover, the statement is not much affected by the conjecture that the rate of change of wages and prices is higher than it has been for even lower levels of unemployment in the recent past because the public are now beginning rapidly to adjust their expectations to the possibility that the current rate of inflation may continue into the foreseeable future and are adjusting their

* A. G. Hines is Professor of Economics at the University of Durham.

monetary claims accordingly. For, contrary to what this would imply, the data reveal no evidence of an upward-shifting Phillips curve (whose slope may or may not remain unchanged), the parameter of shift being some proxy for the expected rate of change of prices.

We therefore propose to discuss three matters. The first is the conventional theory of the Phillips curve and our fundamental objections to it. The second is a proposed alternative framework for the analysis of the relationship between the rate of change of money wage rates and the level of unemployment. The third is the state of empirical knowledge concerning the determinants of the rate of change of money wage rates and the effects of incomes policy upon it.

THE CONVENTIONAL THEORY OF THE PHILLIPS CURVE

A logically valid theory of the Phillips curve may be developed within the framework of neo-classical theory.

We have as equilibrium relationships

$$N^d - N^s = f\left(\frac{W}{P}, \mid Y\right) - g\left(\frac{W}{P}, \mid Z\right) = 0 \quad (1)$$

where $N^d = E+V, N^s = E+U = L$.[1]

Y and Z are vectors of exogenous variables the elements of which are parameters of shift of the demand and supply functions, $\frac{W}{P}$ is the real wage rate E, V, U and L are the levels of employment, vacancies, unemployment and the labour force respectively.

The neo-classical dynamic adjustment hypothesis is

$$\left(\frac{\dot{W}}{P}\right) / \left(\frac{W}{P}\right) = \lambda[(N^d - N^s)/N^s] = \lambda(X) \quad (2)$$

where $X = (V - U)/L$ is the level of excess demand.

$$\text{Now, } \left(\frac{\dot{W}}{P}\right) / \left(\frac{W}{P}\right) = \dot{W}/W - \dot{P}/P \quad (3)$$

$$\text{Hence, } \dot{W}/W = \lambda(X) + \beta\dot{P}/P \quad \beta = 1. \quad (4)$$

If data on excess demand were always available, equation (4) could be estimated directly. But the data are not always available. Consequently, Phillips [9] proposed that the proportion of the labour force which is unemployed should be used as a proxy for excess demand. We must therefore analyse the relationship between unemployment and excess demand.

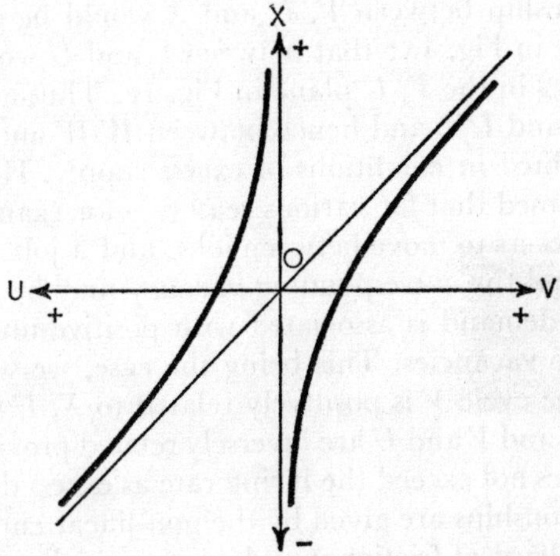

Fig. 1A

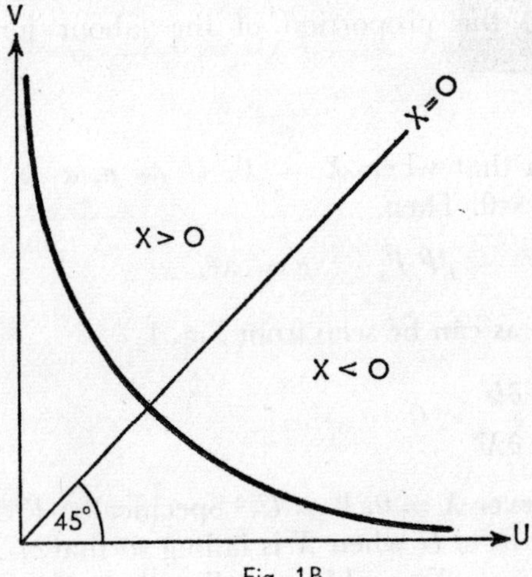

Fig. 1B

In a frictionless labour market, equilibrium would occur at zero vacancies and zero unemployment, and if the market is cleared along the supply curve when excess demand is positive and is cleared along the demand curve when it is negative,

$$X = -\frac{U}{L} \text{ for } X < 0 \text{ and } X = \frac{V}{L} \text{ for } X > 0.$$

The relationship between V, U and X would be given by the straight line in Fig. 1A; that between V and U would coincide with the axes in the V, U plane in Fig. 1B. Thus a relationship between X and U/L and hence between $\dot{W}/W$ and U/L would only be defined in conditions of excess supply. However, it is usually assumed that for various reasons – for example, it takes time for workers to move between jobs, and a job may exist in one place and the corresponding vacancy may be in another – zero excess demand is associated with positive unemployment and positive vacancies. This being the case, we would expect that over the cycle V is positively related to X, U is negatively related to X and V and U are inversely related provided that the quit rate does not exceed the hiring rate as excess demand rises. These relationships are given by the non-linear curves in Fig. 1 for a given level of frictional and/or structural unemployment and vacancies at zero excess demand. If therefore we now assume that there is a stable non-linear transformation between excess demand and the proportion of the labour force which is unemployed,

$$X = \theta(U) \tag{5}$$

θ being such that when $X \to 0$, $U \to a$, $a > 0$ and when $X \to \infty$, $U \to 0$. Then,

$$\dot{W}/W = \alpha(U) + \beta\dot{P}/P, \qquad \alpha = \lambda\theta. \tag{6}$$

Moreover, as can be seen from Fig. 1,

$$\frac{\partial V}{\partial X} > 0 \text{ and } \frac{\partial U}{\partial X} < 0$$

so that whenever $\dot{X} \neq 0$, $\dot{V} \neq \dot{U}$.[2] Specifically, $\dot{V} > \dot{U}$ when X is rising and $\dot{V} < \dot{U}$ when X is falling so that $|\dot{X}| > |\dot{U}|$ whenever $X_t \neq X_{t-1}$. This implies that X will be higher (lower) when U is falling (rising) than when it is rising (falling) for any given level of U, i.e. X is underestimated when U is falling and overestimated when U is rising. But this means, as Phillips argued, that if employers bid for labour on the basis of the level of excess demand, they will bid more for labour when U is falling than when it is rising for any given level of U. To the extent that such bidding is successful, it reduces both U and V. However, given that the relationship between V and U is non-linear, it reduces U *by less* than it reduces V. Hence $\dot{W}/W$ will be greater when U is falling than when it is rising for any given level of U. Moreover, the misstatement of X by U varies in a manner which is determined by the non-linearity in the relationship between V and X, U and X as well as by the pattern of cyclical variations in X. Define the misstatement of X by U as M.

$$M = \frac{\partial V}{\partial X}\dot{X},\ \dot{M} = \frac{\partial^2 V}{\partial X^2}\dot{X} + \frac{\partial V}{\partial X}\ddot{X} \text{ where } \frac{\partial^2 V}{\partial X^2} > 0$$

but tends to a limit of zero. Assume that on the upswing of the cycle ($\dot{X} > 0$), $\ddot{X} > 0$ for $X < 0$ and $\ddot{X} < 0$ for $X > 0$. Assume that the upswing and the downswing are symmetrical. It is then readily seen that there will be anticlockwise loops whenever X is not constant. Thus if vacancy statistics are not available so that X is not directly measurable, in *non-stationary* situations, $\dot{U}/U$ is a valid proxy with U/L for the level of excess demand. We therefore have

$$\dot{W}/W = \alpha(U) + \gamma(\dot{U}/U + \beta\dot{P}/P \tag{7}$$

This completes the formal theory of the usual version of the Phillips curve. It raises several questions of which we shall discuss three.

(i) We have just established that in non-stationary situations, $\dot{U}/U$ is a valid proxy with U for the level of excess demand. However, excepting the nineteenth-century data, investigators have not generally found a significant regression coefficient on $\dot{U}/U$ in equations of the type $\dot{W}/W = f(U, \dot{U}/U)$. And it cannot be said that since the nineteenth century the level of unemployment has been stationary.

It will be recalled that Phillips [9] introduced $\dot{U}/U$ to account for the loops which he observed in the nineteenth-century U.K. data on the hypothesis that in anticipating cyclical phases in the labour market, employers overbid for labour when unemployment is falling and underbid when it is rising for any given level of unemployment. Lipsey [6] rejected this on the grounds that such over- and underbidding affected both $\dot{W}/W$ and the level of unemployment simultaneously. He put forward his by now familiar aggregation hypothesis according to which the loops are the results of aggregation over identical sector Phillips curves with varying levels of unemployment and hence varying rates of change of money wage rates over the cycle, the upswing affecting different sectors differently while the downswing is more evenly synchronised. According to this hypothesis, $\dot{U}/U$ is a proxy for the dispersion of unemployment (σ_u^2) in each market around the average for the whole economy. This implies that $\dot{U}/U$ and σ_u^2 should be significantly and negatively correlated, that $\dot{U}/U$ and $\dot{W}/W$ should be negatively correlated, that σ_u^2 and $\dot{W}/W$ should be positively correlated and that either but not both should contribute significantly to the explanation of the variance in $\dot{W}/W$.

It is clear from what has been established above that the Lipsey criticism of Phillips's rationalisation of the inclusion of $\dot{U}/U$ in the wage equation is invalid. This being the case, Lipsey's aggregation hypothesis is to be regarded as an alternative to another which is also logically admissible. Which is to be preferred is to be settled by an appeal either to their wider implications or to the empirical evidence. However, as has been shown in [5], there are severe difficulties with the aggregation hypothesis. The conditions under which the sign of the dispersion effect $\left(\dfrac{\partial \dot{W}/W}{\partial \sigma_u^2}\right)$ is unambiguously positive – identical non-linear Phillips curves with constant second derivatives in each sector – is very restrictive. These conditions are clearly not met in the data given the assumption that the sectors which have been treated in empirical analysis can be said to correspond to 'true' sectoral labour markets. Moreover, it has been shown [5], on post-war data, that $\dot{U}/U$ and $\dot{W}/W$ are not significantly correlated, that $\dot{U}/U$ and σ_u^2 are not significantly correlated, but that $\dot{W}/W$ and σ_u^2 are significantly correlated. This has led us to rationalise the observed relationship between the variance of unemployment and the rate of change of money wage rates in terms of the *transfer mechanism* hypothesis according to which groups in the bargaining process in different sectors are related in such a way that wage changes in lead sectors are transmitted to following sectors. This hypothesis is consistent with the data and is not open to the objections which we have made to the aggregation hypothesis.

One conclusion of this is that neither the theory of the Phillips curve nor the available evidence unambiguously indicate that a policy of reducing the sectoral distribution of unemployment – a policy which is to be encouraged on many grounds and in its own right – will reduce the aggregate rate of change of money wage rates.

(ii) In equation (2), instead of writing $\left(\frac{\dot{W}}{P}\right) / \left(\frac{W}{P}\right) = \lambda(X)$, we could have written

$$\left(\frac{\dot{W}}{P}\right) / \left(\frac{W}{P}\right) = \lambda h\left(\frac{W}{P} \mid Y, Z\right) \tag{8}$$

The elements of the vectors Y and Z are parameters of shift of the demand and supply functions such as tastes concerning leisure and goods, productivity, the degree of monopoly power in factor markets, etc. (We can also write

$$\left(\frac{\dot{W}}{P}\right) / \left(\frac{W}{P}\right) = f(X \mid Y, Z) \tag{9}$$

if we assume that, given the inclusion of the elements of Y and Z, X refers to those levels of excess demand which are associated with the adjustment of W/P to its equilibrium level as of given demand and supply curves. But we cannot have $\left(\frac{\dot{W}}{P}\right) / \left(\frac{W}{P}\right) = \lambda h\left(\frac{W}{P} \mid Y, Z, U\right)$. The one formulation relates $\dot{W}/W$ to an adjustment mechanism (given $\dot{P}/P$), the other relates $\dot{W}/W$ to the underlying structural parameters of the labour market. Which we choose to have depends on the problem in hand. Thus we might assume a stable relationship between $\dot{W}/W$ and $X = f(U, \dot{U}/U)$ if we simply wish to predict $\dot{W}/W$ conditional on X. However, we might wish to investigate the *causes* of inflation in order to be able to say something about the relative importance of the various impulse factors in the inflationary process over some given period. (The writer hazards the guess that it is this interest in the causes of inflation, as evidenced by the demand-pull/cost-push debate, which has stimulated much of the work of the past fifteen or so years.) However, knowledge of the form of an adjustment function which is assumed to be stable does not allow one to distinguish between causes of disequilibrium. But we do wish to know something about the causes of inflation. And to obtain this information, we require an explicit specification of the wage equation in terms of the variables which constitute the parameters of shift of the supply and the demand functions.

Thus, contrary to what has become almost standard doctrine, such variables as the rate of change of productivity and the rate of change of unionisation as well as the rate of change of unemployment and the rate of change of prices are *not* 'intruders' in the wage equation.

If this is correct, it shows the importance of distinguishing between a procedure according to which we express the relationship between $\dot{W}/W$ and excess demand (given $\dot{P}/P$) in terms of some one proxy variable such as the level of unemployment or vacancies minus unemployment, a procedure which enables conditional prediction but no explanation, and one in which we express the relationship in terms of variables which correspond to the parameters of the structural equations and from which we can not only predict $\dot{W}/W$ conditional on knowing the exogenous variables, but from which we can also learn something about the causes of inflation. The writer has no doubt that the latter specification is the more fruitful so long as one wishes to operate within this kind of framework. Moreover, this distinction should go some way towards rationalising the diverse empirical findings concerning the significance of the level of unemployment in wage adjustment equations which have been reported in the literature. For it implies that if in a fitted regression model we were to include all the relevant variables which influence supply and demand as well as the level of the real wage rate, the coefficient of U should take on a value which is not significantly different from zero. Indeed, if such a model were fitted to adequate data and a coefficient on U was obtained which was significantly different from zero, it would simply imply that some relevant determining variable had not been included in the appropriate form among the set of regressors. However, the level of unemployment could be significant if it replaced W/P in the wage equation, it being assumed that U governs the adjustment of W/P from a disequilibrium position to its equilibrium level as of given values of the elements of Y and Z. In that case an insignificant coefficient on U would imply that over the sample period changes in wage rates which are the result of shifts in the schedules predominated over changes which eliminate excess demand as of given values of the exogenous variables.

The available empirical evidence for the U.K. is consistent with these views. Thus, as has been shown in previous studies and as can be seen from Table 1, whenever the equation $\dot{W}/W = f(U, \dot{P}/P)$ is fitted to aggregate post-war data, the coefficient on U is invariably significant (the coefficient on $\dot{P}/P$ is also significant). But whenever variables such as the rate of change of the proportion of the labour force which is unionised ($\dot{T}/T$), a proxy for changes in union militancy, are included either in single equations as in the table or in simultaneous equation systems as in [2], the coefficient on the unemployment variable is usually insignificant, at any rate in annual data. However, there is a snag.

The argument which we have been advancing implies that the proportion of the variance in $\dot{W}/W$ which is explained when the parameters of shift of the supply and demand functions are explanatory variables cannot exceed that which is explained by the proxy for excess demand. However, as can be seen from the table, this is not the case. $\bar{R}^2$ increases noticeably when $\dot{T}/T$ is added as an explanatory variable, which suggests that union militancy accounts for some of the variance in $\dot{W}/W$ over and above that which is explained by the level of excess demand. (The position is not altered if both U and $\dot{U}/U$ are used as joint proxies for X.) In [5], we have explored various rationalisations of these findings. However, we have been unsuccessful in

TABLE 1. DEPENDENT VARIABLE IS $\dot{W}/W$, $N = 16$

Equation	*Constant*	U^{-1}	$(\dot{P}/P)_{t-\frac{1}{2}}$	$\dot{T}/T$	σ^2_{UR}	σ^2_{UI}	$\bar{R}^2$	D.W.
(1)	1·385	6·571 (2·960)					0·341	1·690*
(2)	1·084	3·617 (1·761)	0·588 (0·201)				0·572	2·332*
(3)	2·124	2·873 (1·789)	0·436 (2·681)	2·525 (3·124)			0·744	2·833*
(4)	−4·334	8·655 (3·840)				41·909 (2·032)	0·461	1·668*
(5)	−1·382	5·078 (1·874)	0·480 (1·997)			18·480 (0·840)	0·562	2·160*
(6)	−0·113	5·883 (2·687)		2·697 (2·528)		18·516 (0·942)	0·619	2·529*
(7)	2·422	2·695 (1·161)	0·446 (2·322)	2·564 (2·803)		−2·108 (0·110)	0·721	2·852*
(8)	−2·733	5·253 (2·026)			24·966 (0·986)		0·340	1·633*
(9)	−2·742	2·426 (1·065)	0·581 (2·925)		23·215 (1·153)		0·583	2·328*
(10)	5·048	5·200 (2·586)		3·541 (3·102)	−14·025 (0·602)		0·603	2·744*
(11)	3·186	3·131 (1·672)	0·428 (2·493)	2·696 (2·666)	−6·015 (0·305)		0·723	2·885*

Notes:

1. The data are for the period 1951–66 ($N = 16$). The sources and methods of computation of $\dot{W}/W$, $\dot{P}/P$, $\dot{T}/T$ and U are described in Hines [4]. Data for σ_{UI} and σ_{UR} were kindly supplied by Mr A. P. Thirwall.
2. 't' values are in parenthesis beneath the regression coefficients.
3. D.W. statistic: * Indicates that the test showed no autocorrelation at the 1 per cent probability level. † Indicates that the test was inconclusive. For other values the term showed positive autocorrelation.
4. Results including $\dot{U}/U$ are not shown. The coefficient on this variable is invariably insignificant by conventional stan-

generating a rationalisation within the framework of the excess demand model which is both *a priori* plausible and consistent with the relevant empirical evidence.

(iii) In equation (2) we formulated the dynamic adjustment function in terms of real wages and transformed it into a function in money wages by assuming that $\beta = 1$. This formulation is suggested by neo-classical theory which is concerned with the dynamic stability of markets rather than with the disequilibrium dynamics of ongoing processes. Alternatively, we could have postulated an adjustment function which is stated directly in terms of money wages and which is concerned with how the participants in the wage bargain respond to a state of disequilibrium irrespective of whether the responses are or are not equilibrating. Thus the adjustment function $\frac{\dot{W}}{W} = \lambda(X)$ simply states that when, for example, there is excess demand for labour, money wages are bid up by buyers or advanced by sellers, the percentage rate of rise being proportional to the excess demand. On this view the wage bargain in a non-tâtonnement situation is necessarily conducted in money terms whatever is the objective of the participants. Money wages are the only variable which the workers can control or influence directly. This being the case, if the wage bargain (necessarily conducted in money terms) is a bargain for real wages, the expected rate of change of prices enters the adjustment function. In place of equation (6), we would then have

$$\frac{\dot{W}}{W} = \theta(U) + \kappa(\dot{P}/P)^*, 0 < \kappa \leqslant 1. \tag{10}$$

Suppose that the adaptive expectations hypothesis is appropriate to the formation of expectations about price changes. Then, using p to denote $\dot{P}/P$ and p^* to denote $(\dot{P}/P)^*$,

$$p_t^* = p_{t-1}^* + \psi(p_{t-1} - p_{t-1}^*) = \ldots = \sum_{i=0}^{\infty}\psi(1 - \psi)^i p_{t-1-i}. \tag{11}$$

If, as is assumed in the real wage formulation in [2], the elasticity of expectations is unity, $\psi = 1$ so that $\kappa = \beta = 1$ and if there is no lag in the adjustment of $\dot{W}/W$ to excess demand so that $p_t = p^*_{t-1}$ all t, the relationship between $\dot{W}/W$ and U would always be a vertical line in the $\dot{W}/W$, U plane. However, empirical work usually yields historical Phillips curves with a non-vertical slope. This suggests that there is some lag in the adjustment of money wages to the level of excess demand and that the elasticity of expectations is not unity within the unit period. Hence, in the more usual case $0 < \psi < 1$ and p^*_t is some weighted function of all past values of p_t. Now consider the behaviour of a system to which the adaptive expectations hypothesis applies and in which $0 < \psi < 1$ so that

$$\frac{\dot{W}}{W} = \alpha(U) + \kappa \sum_{i=0}^{\infty} \psi(1 - \psi)^i p_{t-1-i}. \qquad (12)$$

In a situation in which $p^*_t \neq p_{t-1}$, the Phillips curve is downward-sloping. But if $p^*_t = p_t$, i.e. given sufficient time such that the actual rate of inflation comes to be expected, $\kappa = \beta = 1$ and the Phillips curve becomes a vertical line in the $\dot{W}/W$, U plane. As Friedman [1] put the matter, the trade-off between $\dot{W}/W$ and U is temporary and is due to lags in the adjustment of expectations to the actual state of affairs.

Investigators such as Solow [11] have analysed U.K. and U.S. data to see if this conclusion holds. They have estimated β for a wide range of values of ψ between zero and unity and have invariably found that in the long run as well as in the short run, $0 < \beta < 1$. (However, the value of β is greater in the long run than in the short run, indicating that the trade-off between $\dot{W}/W$ and U is less favourable in the long run.)

Such findings pose serious difficulties for those who rationalise the Phillips curve within the neo-classical paradigm. Thus, Solow accepts that the hypothesis which generates the vertical long-run Phillips curve is grounded in the theory of rational conduct. He therefore has to explain away what is observed in the data. Accordingly, he postulates the existence of some threshold – a minimum sensible – below which individuals do not adjust their expectations to irregular rates of inflation. In the same vein, Rees [10] has argued that costs of change prevent the full adjustment of monetary contracts even when the actual rate of inflation comes to be expected. He also maintains that a part of the reduction in unemployment which is associated with an increase in the actual rate of inflation may be permanent in so far as it consists of a reduction in structural unemployment among workers whose skills were previously adapted to industries which are in decline and/or among members of minority groups against whom there is social discrimination. Such reductions in unemployment are said not to be reversed when expectations become adjusted because the marginal product of these workers is increased by the experience of employment in non-depressed trades and/or because employers may learn that their prior estimate of the marginal products of members of minority groups was wrong.

Such 'explanations' are clearly plausible and can account for the discrepancy between theoretical expectation and what is observed in the data. However, they do appear to be *ad hoc*. Reaction functions are assumed to be quadratic; costs of adjustment functions and the mapping from excess demand to unemployment are assumed to have specific forms. The sole purpose of this is to reconcile the theory with what is observed in the time series. The question therefore arises whether there exists a more satisfactory framework in which to interpret the negatively sloped relationship between $\dot{W}/W$ and U which has been observed in the 'long-run' time-series data. Such a framework is also necessary in view of the problems of reconciling the evidence with the excess demand model which we also encountered in (i) and (ii). Fortunately, an alternative framework does exist. To utilise it we must drop the assumption of an invariant level of full employment upon which the neo-classical model rests. For it is only in a situation of full employment that the marginal product curve can be taken to be the demand curve for labour. As we have seen, in such a framework changes in money wage rates either reflect the adjustment of factor proportions to that which is optimal as of a predetermined level of output or are associated with the existence and resolution of the conflicting *ex-ante* demands which are assumed to be the result of differential foresight as between employers and employees such that they evaluate a given exogenous change in money wages at different expected price levels.

AN ALTERNATIVE FRAMEWORK FOR THE ANALYSIS OF THE RELATIONSHIP BETWEEN THE RATE OF CHANGE OF MONEY WAGE RATES AND THE LEVEL OF UNEMPLOYMENT

The alternative framework is the Keynesian model. It is a model of a system of interdependent markets in which there is no guarantee that full employment will be maintained. It assumes that states of under-full employment are quite normal and that the level of aggregate demand fluctuates over time. If this is the case it is more fruitful to think of the aggregate demand for labour as being derived directly from the aggregate demand for goods rather than from the substitutability between the services of labour and the services of other inputs as of a given level of final demand. As aggregate demand varies, the relationship between employment and the real wage rate will depend on technology, market structures and the employment policies of firms. Thus, given the dominance in the economy of technologies which exhibit constant or falling cost with output and/or given the prevalence of oligopolistic structures in the key sectors of the economy together with the overhead characteristics of much labour (implying a lagged response of employment to changes in output), output per man and the real wage rate actually increase with a rise in output and employment. Thus, if we are to offer an analysis which is consistent with the inflationary processes which are observed in actual economies, we must abandon the framework of the perfectly competitive labour market together with the assumption of an invariable full-employment level of output.

We should therefore start the other way round and regard the money wage rate as the independent variable in the observed relationship between the rate of change of money wage rates and the level of unemployment. The Keynesian system is then viewed as a reduced form in which the level of demand and hence the level of unemployment depend on the level of the money wage rate.[3] At any moment of time, it is assumed that there exists some positive unemployment which consists of demand-deficient as well as structural components and which can be reduced by an increase in effective demand. The money wage rate is assumed to be determined in a manner which is substantially independent of the level of aggregate demand. It is regarded as the outcome of bargaining in labour markets in which the situation corresponds most nearly to bilateral monopoly and in which the determination of the money wage rate requires explicit recognition of bargaining strategy and market power even though the bounds to a settlement may be set by 'economic' forces. The problem then is to find some way of representing in an operational form those forces which exert pressure upon the money wage rate independently of the level of demand for labour. It was hypothesised in [2] that autonomous pressure to maintain or to increase money wage rates is related to union militancy and that the rate of change of unionisation be taken to be a proxy for militancy, which is not a directly observable variable. For workers do not regard the value of their human wealth as being perfectly variable. Consequently, in a state of mass unemployment, they resist cuts in their money wages. In a growing economy (which may or may not be in a state of full-employment) workers, as well as other agents, expect that the value of their wealth and hence their real income should rise as national income rises. If Walras's auctioneer or his equivalent were available to ensure that all transactors were made aware of the feasible increases in real incomes and to ensure that these increases are distributed in a manner which is not only acceptable to each transactor but which also yields a level of aggregate demand which is consistent with actual transformation possibilities, all would be well. But there is no auctioneer. Moreover, in this situation individuals cannot rely on a fall in the aggregate price level to bring about the requisite increase in their real income. The transactor has no direct control over the price level. He does, however, have some control over the price of the services of the productive resource which he owns. It is therefore quite rational that workers, for example, should take steps, e.g. by combining in trade unions, to raise their money rates of remuneration. And since there is no guarantee that the sum of those claims which are successful and the resulting level of aggregate expenditure (including government expenditure) will mesh with productive potential, the situation is clearly inflationary. We therefore see that whereas in the neo-classical model of full-employment quantities the expectations of transactors are only concerned with prices, in a system in which the level of aggregate demand and output fluctuates over time transactors form expectations concerning *quantities* as well as prices. Specifically, it is *a priori* reasonable that workers should form expectations concerning real incomes and hence the real wage rate and that their monetary claims should be influenced by the discrepancy between the expected level and rate of growth of real wages and the actual level and rate of growth of real wages.

Suppose that in this setting owners of productive services put upward pressure upon the prices of their services in an attempt to raise their real incomes. Specifically, suppose that there is an autonomous push on money wage rates. If the necessary finance is forthcoming, the increase in aggregate demand will generate an increase in output and a reduction in unemployment. However, given the existing level of excess capacity, the interdependence of changes in factor and product prices as well as the trend rate of growth of productivity, the resulting increase in real incomes may fall short of the expected increase. (In addition income may be redistributed between transactors according to their market and bargaining power and according to the relative fixity of contracts which are made in money terms.) If this is voluntarily accepted by all agents, the process comes to an end. If it is not accepted, and the push on prices of factors and products is maintained or accelerated, and there are no monetary and/or fiscal restraints, money incomes, wages and prices continue to rise at an accelerating rate while real output and real wages increase and unemployment falls at a decreasing rate. Thus asymptotically, unemployment approaches zero or some positive constant, the rate of change of prices and money wages approaches infinity and real wage and real output tend to levels which are determined by the real forces of productivity, thrift and technical progress. Such a sequence of events would clearly generate a Phillips-curve-like relationship between the rate of change of money wage rates and the level of unemployment. Moreover, such a curve would not have the expected rate of change of prices as a parameter of shift. In this framework, the expected rate of price change is a factor which determines the force of the exogenous push on money wage rates through its effect upon the discrepancy between the actual and the real wage rate. Thus even if expectations were to become fully adapted to the going rate of inflation – an unlikely state of affairs in this model since uncertainty is assumed always to be present in a fashion which influences behaviour significantly – the curve would not shift to become vertical throughout its length as in the neo-classical case where full employment is invariably maintained. We do, however, reach the conclusion that as $\dot{W}/W \rightarrow \infty$, $U \rightarrow a$, $a > 0$, where a is some irreducible amount of frictional and/or structural unemployment.

This does not mean that money wages might not vary in response to a change in the level of unemployment which is the result of changes in aggregate demand which are brought about by changes in autonomous expenditure including government expenditure and the trade balance in an open economy. Nor do we wish to deny the possibility that the rate of change of money wage rates might be modified by an increase in unemployment which is the result of countervailing monetary and fiscal policy. However, it is likely that the magnitude of the effect of the rate of change of money wages on the level of unemployment is greater than the magnitude of the effect of the level of unemployment upon the rate of change of money wage rates. Moreover, it is possible that a policy of increasing the level of unemployment which is intended to slow down the rate of inflation may at best have no effect on the rate at which money wages and prices are pushed up and might even result in an increase in the rate of inflation inasmuch as an increase in unemployment increases the gap between the actual and the expected real wage rate. Hence, it is quite possible that we may observe, as we do in fact observe, a strong positive relationship between the rate of change of money wage rates and some index of autonomous pressure on wage rates–say an index of union militancy – associated with a positive or a negative relationship between the level of unemployment and the rate of change of money wage rates according as monetary and fiscal policy are passive in the face of autonomous increases in wages and prices or as a countervailing policy results in an increase or a slowing down of the rate of change of money wages and prices. Thus, suppose that fiscal and monetary policy has no effect upon the rate of change of wages and prices. In periods of monetary and fiscal ease we should therefore observe a negative relationship between $\dot{W}/W$ and U. We should observe a positive relationship if, given autonomous pressure on wages and prices, an active fiscal and monetary policy is sufficiently strong to more than offset the reduction in unemployment which would be the consequence of increases in money wage rates. If policy just offsets the increase in aggregate demand which would flow from an increase in wage rates, the relationship between $\dot{W}/W$ and U would not be significantly different from zero. In periods in which policy only partially offsets the expansionary effects of an increase in wages, the relationship between $\dot{W}/W$ and U would be negative but the size of the regression coefficient should be significantly smaller than it would be in periods when policy is passive. Moreover, our hypothesis concerning the determination of $\dot{W}/W$ would imply that whatever is the difference in the sign or the magnitude of the coefficient on unemployment in the regression of $\dot{W}/W$ on U as between such periods, there should be a strong and positive association between $\dot{T}/T$ and $\dot{W}/W$.

What is now required is the specification of an appropriate model (in which U is an endogenous variable) in which the implications of our hypothesis concerning the relationship between the level of unemployment and the rate of change of money wage rates can be explored. We hope to report on this matter at a later date.

SOME EMPIRICAL EVIDENCE ON THE DETERMINATION OF THE RATE OF CHANGE OF MONEY WAGE RATES

Table 2 shows the results of fitting the equation $\dot{W}/W_t = f(U_{t-a}, \dot{P}/P_{t-b}, \dot{T}/T_{t-c})$ to all post-war data and to 'off' and 'on' periods separately. (The lags *a*, *b* and *c* are to be determined from the data.) The division of the data into 'policy off' and 'policy on' periods was suggested by Lipsey and Parkin [7]. They were concerned with investigating the effect on $\dot{W}/W$ and $\dot{P}/P$ of incomes policy by fiat or exhortation as distinct from incomes policy which is based on demand management. (They consider that the use of shift and/or slope dummies is not appropriate to the task.) The equations that were fitted to the data which were used by Lipsey and Parkin are labelled L/P.

The equations which were fitted to our own quarterly and annual data are labelled H and H_A respectively.

The results show that in 'off' periods the coefficient of U is significantly negative whereas in 'on' periods it is either negative or positive but is in any case not significantly different from zero. This is consistent with our hypothesis concerning countervailing fiscal and monetary policy. The coefficient on $\dot{P}/P$ has the expected sign but is sometimes not significantly different from zero. In the entire post-war period as well as in 'off' and 'on' periods the coefficient of $\dot{T}/T$ is significant and positive. Indeed, as can be seen in the relevant cells of the table, it is usually the most significant of all the explanatory variables. This is consistent with the hypothesis that there should exist a significantly positive relationship between $\dot{W}/W$ and $\dot{T}/T$ independently of the significance of the relationship between U and $\dot{W}/W$.

Our findings, particularly those concerning the significance of $\dot{T}/T$, are directly opposite to that which was reported by Lipsey and Parkin [8]. They report that $\dot{T}/T$ is significant when the equation is fitted to the whole period, is nearly significant in the 'policy on' periods, but is totally insignificant in the 'policy off' periods. As can be seen from the table, there are also some differences with respect to the coefficients of other explanatory variables. Thus in two of the equations which are fitted to data for the entire period we find that the coefficient of U is negative and significant. The coefficient of $\dot{P}/P$ is usually less well determined than it is in their study. However, the divergence of results is most marked in the case of the trade union variable.

There are three reasons for the marked divergence between our results and those of Lipsey and Parkin. The first concerns the specification of the wage equation which is estimated by O.L.S. The second concerns the choice of estimating techniques. The third concerns the data which are used.

In almost all studies of wage inflation in the post-war period, the interdependence between price change and wage change and its consequences for O.L.S. estimates of parameters is recognised. In consequence, most investigators have either employed a simultaneous method of estimation or have introduced an initial delay in the response of wage changes to price

TABLE 2. DEPENDENT VARIABLE IS $\dot{W}/W_t$

Period	*Equation*	*Constant*	U_t	$(\dot{P}/P)_t$	$(\dot{P}/P)_{t-\frac{1}{2}}$	$(\dot{T}/T)_t$	R^2	D.W.
The model fitted to the entire period	(1) L/P	4·147	−0·891	0·482		3·315	0·616	0·742
			(1·77)	(5·76)		(2·09)		
	(2) L/P	5·580	−1·272		0·277	7·911	0·571	0·702
			(2·42)		(3·43)	(4·63)		
	(3) H	6·076	−0·918	0·229		8·900	0·656	0·979
			(2·08)	(2·43)		(4·62)		
	(4) H	6·940	−1·197		0·136	11·103	0·649	1·026
			(2·96)		(2·09)	(7·51)		
	(5) H_A	5·051	−0·346		0·338	0·395	0·775	2·672
			(0·78)		(1·97)	(4·56)		
The model fitted to the 'policy off' period	(1) L/P	6·672	−2·372	0·457		0·136	0·856	1·231
			(3·64)	(6·25)		(0·07)		
	(2) L/P	9·293	−3·490		0·231	4·451	0·760	0·655
			(4·42)		(3·06)	(2·07)		
	(3) H	7·145	−1·384	0·211		7·844	0·840	1·565
			(2·50)	(2·38)		(3·78)		
	(4) H	8·412	−1·848		0·101	10·266	0·830	1·472
			(3·61)		(1·83)	(6·44)		
	(5) H_A	6·147	−0·628		0·194	3·628	0·898	3·293
			(0·89)		(0·99)	(3·79)		

TABLE 2 (*cont.*)

The model fitted to the 'policy on' period	(1) L/P	3·919	−0·404 (0·56)	0·227 (0·93)		3·764 (1·61)	0·138	0·724
	(2) L/P	2·464	0·192 (0·24)		0·408 (1·56)	6·505 (2·37)	0·288	0·910
	(3) H	5·165	−0·589 (0·81)	0·258 (0·92)		9·793 (3·01)	0·382	0·815
	(4) H	3·809	−0·173 (0·26)		0·412 (2·12)	10·758 (4·01)	0·441	0·985
	(5) H_A	−0·276	0·870 (1·12)		1·063 (2·47)	1·319 (1·11)	0·691	2·553

Notes:

1. The equations labelled L/P employ the data which were used by Lipsey and Parkin [7]. The sources are described therein. In particular, the wage variable is an index of weekly wage rates. The data were kindly supplied by Professor Parkin.

The equations labelled H use an index of hourly wage rates which was kindly supplied by the Department of Employment and Productivity. The other variables were obtained from the same sources as were used by Lipsey and Parkin.

The equation labelled H_A employs annual data. The sources are described in Hines [5].

2. The methods by which the raw data are transformed are reported in [11] and [6]. In all the equations excepting those which use annual data, $U = 1/3(U_t + U_{t-1} + U_{t-2})$. For the equations in annual data $U + U_{t-7/12}$. In equations H, $\dot{T}/T$ for each quarter in a given year is obtained from a quarterly linear interpolation of the one available observation for that year. We have not succeeded in locating the source of Lipsey and Parkin's semi-annual data on unionisation. Their quarterly data are linear interpolations.

3. '*t*' values are in parenthesis beneath the regression coefficients.

changes in the wage equation when O.L.S. is employed. (Careful prior study of the data by many investigators has usually shown the lag on the price variable in the wage equation to be between three and six months and the lag on the wage variable in the price equation to be between zero and three months.) However, Lipsey and Parkin introduced $\dot{P}/P$ into the wage equation with a zero lag, obtaining the results reported in their paper and reproduced in the first row of each subsection of Table 2. When $\dot{P}/P$ is lagged by six months and their data are used, as can be seen in the second row of each subsection of the table, there is the 'dramatic' reversal in the results which we have described above.

The reasons why Lipsey and Parkin decided not to use a simultaneous technique of estimation are not persuasive. They argue that variables such as the rate of change of unionisation, the rate of change of productivity and the level of unemployment cannot be regarded as exogenous to the system. However, taken literally, their argument implies that there can be no stopping-place between a single equation and a model of the whole economy. The question then is whether there exist gaps in the degree of interdependence which holds among the variables and equations that describe the economy, which are sufficiently marked to allow us to estimate a subset of equations which correspond to a given sector. Be that as it may, since our objective is the strictly limited one of dealing with the interdependence between wages, prices and unionisation, we used quarterly data to estimate the three-equation model which was introduced in [2]. The results are reported in Table 3. They show that, excepting the case of $\dot{P}/P$, the coefficients of *all* the variables are well determined in 'on' and 'off' quarters as well as in the entire period.

Further, the wage series which is used by Lipsey and Parkin is an index of weekly wage rates. The annual data which were used by Hines in [2], [3] and [4] is in the form of an index of hourly wage rates. The index of hourly wage rates is the index of weekly wage rates normalised for changes in normal hours worked per week. And since Lipsey and Parkin eschew simultaneous estimation techniques, they are precluded from having an equation in hours worked in an appropriately chosen subset of equations. Be that as it may, since our primary objective is to

TABLE 3

The Model Fitted to the Entire Period

$$\dot{W}/W_t = 6{\cdot}234 + \underset{(10{\cdot}682)}{8{\cdot}800}\ \dot{T}/T_t + \underset{(5{\cdot}191)}{0{\cdot}214}\ \dot{P}/P_t - \underset{(7{\cdot}051)}{0{\cdot}982}\ U_t, \qquad R^2 = 0{\cdot}953$$

$$\dot{P}/P_t = -0{\cdot}675 + \underset{(26{\cdot}043)}{0{\cdot}852}\ \dot{W}/W_t - \underset{(14{\cdot}635)}{1{\cdot}108}\ \dot{X}/X_t + \underset{(19{\cdot}636)}{0{\cdot}086}\ \dot{M}/M_{t-1}, \qquad R^2 = 0{\cdot}984$$

$$\dot{T}/T_t = 4{\cdot}555 - \underset{(27{\cdot}854)}{0{\cdot}421}\ T\%_{t-1} + \underset{(53{\cdot}333)}{0{\cdot}032}\ \dot{P}/P_t - \underset{(15{\cdot}744)}{0{\cdot}067}\ D_{t-2}, \qquad R^2 = 0{\cdot}982$$

The Model Fitted to the 'Policy off' Period

$$\dot{W}/W_t = 6.394 + \underset{(15{\cdot}868)}{7{\cdot}850}\ \dot{T}/T_t + \underset{(13{\cdot}806)}{0{\cdot}264}\ \dot{P}/P_t - \underset{(10{\cdot}436)}{1{\cdot}048}\ U_t, \qquad R^2 = 0{\cdot}994$$

$$\dot{P}/P_t = 0{\cdot}325 + \underset{(5{\cdot}260)}{0{\cdot}704}\ \dot{W}/W_t - \underset{(6{\cdot}445)}{0{\cdot}194}\ \dot{X}/X_t + \underset{(6{\cdot}477)}{0{\cdot}113}\ \dot{M}/M_{t-1}, \qquad R^2 = 0{\cdot}973$$

$$\dot{T}/T = 5{\cdot}555 - \underset{(16{\cdot}350)}{0{\cdot}508}\ T\%_{t-1} + \underset{(32{\cdot}555)}{0{\cdot}029}\ \dot{P}/P_t - \underset{(7{\cdot}556)}{0{\cdot}080}\ D_{t-2}, \qquad R^2 = 0{\cdot}980$$

The Model Fitted to the 'Policy on' Period

$$\dot{W}/W_t = 12.983 + \underset{(5{\cdot}590)}{17{\cdot}750}\ \dot{T}/T_t - \underset{(2{\cdot}398)}{0{\cdot}979}\ \dot{P}/P_t - \underset{(3{\cdot}617)}{2{\cdot}550}\ U_t, \qquad R^2 = 0{\cdot}672$$

$$\dot{P}/P_t = 1{\cdot}427 + \underset{(4{\cdot}182)}{0{\cdot}436}\ \dot{W}/W_t - \underset{(1{\cdot}905)}{0{\cdot}052}\ \dot{X}/X_t - \underset{(0{\cdot}098)}{0{\cdot}002}\ \dot{M}/M_{t-1}, \qquad R^2 = 0{\cdot}411$$

$$\dot{T}/T_t = 4{\cdot}208 - \underset{(5{\cdot}580)}{0{\cdot}396}\ T\%_{t-1} + \underset{(5{\cdot}567)}{0{\cdot}041}\ \dot{P}/P_t - \underset{(2{\cdot}944)}{0{\cdot}058}\ D_{t-2}, \qquad R^2 = 0{\cdot}768$$

Notes:

1. $\dot{T}/T$, $T\%$ and D for each quarter in a given year is obtained from a quarterly linear interpolation of the one available observation for that year.
2. $T\%$ is the percentage of the labour force which is unionised and D is a deflated index of the gross trading profits of companies.
3. $\dot{W}/W$ is an index of *hourly* wage rates.
4. 't' statistics are given in parenthesis.

see how our chosen explanatory variables affect wage rates rather than how they may affect the length of the working week, and in order to achieve comparability with our previous work which used annual data, it was decided to re-estimate the equations which were fitted to quarterly data using an hourly wage-rate series. The results are reported in the third and fourth rows of each subsection of Table 2. They show that $\dot{T}/T$ is significant *even when the price variable is unlagged*, although the '*t*' statistics are larger when the price variable is lagged.

We have also found, as did Lipsey and Parkin, that there is marked first-order serial correlation in the residuals of the equations fitted to quarterly data. We are re-estimating these equations using a non-linear constrained least squares estimation. However, the first-order serial correlation might very well be due to the level of time aggregation. For, as can be seen in the last row of each subsection of Table 2, when the equations are fitted to annual data, the serial correlation disappears.

INCOMES POLICY AND THE RATE OF WAGE INFLATION

Let us now turn to a brief consideration of the effects of incomes policy on the rate of change of money wage rates.

Lipsey and Parkin divide the post-war data into 'policy on' and 'policy off' periods and use the equation which is estimated from the data of the 'policy off' period to predict $\dot{W}/W$ in the 'policy on' period. The efficacy of the policy is then to be inferred from the pattern of the residuals. We will follow their procedure without questioning their contention that shift and slope dummies cannot adequately capture the effects of incomes policy.

Table 4 and 5 and Figs. 2 and 3 report results which are derived from the comparable equations which we have fitted to the data. To facilitate comparisons, the Lipsey–Parkin results are reproduced in Table 6. In assessing the impact of incomes policy on the rate of change of money wage rates, Lipsey and Parkin conclude that, excepting the Cripps period when 'policy did exert a significant average downward pressure on wages', in all other periods the mean prediction errors are positive. For all incomes policy periods taken together, Parkin [8] concludes that

Table 4. Estimated effects of incomes policy on the rate of wage inflation

$$\dot{W}/W_t = 8{\cdot}412 - 1{\cdot}849\, U_t + 0{\cdot}101\, \dot{P}/P_{t-\frac{1}{2}} + 10{\cdot}266\, \dot{T}/T_t$$

Incomes Policy years	A Actual U			B $U \leqslant 1{\cdot}8\%$			C $U \leqslant 1{\cdot}5\%$			D $U \leqslant 1{\cdot}0\%$		
	(+)	(−)	($\bar{e}$)	(+)	(−)	($\bar{e}$)	(+)	(−)	($\bar{e}$)	(+)	(−)	($\bar{e}$)
1. 1949(I)–1950(II)	0	7	−1·087	0	7	−1·807	0	7	−1·141	0	7	−1·574
2. 1956(I)–1956(IV)	2	2	−0·085	2	2	−0·085	2	2	−0·085	2	2	−0·158
3. 1961(III)–1964(III)	8	5	−0·065	3	10	−0·209	1	12	−0·307	0	13	−0·512
4. 1964(IV)–1968(II)	11	4	+0·008	8	7	−0·056	8	7	−0·093	3	12	−0·239
5. 1964(IV)–1969(IV)	13	8	−0·023	9	12	−0·121	9	12	−0·174	3	18	−0·321
(i) All periods (1)+(2)+(3)+(4)	21	18	−0·222	13	26	−0·295	11	28	−0·352	5	34	=0·561
(ii) All periods (1)+(2)+(3)+(5)	23	22	−0·206	14	31	−0·293	12	33	−0·355	5	40	−0·556

Standard deviation for the residuals of the 'policy off' equation = 0·774

(+) = number of positive prediction errors.
(−) = number of negative prediction errors.
($\bar{e}$) = mean percentage prediction error.

TABLE 5. ESTIMATED EFFECTS OF INCOMES POLICY ON THE RATE OF WAGE INFLATION

$$\dot{W}/W_t = 9{\cdot}117 - 1{\cdot}989\ U_t + 0{\cdot}012\ \dot{M}/M_{t-\frac{1}{4}} - 0{\cdot}027\ \dot{X}/X_t + 11{\cdot}050\ \dot{T}/T_t$$

(reduced form of equations estimated by O.L.S. with lag on $\dot{P}/P_t$)

Incomes policy years	A Actual U (+)	(−)	($\bar{e}$)	B $U \leqslant 1{\cdot}8\%$ (+)	(−)	($\bar{e}$)	C $U \leqslant 1{\cdot}5\%$ (+)	(−)	($\bar{e}$)	D $U \leqslant 1{\cdot}0\%$ (+)	(−)	($\bar{e}$)
1. 1949(I)–1950(III)	0	7	−1·165	0	7	−1·165	0	7	−1·224	0	7	−1·689
2. 1956(I)–1956(IV)	2	2	−0·089	2	2	−0·089	2	2	−0·089	2	2	−0·167
3. 1961(III)–1964(III)	7	6	−0·065	3	10	−0·221	1	12	−0·327	0	13	−0·547
4. 1964(IV)–1968(II) ...	11	4	+0·001	8	7	−0·068	8	7	−0·108	3	12	−0·265
5. 1964(IV)–1969(IV)	13	8	−0·026	9	12	−0·131	9	12	−0·188	3	18	−0·347
(i) All periods (1)+(2)+(3)+(4)	20	19	−0·240	13	26	−0·318	11	28	−0·379	5	34	−0·604
(ii) All periods (1)+(2)+(3)+(5)	22	23	−0·220	14	31	−0·314	12	33	−0·380	5	40	−0·597

$Z(i)$ 0·040
$Z(ii)$ 0·119

(+) = number of positive prediction errors.
(−) = number of negative prediction errors.
($\bar{e}$) = mean percentage prediction error.

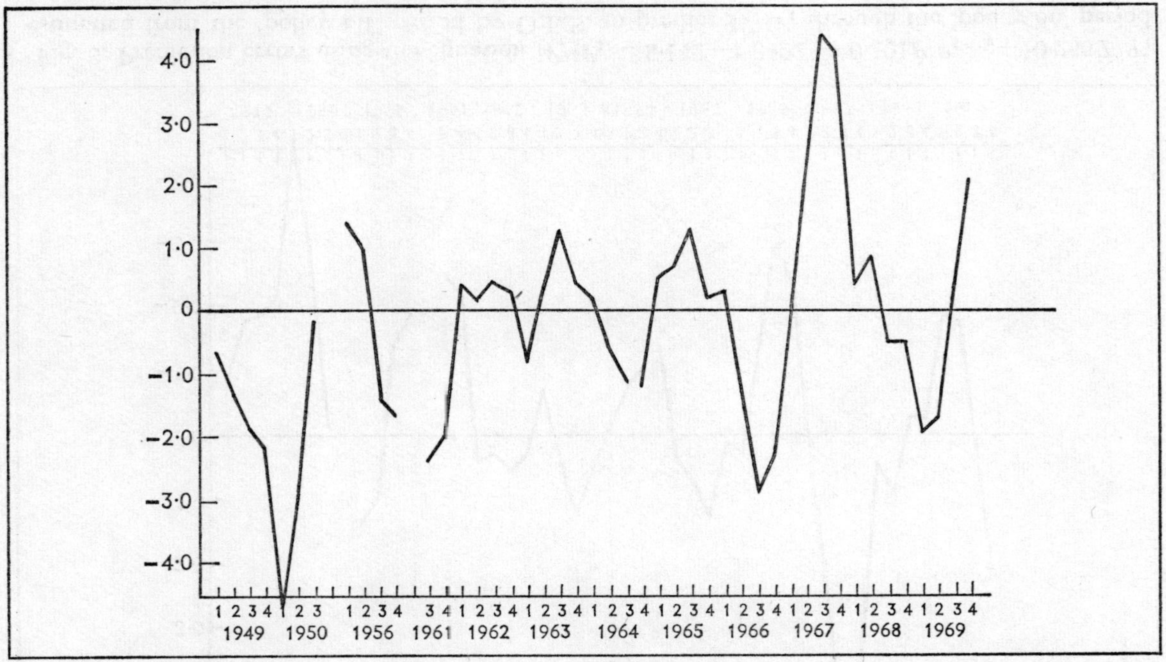

Fig. 2. Prediction errors using the reduced form of the price and wage equations with a six-month time-lag on the price variable $\dot{W}/W_t = 9{\cdot}117 - 1{\cdot}989\, U_t + 0{\cdot}012\dot{X}/X_{t-\frac{1}{2}} - 0{\cdot}027\dot{X}/X_t + 11{\cdot}050\dot{T}/T_t$ estimated from the 'policy off' period by O.L.S. to predict $\dot{W}/W_t$ through the 'policy on' period.

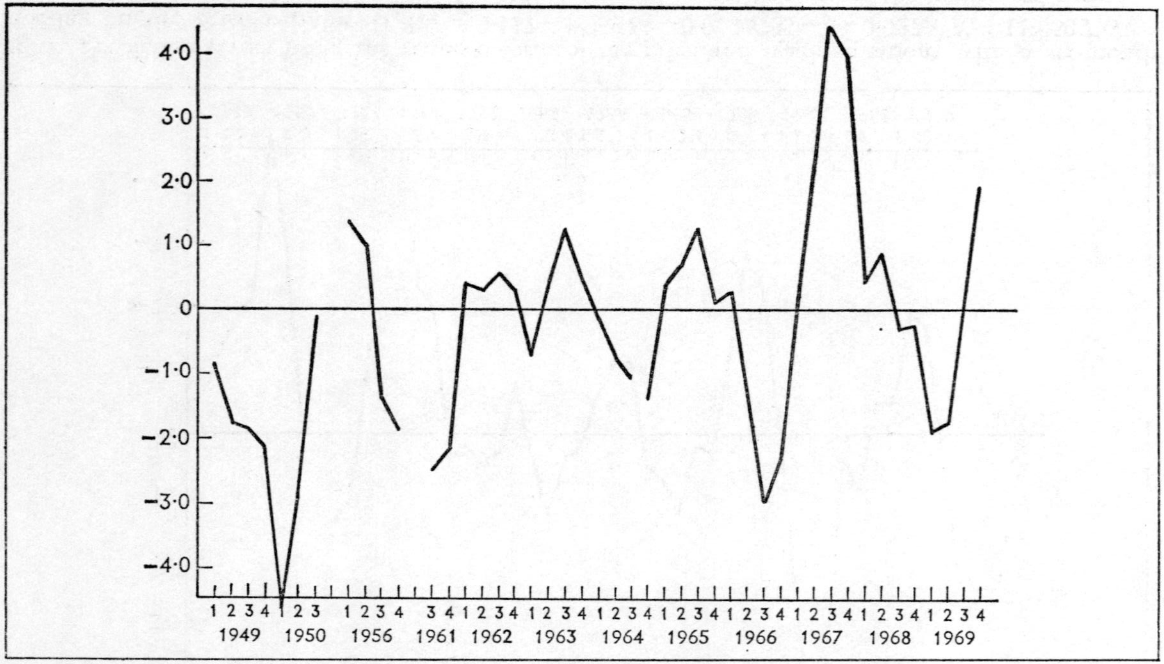

Fig. 3. Prediction errors using the equation $\dot{W}/W_t = 8{\cdot}142 - 1{\cdot}849\,U_t + 0{\cdot}101\,\dot{P}/P_{t-\frac{1}{2}} + 10{\cdot}266\,\dot{T}/T_t$ estimated from the 'policy off' period by O.L.S. to predict W/W_t through the 'policy on' period.

TABLE 6. ESTIMATED EFFECTS OF INCOMES POLICIES ON THE RATE OF WAGE INFLATION

Incomes policy years	(+)	(−)	($\bar{e}$)
1. 1948(III)–1950(III)	1	8	−1·778
2. 1956(I)–1956(IV)	2	2	+0·290
3. 1961(III)–1964(III)	9	4	+0·220
4. 1964(IV)–1968(II)	7	8	+0·322
All periods	19	22	−0·174

Standard deviation of residuals for 'policy off' equation = 0·774

Source: Lipsey and Parkin [7].
Key: (+) = number of positive prediction errors.
(−) = number of negative prediction errors.
($\bar{e}$) = mean prediction error.

'*the mean effect of incomes policy is nil*'. As can be seen from column A of Tables 4 and 5, our results differ from theirs both with respect to the number of negative and positive predictions as well as the magnitude of the mean prediction error. The differences are due primarily to the same factors which account for the divergences between the estimates of the parameters which were discussed in the previous section. Thus, in Table 6 not only is the wage variable an index of hourly wage rates but the price variable enters the wage equation with a six-months time-lag. As can be seen, in only one period, namely 1964–8, is the mean prediction error positive. (If we divide this period into two sub-periods – 1964(IV) –1966(IV) and 1967(I)–1968(II) – in the former the mean percentage prediction error ($\bar{e}$) is 0·556, in the latter it is −1·803.) The results in Table 5 follow from the correction of a failure appropriately to transform the equations from which the predictions have up until now been made. Even if the price and wage equations are estimated by O.L.S., when one comes to predict the effects of incomes policy one must allow for the feedback effect – wages affect prices which in turn affect wages. This means that the appropriate predictors are the solved reduced forms of the structural equations in the rates of change of prices and wages and not the estimates of the structural equations which were used by Lipsey and Parkin [7].[4] The main effect of this correction is that the one positive value of $\bar{e}$ in the period 1964(IV)–1968(II) is now almost zero. The equations on which Table 5 is based and which were estimated by O.L.S. are the best that are currently available. (Predictions from equations estimated by 2S.L.S. and by other techniques will be reported in a subsequent paper.) Hence, we may conclude that on average incomes policy has, in fact, reduced the rate of change of money wage rates by approximately 1·15 per cent per annum (23 per cent of 5 per cent = 1·15 per cent) over the entire period when such policies have been in operation, with substantial variations within each sub-period. Thus the data reject Parkin's conclusion that 'the mean effect of incomes policy is nil'.

Lipsey and Parkin report that the reduced form of the Phillips curves for 'policy on' and 'policy off' intersect at a level of unemployment of 1·8 per cent. This result must be treated with some caution. In the 'on' equation, U is not significantly different from zero. However, if we waive this point, what is really implied is that, except in the Cripps period, Governments have often treated demand management policies and incomes policy by fiat, exhortation and/or by holding back the rate of wage increase in the public sector as complementary rather than as alternative instruments of policy. Thus they have simultaneously adopted incomes policies and have taken fiscal and monetary action to reduce the level of aggregate demand. This being the case, we might ask whether incomes policy would have had a greater effect on wages if lower levels of unemployment were held. As a preliminary approach to this question we used the 'off' equation to predict $\dot{W}/W$ in the 'on' periods subject to the constraint that $U = 1{\cdot}8$ per cent for actual $U \geqslant 1{\cdot}8$ per cent, 1·8 being suggested by the intersection point of the Lipsey–Parkin 'on' and 'off' equations, $U = 1{\cdot}5$ per cent for actual $U \geqslant 1{\cdot}5$ per cent, 1·5 being the average level of unemployment for the entire sample period, and $U = 1$ per cent for actual $U \geqslant 1$ per cent. The results are reported in sections B, C and D of the table. They show that in *all* sub-periods $\bar{e}$ is now negative, and that the number of negative predictions are greater when unemployment is constrained and increase for a decrease in the level at which unemployment is constrained. The magnitudes of the negative prediction errors are also increased.

These results suggest that if in those quarters of the post-war period in which incomes policies were operated the level of unemployment had been held at 1·5 per cent, 1·5 per cent being the average level of unemployment over the entire post-war period, the rate of change of money wage rates would have been reduced on average by 1·9 per cent per annum. Since over the same period the *average* rate of change of money wage rates has been 5 per cent per annum, this would have meant a rate of rise which would have been roughly in line with the growth in productive potential. If unemployment had been held at 1 per cent the average reduction in the rate of change of money wage rates would have been as much as 3 per cent per annum.

That this would have been the case is consistent with the hypothesis which we have advanced in this paper. The higher level and faster rate of growth of output which is implicit in lower levels of unemployment would have substantially reduced the gap between actual and expected real wages and hence would have reduced union pressure on money wage rates. The simultaneous operation of an incomes policy as well as a public sector expenditure policy geared in a satisfactory fashion to the growth in productive potential would have helped to make the sum of all monetary claims and the resulting aggregate expenditure mesh with productive potential. Thus past incomes policies have had some success in ameliorating the rate of rise of money wage rates. (Work in progress indicates that they have also had a similar success in slowing down the rate of change of prices.) Moreover, this study suggests that an incomes policy might even be more successful than such policies have been in the recent past, provided that it does not rely on the maintenance of a large and increasing pool of unemployed labour and other resources, and provided that workers are not persuaded that it will operate against their interest, for example if it allows for a planned growth in real incomes which is in line with reasonable expectations and is not designed to or operates in such a way as to shift the distribution of income in favour of other groups, even if at the same time it has the unlikely, even though desirable, consequence of reducing the inequality of incomes as between different groups of workers.

p112.

NOTES

1. Except in this section where it refers to the number of unemployed workers, U represents the proportion of the labour force which is unemployed $\left(\frac{U}{L}\right)$.

2. A dot over a variable indicates a time derivative $\frac{d}{dt}$.

3. Any standard version of the Keynesian model can, given the stock of capital and the stock of money, be reduced to an equation in which the level of demand depends on the level at which the money wage rate is set. However, the Phillips curve relates the rate of change of money wages to the level of unemployment:

$$\frac{\dot{W}}{W} = f\{(N^d - N^s)/N^s\} = g(U).$$

We can get to the right-hand side of this relation by assuming that the labour supply is fixed or that it grows at the same rate as full-employment aggregate demand. We can get to the left-hand side by noting that since 1933 the level of money wage rates in the U.K. is a trended variable which has never been negative. A variable and its rate of change are correlated if the variable is trended.

4. The relevant price equation fitted to the 'policy off' data is

$$\dot{P}/P_t = 0{\cdot}579 + \underset{(3{\cdot}855)}{0{\cdot}699\dot{W}/W_t} + \underset{(3{\cdot}824)}{0{\cdot}106\dot{M}/M_{t-1}} - \underset{(3{\cdot}797)}{0{\cdot}244\dot{X}/X_t}$$

$R^2 = 0{\cdot}836$, D.W. $= 1{\cdot}057$

( ) = t statistics.

REFERENCES

[1] Friedman, M., 'The Role of Monetary Policy', *American Economic Review* (May, 1968).

[2] Hines, A. G., 'Trade Unions and Wage Inflation in the United Kingdom 1893–1961', *Review of Economic Studies* (Oct 1964).

[3] Hines, A. G., 'Unemployment and the Rate of Change of Money Wage Rates in the United Kingdom 1862–1963: A Reappraisal', *Review of Economics and Statistics* (Feb 1968).

[4] Hines, A. G., 'Wage Inflation in the United Kingdom, 1948–1962: A Disaggregated Study', *Economic Journal* (Mar 1969).

[5] HINES, A. G., 'The Phillips Curve and the Distribution of Unemployment', (mimeograph, 1970).

[6] LIPSEY, R. G., 'The Relation between Unemployment and the Rate of Change of Money Wage Rates in the United Kingdom: A Further Study', *Economica* (Feb 1960).

[7] LIPSEY, R. G. and PARKIN, J. M., 'Incomes Policy: A Reappraisal', *Economica* (May 1970).

[8] PARKIN, J. M., 'Incomes Policy: Some Further Results on the Determination of the Rate of Change of Money Wages', *Economica* (Nov 1970).

[9] PHILLIPS, A. W., 'The Relation between Unemployment and the Rate of Change of Money Wage Rates in the United Kingdom, 1961–1957', *Economica* (1958).

[10] REES, A., 'The Phillips Curve as a Menu for Policy Choice', *Economica* (1970).

[11] SOLOW, R. M., *Price Expectations and the Behaviour of the Price Level* (Manchester U.P., 1970).

PART THREE

Panel: Opening Statements

9 External Influences and Inflation in the United Kingdom

LESLIE DICKS-MIREAUX*

I have been asked to try to strike some sort of balance between the external and internal factors which might be considered the prime movers of the present wave of wage and price inflation in the United Kingdom. As we have discussed all morning many of the internal factors that may or may not be at work, I shall not dwell at length on these now. Nor am I going to seek out any common factor behind what I believe to be an extraordinary accident, in that the present wave of wage and price inflation appears to have beset so many industrialised countries at about the same time. Instead, I shall set out four fairly obvious routes by which inflation may be imported – there may be others which may be suggested from the floor – and consider each of these from the standpoint of the United Kingdom.

The first, and perhaps most obvious way, by which inflation may be imported is through rising import prices. The second is via the foreign trade multiplier relating only to international trade in goods and services, i.e. the current account of the balance of payments. The third represents little more than an extension of the second by embracing the overall balance of payments position and can be called the international monetary multiplier. The fourth and last is perhaps the least obvious; I have called it the export sector wage/national wage spiral. I need hardly dwell on the way these different transmission mechanisms might be expected to work, but I will try to set out some facts, in the time I have, bearing on each of them as far as the United Kingdom is concerned.

For this purpose, I shall refer occasionally to the O.E.C.D.

* Leslie Dicks-Mireaux is Deputy Chief of the Economic Intelligence Department and Head of the Economic Section of the Bank of England.

document (*Inflation: The Present Problem*[1]) which we have as one of the background papers to this Conference; and in particular, I would draw your attention to the charts on p. 21. These charts define for a number of industrialised countries the periods of excess demand for goods and services experienced over the last decade. For the United States, the most recent period of excess demand ran from 1964 through to 1969; for the United Kingdom, excess demand was experienced over a much briefer period running from 1964 to the end of 1966. As the behaviour of the United States economy is the predominant international influence on other industrialised economies, I want, therefore, to concentrate upon the behaviour of the United Kingdom economy from 1966 to 1969. Here is a period during which excess demand was present in the United States economy but not in the United Kingdom; and although I have not included the year 1970, by which time wage and price inflation in the United Kingdom had got well under way, we may be able to judge whether the events of this year can be regarded as a lagged response to those of earlier years. In sum, I shall be quoting annual averages or average changes from 1966 to 1969.

Let us first look then at import prices into the United Kingdom. Total import prices rose on average by 5 per cent a year and, as I am referring to sterling prices, this increase will include the effects of the 1967 devaluation. Taking an average import propensity of 20 per cent, we might expect that final prices in the United Kingdom would be 1 per cent a year higher on account of import prices, in the first round. Assuming also that wage increases fully compensate for previous price increases – an extreme assumption, I believe – wages would also be 1 per cent a year higher on account of the increase in import prices. In the longer term and with as rigid a wage–price relationship as outlined above, the full increase in import prices would show up in United Kingdom final prices; but this extreme specification of the model is going farther than I would wish, especially without greater knowledge of what lags might be involved. Earlier this morning, we spoke particularly of the manufacturing sector as being possibly the seat of inflationary wage movements. In this respect, we should perhaps look at import prices of manufactured goods which have risen on average by 8 per cent a year, faster than the average price of all imports into the United Kingdom. This sharp rise in the prices of internationally traded manufactured goods is a distinguishing feature of the present wave of inflation. It will be recalled that at the time of the Korean War, 1950–1, the very sharp rise in international commodity prices, i.e. raw materials, did lead in part to the import of wage and price inflation into the United Kingdom. In the present wave of inflation, we have seen no such upward pressure on raw material prices, which might perhaps have been expected via speculative stockbuilding if inflation were being internationally transmitted. But whether we should confine our attention to import prices of manufactured goods or of goods more generally, it seems certain that the sharp increase in import prices – exacerbated by the 1967 devaluation – has made some contribution to the inflation we have been experiencing in this country. However, this contribution hardly accounts for the major part of our inflation; and because the 1967 devaluation raised only import prices into the United Kingdom, rising import prices do not seem to have been a significant route leading to the international transmission of inflation among the major industrialised countries.

Having dealt with the first cost-inflation route, the second possibility I set out was the transmission of inflation via the foreign trade multiplier. It is sometimes argued that the foreign trade sector – goods and services – of the United States is so small that changes in the current account may have only a moderate influence on trade with the rest of the world. This is misleading, for what we should be considering is the *marginal* import propensity of the United States; and as the experience of 1966–9 has shown, this marginal propensity can swing quite violently, reaching a figure as high as 20 per cent. But for there to have been an inflationary effect imported into the United Kingdom by this means, we must suppose that a sharp increase in the American import propensity led first to an upsurge in United Kingdom exports – true – but second to excessive pressure of demand on the productive resources of the United Kingdom. It is this last conclusion which is not substantiated by the facts. As I said at the outset, the chart on p. 21 of the O.E.C.D. study shows that from 1966 to 1969 there was no overall excess demand in the United Kingdom. The growth of productive potential in the United Kingdom is officially estimated to be in the region of 3 per cent a year. Since 1966 G.D.P. has increased by no more than 2¼ per cent a year. On the basis of these figures, slack rather than an aggregative excess demand was generated in the United Kingdom economy. This conclusion seems also to be borne out when we look at the labour market indicators. In 1966 the level of unemployment jumped to 2½ per cent and has remained there or above ever since. It is true that the increase in unemployment in 1966 cannot entirely be explained in terms of aggregate demand changes. None the less, if an allowance of as much as one-half of a percentage point of unemployment is made to adjust for this 'non-demand' increase in unemployment, the percentages ruling over the period 1966 to 1969 hardly point to aggregate excess demand in the economy – a conclusion also supported by the figures for unfilled vacancies. Thus, it is difficult to single out imported excess demand as a factor accounting for the recent inflation in the United Kingdom. I would not deny that such a possibility might help to explain the recent inflation in Germany, for example, but not in the United Kingdom.

Extending the current account to take in the overall balance of payments, I come to my third route, the international monetary multiplier. Accruals to international reserves, representing high-powered money, may, it is argued, generate activity through some form of monetary multiplier. Certainly it is true that we have taken in reserves over the period 1966 to 1969 – substantial on occasion – but the money supply has not grown all that fast. There was one year, 1967, in this period when the growth of the money supply reached double figures. With the variable lag that seems accepted by those who believe in the direction of causation implied by a monetary multiplier, it is arguable that the increase in the money supply during 1967 could be held responsible for part of the present inflation – but I think not. In the other years, the growth of the money supply has been much smaller than in 1967, falling between 3 and 6 per cent; and for those who subscribe to the time-lag of nine to eighteen months, the fact that the money supply grew by only 3 per cent in 1969 must be rich with immediate promise.

So I turn to the last route I enumerated. One way of interpreting this argument is that excessive pressures of demand in one or a number of economies leads to a particularly fast rate of growth in world trade, such as we have seen in the case of manufactured goods over the last few years. This, in turn, leads to a faster than average growth in the exporting sector of a given economy, followed by large wage claims and settlements in that sector. Thereafter, some contagion effect through attempts to maintain wage differentials – which might, for example, stem from the structure of the trade union movement – generates large wage claims and settlements elsewhere in the domestic sector of the economy. Studies somewhat along these lines have been made for Norway[2] and for Sweden.[3] In these two economies, large swings in the world prices of raw materials, such as wood and woodpulp, do seem to have generated domestic inflation via a route such as I have outlined. But it is important to bear in mind the fact that this generative process of inflation resulting initially from external factors is not necessarily accompanied by aggregate excess demand in the domestic economy concerned. In the particular case of the United Kingdom, there are few firm facts to which I can appeal to illustrate the possibility of such a process having occurred here. None the less, it does seem possible that such a process has a ring of credibility about it. Recent large wage claims and settlements are either under way or have been made in the motor-car industry – a major exporting industry. Moreover, the devaluation of 1967 meant that in sterling terms at least there was a sharp lift in the profitability of British exporting industries. This effect of devaluation may, therefore, have compounded with the more general effect of extremely buoyant world trade in manufactured goods. Some rough guidance, perhaps, to the growth of export profits is provided by the fact that over the three years 1966 to 1969 nominal national income rose by 5½ to 6 per cent, whereas exports of goods and services, at current prices, rose at more than twice this rate, by as much as 13 per cent.

Having outlined the four ways I enumerated by which external factors may be considered responsible in part at least for the present wave of inflation, I must conclude that none seems likely to me to have played a significant role. The few facts I have presented to you do not, in my view, support either the foreign trade multiplier or the international monetary multiplier as routes by which the recent inflation in the United Kingdom has been sparked off. Undoubtedly, rising import prices – especially of manufactured goods – have contributed to a price–wage spiral, but hardly enough to account for the very large settlements we experienced in late 1969 and throughout 1970; and in the particular case of the United Kingdom, the 1967 devaluation must be held responsible for much of the rise in import prices. It is perhaps the last route, namely via the exporting sector, which would seem to represent the most potent external force contributing to our recent inflation. Moreover, since the presence of aggregate excess demand is not necessary to this argument, it may go some way to helping to explain the extraordinary coincidence of inflationary trends we have seen recently in a number of industrialised countries. But I would not argue that there is an overriding external factor common to the recent inflation; indeed, we must probably look to factors closer at home not all of which, perhaps, are economic.

NOTES

1. Report by the Secretary-General, O.E.C.D., Dec 1970.
2. O. Aukrust, F. Holte and G. Stoltz, *Instilling fra Utredringsutvalget for inntektsoppgjørene 1966*, (Oslo, 1966).
3. Gösta Edgren, Karl-Olaf Faxèn and Clas-Erik Odhner, 'Wages, Growth and the Distribution of Income', *Swedish Journal of Economics*, (1969).

10. Some Observations on Inflation and Incomes Policy

SIR FREDERICK CATHERWOOD*

Up to a very short time ago I was a great sceptic about incomes policies, and on the basis of what has just been said, there was no discernible evidence that they worked. In fact, I think I would have gone even further at one point and said that if you put on an incomes policy, there would be some anticipation of that policy and in fact you would get a slightly worse result having an incomes policy than otherwise. I think we ought to be clear, however, that that was that particular incomes policy. People talk about incomes policy as if there is only one incomes policy and that the first one we tried was the only one that could be tried, and that the way we worked it is the only way ever to work it.

But recently I must say I have rather come back from that position on the basis of looking at the situation in a company and what is from our point of view the prime cause of cost-push inflation. I think the trouble is that a lot of people did not believe there could be such a thing as cost-push inflation because all inflation tended to arise from an excess demand somewhere. But we have talked a great deal to companies to try to find out the great question, and that is why they give in when they patently cannot or should not be able to afford it. In other words when the economy is running slack, and they are tight on cash, why do they concede these colossal wage increases which average around 14 per cent now, and we are driven fairly inexorably to the conclusion that there is a very fundamental imbalance of bargaining power, at any rate in the private sector, and this evidence is borne out by company chairman after company chairman whom I to go see.

Now I do not obviously believe everything a company

* Sir Frederick Catherwood is Director-General of the National Economic Development Office.

chairman tells me, but it has been my job for the last six years to try to interpret company chairmen in an economically articulate way to chaps like you, so I hope I have got the correct answers. But roughly speaking, the company chairman looking at a big wage claim can find very many reasons why, so far as he personally is concerned, it will pay him to concede it.

Let me just give you an example. I belong to a small dining club in which there are protagonists of the rather hard-line view at the moment that business had better stand on its own two feet. Now one of the members of this dining club runs a sweet factory in North London, and shortly after this Government got in this chap was faced with a colossal swingeing wage claim, or what was then regarded as a swingeing wage claim, of about 15 per cent or something. So we were all relaxed together and he said, 'I've got this 15 per cent wage claim and what ought I to do about it? In the national interests I ought to say no, but if I do say no, I will simply lose all my chaps, who will push off elsewhere and get other jobs.' So the hard-liner said to him, 'Well, it's up to you, stand on your own two feet, that is what management is about, etc.' But you can see that the logical conclusion of this argument is that he was faced with the loss of a very large chunk of his business to competitors if he did not give in. Admittedly in a fairly high employment area such as London, his chaps could go and get another job, and so the logic of the situation was that he should give in. I have not heard that he has gone bust and I imagine that he did give in.

You may say that is simply the question of the employment rate in London being a shade too high. Let us then take another example, the motor industry. Take the case of a company which has got a very good car which has notched up a certain increase in its market share in this country and has also got a long-term deal with export customers. The view that the company will take – especially if it is tight for money – will be a very simple one, and that is if they have a strike they will be faced with a colossal reduction in their cash flow. They have major customers and if they have a good place in the market share they dare not, especially if they are tight for cash, lose out and therefore, as far as they are concerned, they will take the view (*a*) 'I have no mandate from my shareholders to commit hara-kiri', (*b*) 'I don't mind having an incomes policy where everyone holds it down, but I'm hanged if I'm going to be made a stalking-horse for this incomes policy and I don't like Ministers hauling me around the corner and telling me to stand firm', and so they will concede their wage increase and stay in business. The other thing is, of course, that they have an expectation, that is to say if they are told to stand on their own two feet and it is up to them and so on, they realise that by giving these major wage increases they are not going to have a major strike which nobody is going to bail them out of and they pass a part of the cost on to the Government in the form of a general inflation and then it is back on the Government's plate, and that is what the Government asked them to do – to stand on their own two feet and look after their own interests – and that is what they are doing, passing the problem back to the Government again.

Now the pattern that I meet when I go around to see these chairmen is an absolutely consistent pattern. Take the food industry, which is a highly competitive industry, not particularly competitive internationally but very highly competitive from a market point of view. A chairman of a very large food-manufacturing company again said to me, 'I simply cannot afford to have a strike because I cannot afford to lose my market share. If I lost my market share in this particular brand from 30 per cent, say, down to 20 per cent or 15 per cent, the cost of buying back that market share would be about ten times the cost of a strike, and therefore I don't propose to have a strike,' and he does not have a strike.

These are the kinds of arguments that go round in what I would call the leading companies, the companies which determine the thing. Because when you go to a lot of the other companies they then follow from the leader. For instance, I happened to be chairing the Machine Tool Economic Development Committee about three or four weeks ago and I put this to them and they said, 'Whatever the motor-car companies do, we do. We have a differential between ourselves and the motor-car companies but we cannot afford to let that differential get too wide otherwise we tend to lose chaps to the motor-car industry.' So, in other words, what you have is an imperfect market looked at from a point of view of labour as a factor of production, which is only one way of looking at it of course, but looked at from that point of view you have an imperfect market, and the reason for this imperfect market is that companies have an enormous investment in what are more or less sunk costs. That is to say their market share is of enormous value to them. Their distributor network is of enormous value to them.

Take the motor-car industry, for instance. The motor-car market share is determined very largely by the distributor network, so I am told, and, of course, you have people coming in from the outside like B.M.W., Fiat and so on all nosing around trying to pick up key dealerships. So if you have a major strike you will topple a number of your key dealerships over into the foreign competition and you will have lost that chunk of your market share for a very long time, and this is a very expensive thing to do. This is the kind of thing the motor-car companies tell me. So, if you have your market share, your distributor network, then, of course, if you have tooled up for a good car – and I am just taking cars but this would go for any product that was a major product – if you have sunk an enormous amount in advertising, if you have got literature out on it and so on, your sunk costs not only in the tooling for the car and so on but perhaps the whole layout of the factory, perhaps the kinds of rates that you have negotiated with the unions for doing this, the whole of this is an enormous sunk cost, so you have that colossal sunk cost on the one hand and then you have the marginal extra cost of actually getting the production out. So we are in the position today where industry is tremendously wholly capitalised but is still dependent on labour for actually getting the production out of the gate, that is to say labour is an achieve position, the key blackmailing position in industry as it is set up at the moment, and faced with the possibility that the man whom you pay to turn the key to unlock the cupboard full of gold wants a higher rate for turning the key, you pay him the higher rate for turning the key and do not worry too much about it.

Now, of course, the unions realise perfectly well that this is not a position that necessarily goes on for ever. One very major union leader the other day, who has been much in the news recently, said to me, 'At the point at which industry is heavily capitalised, but still depends on my chaps actually to turn the levers, I've got them, but the logical position for them is to go the whole way and automate the process to the point where I can't get them any longer.' So we are in a position where a key factor of production, which is labour, can be withdrawn and it pays, from a demand and supply point of view, to pay a premium all the time in order to keep the key factor of production in full supply. This to me is the major cause of wage inflation.

I'm not saying that all these mechanisms do not operate, of course; in the case of Rootes, as you have very rightly said, the key factor is that they have a major overseas contract and there was a demand for these motor-cars in the United States, tariffs are coming down and we are becoming more interlocked with other economies, and the marginal costs of production override the tariffs when you are making a marginal calculation. Obviously it is not enough simply to regulate the U.K. economy – you have got the world economy in which these companies have been encouraged progressively to intertwine themselves.

Now this is therefore where I come back to an incomes policy, but to me an incomes policy has got to be realistic. I do not think it can be produced again by a P.I.B. sitting on the sidelines waving a finger at people and telling them what to do. I do not think that is a very good sort of incomes policy. To me an incomes policy will not arise unless you can have a real dialogue with the unions, to whom I say, 'Look you've got them over the barrel at the moment, and you have produced the power to destroy the currency, but you have not got the power to produce a higher real wage. Now you have got, therefore, to decide what you are going to do, whether you think that you can get a higher real wage by continually putting in these inflationary claims on the basis that you may just get a little margin ahead of the thing, or whether you will readily try to do a deal for growth in exchange for a wage restraint which you have then got to enforce yourselves,' because there is no point in having an incomes policy unless the unions themselves undertake to deliver, and this to me is the only realistic policy. I do not think that a policy of the Prices and Incomes Board kind will be any more effective now than it was then and, of course, the problem at this precise moment is not that people do not realise that – I think the Government realise this, the Ministers whom I talk to realise this, the trade union leaders certainly do. The main snag at the moment is that you have a most contentious piece of union legislation going through the House, and while that is going through the House the two sides cannot talk. If that gets through the House without any more upsets than our demonstration today, then I hope the two sides can talk, but then the chief question will be to the Government – 'are you going to be able to deliver the kind of growth that all the other industrial countries have had?' – and this is what the T.U.C. keep coming back to. They say, 'Look at Japan, look at Germany, look at Italy, look at France, Holland, Sweden, Canada and so on. They've all had a rate of industrial growth that we have not had, and why shouldn't we have that rate, as we think that the productive potential in a modern economy is higher than it could be?' On the other hand, the Government will have to say to the unions that they are not going to have the kind of incomes policy that has operated in the past, i.e. 'We don't want an ineffective incomes policy. The only incomes policy we want is one that you undertake to deliver.'

11. The Phillips Curve: A Historical Perspective, Lessons from Recent Empirical Studies and Alternative Policy Choices

MICHAEL PARKIN*

I want to do three things. First, to take a fairly long-period look at inflation in this country and ask how the present experience fits into that. Second, to examine and try to make some sense of the very recent work that has not yet appeared in print. This is the work of Leslie Godfrey, Kenneth Wallis and Professor Hines.[1] Finally, I shall say what bearing I think all of this has on the current policy choice problem.

The first and obvious question I think we ought to ask is: why is it that the last eighteen months have been so far off the Phillips curve? I want to begin tackling that question by asking: is it unique, is it something that has never happened before, are we now experiencing new waters that are totally untravelled and therefore can we get no guidance at all from the past? To answer this question I think we can do no better than go back to Phillips's own work. An examination of Phillips's very helpful scatter diagrams is very revealing. If economists had been looking at the British economy almost exactly one hundred years ago today, they would have been saying 'Why are we so far off the Phillips curve?' In the early 1860s, but again in a more pronounced fashion around 1868–69–70–71, the Phillips curve displayed large positive residuals. They were not quite as big as the positive residuals we have today, but they were of the order of 4 or 5 per cent. That is, the rate of wage inflation was

* Michael Parkin is Professor of Economics at the University of Manchester.

4 or 5 per cent higher than would have been predicted by the Phillips curve given the then level of unemployment. Coming forward in time to 1919 we see that the rate of wage inflation was some 26 percentage points above the Phillips curve. The next interesting period was around the beginning of the Second World War and into the Second World War – 1937 through 1941. Here we see positive residuals of the order of 5 per cent, with the highest being in 1940 with a 12 per cent positive residual (these are all percentage points). In the immediate post-war period, 1946 had an 8 percentage point positive residual; 1951 was 5 percentage points and 1970 has something around 9 percentage points.

All this should certainly be enough to suggest that 1969, 1970 and 1971, whilst a nuisance, are not totally unprecedented. In terms simply of the difference between the Phillips curve's predictions and the actual rate of inflation, it has happened before. Current experience might, however, be unprecedented in terms of *why* it is happening. Let us now look at this. Can we see anything in what has happened before that might give us some clues as to what is currently going on – only clues? I do not say we can get answers.

The first possibility is the obvious one: it is all stochastic. Any econometric model of today's vintage is going to have error terms that sometimes are uncomfortably large. They might also run for a year or two at uncomfortably large levels. Now if it is the case that the current departures from the Phillips curve are purely stochastic departures, then I suppose we have to conclude that it is a bad theory. It may be the best we have got but it is not too good and certainly not good enough for policy purposes. I think, though, that we can do a bit better than that. Implicit in Phillips's formulation of the Phillips curve and also in much recent work is the hypothesis that the rate of inflation affects the wage-determining process in a manner such that, from the point of view of just plotting scatter diagrams, it is possible to ignore prices. That is, the plotted curve is the reduced form which results from transforming out the effects of prices on to wages and wages back on to prices. The reduced form is simply the relationship between the excess demand (measured in the form of unemployment) and the rate of wage inflation. Now, in the middle of all that lot, there is a crucially important hypothesis about anticipated price inflation – or inflation expectations. The hypothesis implicit in the crude Phillips curve is a very dumb beast. It really says that actual and anticipated inflation are one and the same.

In recent years we have done a bit better than that, but not very much better. We have postulated that anticipated inflation is some distributed lag function of past inflation. Now look back to the periods when the Phillips curve performed badly in the past. You will notice that the dates when we had positive residuals are exactly periods when any reasonable man would suppose that a dumb-beast expectation hypothesis would not work. Let us start in 1970 and work back. Looking at the present experience, we have a period when an incomes policy has just been taken off. It seems to be the case that incomes policy, on the average, has no effect (I will say more about this below). Even if incomes policy actually has no effect, if there is a general belief that it is working then to abandon the policy might have the effect of raising inflation expectations.

Going back further we see that the earlier periods – 1951, 1946, 1919 – are all periods when, for one reason or another, one would expect a dumb-beast expectation hypothesis to fail. Just after a war it is most unlikely that one would extrapolate past price behaviour to form a judgement about its future rate of change. I do not offer an alternative explanation.

To summarise the argument so far, I have said that perhaps there is some randomness in the present inflation, and second, some expectations.

A third possibility, of course, is the one that has been raised in quite a lot of the discussion today. It is that the corrective Phillips hypothesis is just plainly wrong and not a viable explanation of inflation. In its strongest form the argument would go on to say that there are better alternative hypotheses. Professor Hines and others have put forward views that suggest alternative formulations based largely on considerations of trade unions' activities. Alternative explanations to the Phillips models seem to have two lines of development.

The first proposition is that 'frustration' is the main cause of inflation. It seems to me that the 'frustration hypothesis' is, properly interpreted, the expectation hypothesis. That is, if we assume that people have in mind a desired share of the national income which they will try to achieve, then we come up with the prediction that the rate of change of money wages will equal the rate of change of prices plus the rate of change of output per head. Now that, of course, is exactly the prediction we get from the Phelps and Friedman expectation hypothesis. The expectation interpretation has at least the advantage that it explains why firms meet unions' demands. The frustration hypothesis is absolutely silent on why firms agree to inflationary wage increases, a simple qualitative test, on which, therefore, we can rule out the frustration hypothesis and banish the term from our vocabulary and get back to serious analysis.

The second line of development of the recent theories concerns the development of monopoly bargaining power. It clearly is true that there may be periods in which the unions are raising the share of labour in the national income as a result of a strengthening of their monopoly power. It does seem to me, however, that there must be severe limits on the effects that this can have on inflation in any but the shortest run.

What, if anything, do we conclude from this long-period look at inflation? My own conclusions are these: first, on the basis of what is, after all, 110 years of empirical evidence, there is a Phillips curve; second, that allowance for random fluctuations combined with an as yet unspecified model of expectations will go a long way to clearing up the present problem.

I would like now to say something about the recent work on the effects of incomes policy. If what I have said so far makes sense, then it does say that we have a choice of either raising unemployment and lowering inflation, or keeping inflation; but perhaps there is another way out. Perhaps incomes policy could help. Let us look at this. Two and a half years ago two pieces of work were done on the effects of incomes policy. One was at the P.I.B. and the other by David Smith as part of the Brookings study of the U.K. Those pieces of work were based on very simple econometrics and they told us that incomes policy worked. The basic prediction was that incomes policy shifted the Phillips curve downwards, significantly, by something like 1 per cent. The Lipsey–Parkin work was the next to appear. The conclusion of that study was that on the average incomes policy had no effect on the rate of change of wages.

Further, there appeared to be a tendency for the Phillips

curve to flatten when policy was on and for there to be a quite well-determined relation when policy was off. What has happened since the appearance of the Lipsey–Parkin results is what I regard as technically superior work on the basic model. I think we should have much more faith in the results of these recent studies than we had in the original results. We must notice, though, that none of the recent studies says that incomes policy works. They all say that incomes policy has no discernible statistical effect on the rate of wage inflation. The work by Leslie Godfrey and Ken Wallis seems to be saying that when the most refined statistical techniques are used, all that emerges unscathed is the proposition that wage and price inflation are correlated but 'not much else is'. Also, incomes policy makes no difference to that relationship.

On the basis and evidence of all this work, what conclusion do we reach? The weight of the evidence seems to say that incomes policy at this moment cannot be regarded as a serious alternative to demand management policies for controlling inflation. It may be possible to devise an incomes policy which will successfully remove, or improve, the trade-off between inflation and unemployment but we do not, at this moment, have such a policy.

The weight of evidence says that there is a trade-off between unemployment and inflation. In the meantime, demand management represents the only remedy we have for inflation.

NOTE

1. The papers by Godfrey and Hines appear in this volume. 'Comments on wages, Prices and Incomes Policy' by K. F. Wallis will appear in a forthcoming issue of *Economica* (1971) – Ed.

12. Some Features of Incomes Policy and Comments on the Current Inflation

RALPH TURVEY*

I agree with much that Sir Fred said in the constructive part of his statement. I think one respect in which he makes his case sound stronger than it really is, is the omission of the fact that trade unions can increase the real incomes of their members at the expense of the real incomes of the aged. This does not apply to the old-age pension, which after all can be put up. But rough estimates of the fraction of consumption which is financed from private pensions and by using up old people's savings come to the order of 10 per cent of total personal consumption. So if the unions double the price and wage level, they can halve the consumption of the old and get 5 per cent of total consumption for themselves. To my mind, if one talks in terms of social equity, that is one of the worst features of inflation. There is some loot to be had for the unions at the expense of the weak, and unions are in business in order to be strong. To some extent they *can* improve their position by being 'bloody-minded'.

Now the other thing I disagree with Sir Fred about is the plausibility of his bargaining-power argument as an explanation of the world-wide character of the present inflation. But let me get to that in time. As Joint Deputy Chairman of the P.I.B. for three and a half years, I have been doing micro-economics all the time and have hardly ever had occasion to join in the sort of discussion we are having now. We only once went macro when we published a single-equation estimate which appeared to show that incomes policy had lowered the rate of wage inflation by 1 per cent per annum. That was done on the back of an envelope; only two envelopes were used, there being another one on

* Ralph Turvey was until recently Joint Deputy Chairman of the National Board for Prices and Incomes.

prices, which apparently showed that the effect of prices and incomes policy had been to *accelerate* the rate of growth of prices! Everybody seized on the first equation, which provided what seemed to be an interesting answer, and ignored the second one. But the presumption is that if half of an exercise is obviously rubbish the other half is probably rubbish too. That was in fact the spirit in which we published the thing, but ever afterwards people went around saying that Aubrey Jones claimed that the P.I.B. slowed down wage inflation by 1 per cent per annum!

Let me now stress four particular features of the micro-economics we have been doing. One of the features, which is really quite new when you look at other bodies, has been the principle of going out and looking. On the occasion when we had to make recommendations about university teachers' pay I actually went to talk to a lot of university teachers! Now this is a radical thing for anybody engaged in this business to do. Similarly we visit factories and workshops and whatnot. I think it would be a pity were this feature of our work lost in any successor body.

Secondly, another important feature which ought to be repeated if there is to be somebody following us in time is that our task was not to determine policy but to apply it. It seems to me that the thing that was wrong with Wilberforce was that it was asked to invent a policy as well as apply it.

Thirdly, a feature which I think will be necessary in any future set-up is concern with efficiency. We took a long-run point of view. This may just reflect my *déformation professionelle* as an economist, but to me the most interesting part of the Prices and Incomes Board's work was the part that wasn't really to do with prices or with incomes, but was to do with structure and efficiency. In fact the two achievements of which I am most proud have really nothing to do with prices and incomes policy. One is the restructuring of forces pay, with the introduction of the military salary, the sort of reform that happens only twice a century which was our doing. The other one, which perhaps appeals more to economists, is that when the Post Office wanted to put up the quarterly rentals for telephones, we demurred. Increase the peak/off-peak differential instead, we said, and see if you can't introduce three rates instead of two, something which just recently they have done. That is a very good example of constructive work which arose as a by-product, in a sense, of prices and incomes policy, and which to my mind had an enduring value.

The last feature of our work was that the policy worked on consent – it may have been grudging consent, it very frequently was; but the point is it worked without all that enormous legal apparatus where people are defensively represented by mendacious Q.C.'s. On the whole people lied to us relatively infrequently and were able to trust us because they knew we were going to trust them. Although 'clients', as we called them, thought we were a frightful nuisance, with very few exceptions we managed to maintain reasonably friendly personal terms. In fact I am reminded of the late Dennis Robertson's remark about economic policy. You may remember a dreadful literary fashion after the war among economists for talking about 'sticks' and 'carrots' in economic policy. Dennis Robertson at last got fed up with this and said didn't we know there were *three* ways of treating a donkey?: the stick, the carrot and ear-stroking. Prices and incomes policy has been ear-stroking.

The conclusions I draw from most of the discussion today, and from that O.E.C.D. document, are (i) that the present post-1969 inflation is not easy to explain in what used to be an orthodox way until the third quarter of 1969, and (ii) that the residuals in the wage equation occur in pretty well all countries. This second point means that no explanation is going to be any good unless it can explain this simultaneity. I think that some of the explanations we have had put before us fail to meet this condition.

First of all, there is the notion of contagion. What I have against that is that similarly convincing mechanisms are to be found for the transmission of the trade cycle in the inter-war period, and all lead to the conclusion that the 1929 slump started in Finland because it had a downturn in exports six months earlier than anyone else! In other words, if inflation is a world-wide phenomenon I want a world-wide explanation, not just a transmission mechanism. Without denying that these mechanisms exist, I do not believe they explain why things have been different since 1969. So though such mechanisms exist, they do not explain the phenomenon at issue.

Secondly, we have Michael Parkin's expectations business–

random fluctuations around a Phillips curve. Well, the interesting point is that they might be random if they had not shown the same timing and the same direction in most of the major industrialised countries of the world. Similarly, although it is great fun reflecting what happened a hundred years ago, I do feel there have been one or two other changes which are relevant.

Then we come to Sir Fred's statement that strikes are more expensive than they used to be. (One reason for this is of course the spread of branding and the proportion of turnover which goes on promotion in the widest sense, advertising being only a part of this. The notion is that promotion builds up invisible, intangible capital, which is an asset which is lost, like a plant, if not continuously watered.) I found his argument quite convincing in itself, but I still do not think that it helps to explain why we have been in a lot more trouble since the last quarter of 1969 than we were before. This clearly invites a little research.

It would be interesting if Sir Fred were now to go and find some of the retired characters who used to run Austin or Morris or similar firms in the 1930s, and ask them what went through their minds thirty years ago when they had to decide whether to face a strike or not. This would show whether the motor industry has become that much more capital-intensive, whether branding and market shares have become that much more important, and whether distributorships are now more crucial than they used to be. On the other hand, and this is no more than a question, if it is true that these characteristics of certain industries explain their readiness to give in to excessive wage demands, should we not find that industries which lack these characteristics are relatively more ready to resist wage demands? If so what is the evidence? You see that I am asking a question and not conducting an argument.

If contagion or Parkin's respect for the persistence of the Phillips curve, or the argument that strikes are more expensive than they used to be, go by the board, what are we left with? Well, I humbly suggest we are left with phenomena which we as economists are not competent to investigate. Why should we assume that all economic phenomena have economic causes and that our rather pathetically small tool-kit of equipment is adequate to explain them? It seems to me that a very important driving force behind the current wage explosion, in other countries as well as this, is strong feelings of social injustice, feelings about the appropriateness of differentials. It is not for the economist to explain these unless he is to be more of a polymath than he has been in the past. My feeling is that it is a question of relative deprivation and the perception of social justice which is the key to understanding what has happened. After all, even as ignorant laymen (which is what we economists are when it comes to social phenomena), it is not too difficult to observe many changes of the social scene which are common to Europe and North America. Some are not relevant perhaps to the wage inflation, but if we ignorant laymen can perceive phenomena that are not relevant, such as the rise in the autonomy of youth, may it not be that there are other things which we are incapable of perceiving but which none the less are important?

So my view, quite frankly, is that not only can we not explain the present bump above the Phillips curve, but that we shall remain incapable of doing so until we become multi-disciplinary. I think what we lack knowledge of is the way people perceive the case for getting more income. We do not know very much about what reference standards people use. We do not know whether there is a lack of transitivity between different people's perceptions of the relative incomes that are appropriate for themselves and their neighbours. It is conceivable that such transitivity used to exist and is now lacking, and that this is the cause of the inflation. So one can think of things to inquire into, but we lack the techniques to do it. If it is the case that it is a newly developed intransitivity in perceptions of appropriate relativities which is at the root of our trouble, the cure must be the generation of a set of appropriate relativities.

Now Arrow's impossibility theorem may lead one to suppose that this will not work, but of course Arrow's book leaves out a most important aspect of the whole social mechanism. This is that, by discussion, people may change their minds. Job evaluation is, in a sense, a contradiction of Arrow's impossibility theorem, in that it is a process which produces mutually acceptable relativities within a relatively small social unit. I think one of the interesting questions is whether we could not attempt something like this on a national scale. I am not convinced, since I have not been able to look into it, by the argument that they tried it in Holland and it didn't work. Why didn't it work? Was it, as someone suggested, excess demand rather than an inherent defect of the approach that caused it to fail?

So I think a long-run incomes policy must be one which involves notions of fairness. None the less, I think an error of past incomes policy has been the attempt to raise the incomes of the low-paid. This has met with great obstacles, and I would wish to separate the problem of the low-paid from the problem of low incomes. If there are certain people who deserve to be low-paid, let them go on being low-paid. On the problem of low incomes, we should say that nobody ought to have a low income beneath a certain level, and see to it that they do not by redistribution, and not by incomes policy.

Those are my general reflections, which were designed less to convince you of any particular line than to stimulate a discussion.

Index